LIVING DONOR ORGAN TRANSPLANTATION: KEY LEGAL AND ETHICAL ISSUES

Living Donor Organ Transplantation: Key Legal and Ethical Issues

AUSTEN GARWOOD-GOWERS

Routledge
Taylor & Francis Group
LONDON AND NEW YORK

First published 1999 by Ashgate Publishing

Reissued 2018 by Routledge
2 Park Square, Milton Park, Abingdon, Oxon, OX14 4RN
52 Vanderbilt Avenue, New York, NY 10017

Routledge is an imprint of the Taylor & Francis Group, an informa business

A Library of Congress record exists under LC control number:

ISBN 13: 978-0-367-14871-3 (hbk)
ISBN 13: 978-0-429-05370-2 (ebk)

Contents

List of Figures and Tables

Table of Legislation

List of Cases

Preface

Within a reductionistic approach to medicine the main therapeutic solution for organ failure is transplantation. In end stage renal failure dialysis can also be used but in most cases it is a supportive measure prior to transplantation and would only be considered a genuine alternative in cases where a patient is not medically suited to transplantation. In certain forms of organ transplantation, such as lung lobe, liver segment and kidney, there may be a choice between obtaining an organ from a cadaveric donor (CDT) or from a living donor (LDT).

Whether LDT or CDT is the best clinical option for the patient will obviously vary according to the circumstances. In kidney transplantation the general rule is that an organ transplanted from a living donor is expected to have a higher graft survival than one transplanted from a cadaver, i.e. the transplant is expected to last longer. Rates will vary according to how well biologically matched the donor and recipient are. Sometimes the level of biological compatibility is high and in these circumstances an LDT will have an expected graft survival rate far in excess of what an average CDT will offer. Where the material is identically matched, as in the case of twins, the expected graft survival is over 4 times that of an average CDT.

If graft survival was the only consideration, living donation would be the standard choice. However, in taking an organ from a living person one causes that person a certain amount of definite physiological harm and exposes him or her to the risk of further harm. The level of this maleficence varies according to the specific circumstances but generally speaking it is greater when an organ or part of an organ is being donated than when tissues, such as blood or bone marrow, are being donated.

The fact that LDT causes maleficence to the donor is probably the main reason why some transplant professionals consider its use unethical. However, others take the view that if harm and jeopardy to the donor is within reasonable limits there are circumstances where use of a living donor is entirely justified. One circumstance is where it produces sufficiently better graft survival to offset the maleficence. Another is where the patient has limited prospects of getting a cadaveric organ within a reasonable space of time and consequently may have diminished health and quality of life unless living donation is used. The latter situation has become typical because nearly all countries that perform transplantation have insufficient supply of organs to meet the demand for them.

Generally the 1990s has seen some improvements in the numbers of organs procured but these have generally been outstripped by increases in demand for transplantation. Waiting lists in most countries are growing year upon year. Most patients are faced with the reality of average waiting times being long enough for living donation to be considered as a realistic option and some patients are faced with the reality that if living donation is not used it is quite possible or even likely that they will die whilst waiting.

These realities have led to calls for living donation to be used more, as well as attempts to increase levels of cadaveric procurement. In the context of the UK, the 1994 King's Fund Institute Report, *A Question of Give and Take: Improving the Supply of Organs for Transplantation,* recommended,

> increased use of genetically related live donors if backed by new Department of Health Guidance.[1]

A year later the Nuffield Council on Bioethics Report, *Human Tissue, Ethical and Legal Issues*, also concluded that there was a need to undertake more living donation.[2] However, the calls for increase have often been fairly cautious. For example, the British Transplant Society Working Party on Organ Donation has recently stated that,[3]

> ..renal units should be encouraged to perform more live donor transplants but with the strict proviso that any increase is not at the expense of a reduction in the strict selection criteria as far as donors are concerned. An increase in the number of live donor transplants will require a more active approach to the families of prospective recipients and this is required to be done with considerable care within nationally agreed guidelines and with reference to legal requirements.[4]

---

[1]Report No 18.
[2]Nuffield Council on Bioethics, 28 Bedford Square, London WC1B 3EG.
[3]Available from the British Transplant Society.
[4]Ibid at p34.

Is a very selective approach to choice of living donors going to yield enough extra organs? Some transplant centres have taken the view that the results of less well matched living donors are sufficiently good to warrant their use under conditions of organ shortage. The Norwegian transplant centre in Oslo has taken a bold approach to the use of living donors and this has led to it consistently achieving the highest rates of LDT per million population in the world. The main features of this approach are:

1. Continuing to use LDT extensively when there are high waiting lists, even if CDT rates have improved;[5]
2. informing the patient and his/her family of the availability of LDT as a matter of course;
3. scheduling a procedure soon after a suitable live donor has willingly offered rather than put or keep the patient on the waiting list in the hope that a cadaveric donor might turn-up (this approach has the added benefit that many LDTs are pre-dialysis, which tends to significantly improve their result);
4. utilising spouses to a significant extent;[6]
5. and accepting all types of tissue mismatch.[7]

There are several ethical and legal issues raised by LDT use in addition to considerations of harm, jeopardy and benefit. Like non-therapeutic research, LDT is not designed to benefit the donor. This, and the fact that it will cause some maleficence, make it especially critical that choices to donate are made on a voluntary basis and are very informed. There is also a case for saying that the prospective recipient should be especially well informed in order to make a sound and ethical choice about whether it is legitimate to use a living donor under the circumstance.

The person considering donation will typically be emotionally linked to the patient. This can make for a high motivation to donate, which in itself is a good thing. However, there are also dangers that decisions to donate will be made impulsively without proper consideration of the implications.

---

[5]Contrastingly, LDT would be rarely used if, as in Eire, demand for organs was being met by cadaveric procurement.

[6]Spouses form up to 6% of living donors in Norway whereas they are rarely used in most countries. See A.Jakobsen, Living Donor Practices and Processes in Europe, in D. Price and H.Akveld (eds.), Living Organ Donation in the Nineties: European Medico-Legal Perspectives, *EUROTOLD*, 1996, 1-12.

[7]Ibid.

Added to this is the potential that a person will be 'maneuvered' into donation or simply, without undue influence, feel constrained to say yes by the plight of the patient. Nonetheless, these are potential dangers in many 'rescue' type situations.

A special set of issues is raised where the prospective donor is an adult incompetent or minor. If someone has the power to consent on behalf of someone else they are legally required to exercise it in that person's best interests. This raises a quandary in relation to living donation. Obviously there are the benefits that can come to a person from expressing compassion through donating but is this benefit alone enough to offset the maleficence and make donation in a person's best interests? Or would the person have to have some special interest in the well-being of the patient? Should consent to donation ever be given on behalf of the person without their agreement?

Another issue that will be examined is the role of money (or money's worth) in relation to the donor. On the one hand there is the concern to pay any reasonable expenses and losses the donor might have but should the donor also be paid. Indeed, what role should payment have in relation to the parties that are providing goods and or services. Should organs themselves be treated as a commodity to be bought and sold?

This book examines the above issues in a global context. An important feature you will see is the discussion of empirical work which helps to put the discussion of law and ethics of living donor transplantation in the context of attitudes, practices and policies. Besides a wealth of data concerning harm, risk and benefit in LDT there has been a significant amount of study of professional attitudes, policies and practice and the perceptions and experience of donors and recipients. This book introduces and evaluates some new data from the empirical programme conducted with professionals, donors and recipients by EUROTOLD in Europe.

EUROTOLD is a 'Multidisciplinary European Study of the Ethical and Legal Aspects of Transplantation of Living Donors' which for several years was contracted with the European Community (Ref : BMH1-CT92-1841). EUROTOLD worked alongside professionals across Europe in disciplines as diverse as medicine, law, ethics, psychology, statistics and economics to encourage cross fertilisation of ideas and views, share experience and gather empirical data from living donor transplant practitioners and participants. In 1996, EUROTOLD submitted its findings to the European Commission in a report entitled, *Questioning Attitudes to Living Donor Transplantation.*

As part of its empirical programme EUROTOLD developed a European Transplant Centre Questionnaire in which we asked European centres for responses to factual questions about transplant practice and centre policies towards LDT. This was followed by a Professional Attitudes Questionnaire in which we asked for individual professional responses from a wide variety of European transplant centre personnel (including surgeons, nephrologists, anesthetists, transplant coordinators and nurses) to hypothetical clinical scenarios with multiple choices given to respondents to select from as solutions. The Professional Attitudes Questionnaire was designed to test current attitudes in action and was coded to test correlations between professional attitudes and centre practice and policy.

After being worked up by a multi-disciplinary team in 1993 and 1994 the questionnaires were distributed in 1995 to 190 centres representing 27 countries across Eastern and Western Europe. 56% of centres responded, the responding centres covering a total of 211.3 million population in Europe with the catchment area of individual centres ranging from 0.5 million (Cyprus) to 10 million (Romania). 86% of responding centres had an LDT programme (85% when weighted by catchment population). The two professional questionnaires were complemented by the development of a scoring system for the restrictiveness/liberality of law in European countries relating to LDT. The scoring was cross correlated with professional attitudes, policy and practice.

EUROTOLD also used a questionnaire/interview strategy for eliciting qualitative and quantitative data from donors and recipients in centres from 7 different European countries concerning their experience in relation to LDT and their perceptions of it. This built on a recent Norwegian study of donor experience and perceptions[8] and the mainly much earlier studies conducted in the US concerning donor - and often recipient and familial - experience and perceptions in relation to LDT. I administered semi-structured interview/questionnaires to a total of 28 donors and 30 recipients in Dublin, Oslo and Leicester. These yielded interesting data which was mainly of a qualitative nature. More extensive quantitive data was derived from a very structured interview/questionnaire process used in Poland, Romania, Slovakia and Slovenia. In these countries EUROTOLDs

[8]L.Westlie et al., Quality of Life in Norwegian Kidney Donors, *Neph Dial Trans,* 1994, 8, 1146-1150.

collaborators gained data from a combined total of 48 donors and 54 recipients.

For more information about the work of the EUROTOLD project and its members see the website on the internet at

http://www.maths.lancs.ac.uk:2080/MedStats/EuroTold

Acknowledgements

From 1991-1996 I was a member of the management group of EUROTOLD. EUROTOLD was a very supportive and stimulating context in which to develop an understanding of the ethical and legal dimensions of LDT and for that I would like to thank not just my colleagues in the management group but also the hundreds of collaborators across Europe. This collaboration formed the background to a PhD thesis I developed entitled,

An Investigation Into the Ethical and Legal Aspects of Living Donor Organ Transplantation.

De Montfort University awarded me a PhD for this investigation in May 1998. I would like to thank the University and Professors David Price and Ronnie Mackay who acted as my PhD supervisors. I am particularly grateful to the hours of collaboration and mentoring of David and the very thoughtful input he and Ronnie gave as experts in medical law. I would like to thank Ashgate for their help publishing this work.

List of Abbreviations

CDT - cadaveric organ transplantation
EUROTOLD - European multidisciplinary study of LDT
EV - elective ventilation
HOTA - Human Organ Transplants Act 1989
LDT - living donor organ transplantation
LURD - living unrelated transplantation
NHBD - non heart beating donor(s)
ULTRA - Unrelated Live Transplants Regulatory Authority

1 Contexts

The Ethical and Legal Basis for Medical Intervention

Medical intervention, including the treatment of organ disease, is influenced by philosophical debates between consequentialism, deontology and rights and also by the so-called four core principles of medical ethics - beneficence, non-maleficence, autonomy and justice.[1] As well as forming an ethical guide to medical professionals, philosophical approaches and principles are at the centre of medical law.

The Ethical Basis for Medical Intervention

Two of the most well known approaches to philosophical thought are consequentialism and deontology. Consequentialism judges the rightness or wrongness of an action by its consequences. A key brand of consequentialism is utilitarianism, which judges consequences in terms of their use value. One of the early proponents of utilitarianism was Jeremy Bentham who stated that the goal of decisions was to maximise happiness and that the rightness of wrongness of action in this sense could be determined by whether, on balance, it produces more pleasure than pain. J.S.Mill subsequently noted a developing trend amongst utilitarians to weigh quality as well as quantity of pleasures.[2] Contrastingly, deontological approaches have held that the rightness or wrongness of an action cannot be determined purely by consequences. Instead it is determined by a system of values. From a deontological perspective Kant suggests that people are ends in themselves as well as means to an end but

---

[1]Developed by Beauchamp and Chidress (see Principles of Biomedical Ethics, *Oxford University Press*, 1994), subjected to a certain amount of criticism (see for instance S.Holm, Not Just Autonomy - The principles of American Biomedical Ethics, *J Med Eth*, 1995, 21, 332-338) but widely accepted and applied and cogently defended by Raanan Gillon who states that, 'very few critics argue that any one of the four principles in incompatible with his or her preferred theory or approach to biomedical ethics' (Defending 'the four principles' approach to biomedical ethics, *J Med Eth*, 1995, 21, 323-324 at 324).
[2]J.S.Mill, Utilitarianism, *Routledge*, 1863 at p15.

one of the main problems with deontology is that systems of values or morality can be formulated in such a way as to support authoritarian control in opposition to the rights of individuals. A similar problem can arise where utility is the overarching concern - as Gillon puts it,

> ...if overall maximisation of welfare is the supreme moral objective the individual seems to be in permanent jeopardy before the overriding interests of society.[3]

Most philosophers accept that rights are intrinsic to being human and must therefore be taken seriously.[4] Some, such as J.S.Mill, go as far as suggesting that a competent adult's rights can only be limited in so far as they conflict with other rights,

> ...the sole end for which mankind is warranted, individually or collectively, in interfering with the liberty of action of any of their number is self-protection.[5]

One of the things that draws most people into being medical professionals is a desire to play a role in encouraging health. Within most traditions a medical professional is seen as having a position of trust with the positive duty to do his best by those in his/her care, known more formally as the duty of beneficence. Almost a part of this is the ethical principle of non-maleficence under which the professional must not harm the patient. The precise combination of these principles within the Hippocratic writings is the injunction to the professional to, 'help, or at least do no harm'.[6] The doctrine of double effect comes into play in saying that if the weight of evidence points toward a course of action having an overall benefit it can be ethical even if it also causes some harm and jeopardy. In reductionistic medicine obvious examples of this principle being applied are the use of mutilating operations and the use of synthetic drugs with side effects.

The principle of beneficence does not support the use of interventions which are non-therapeutic to the person undergoing them. However, from a utilitarian standpoint these interventions can be justified where in a wider

---

[3]R.Gillon, Philosophical Medical Ethics, 1986 at p25.

[4]See e.g. J.Harris, The Value of Life, *Routledge and Kegan Paul*, 1985; Ronald Dworkin, Taking Rights Seriously, *Duckworth*, 1977.

[5]On Liberty, *Penguin*, 1982 at p68.

[6]Edelstein, The Hippocratic Oath: Text, Translation and Interpretation, *Supplements to the Bulletins of the History of Medicine*, 30(1).

sense they have the prospect of being beneficial. For example, non-therapeutic medical research and living donation would be justified on utilitarian grounds where the prospects are of a wider benefit exceeding harm and jeopardy to the subject. From a rights perspective a person should be entitled to volunteer for non-therapeutic interventions even though they offend the principle of beneficence. However, equally they should only be subject to such interventions after making an informed and voluntary choice, i.e. they have a right of refusal.

Where a medical intervention is a treatment in the best interests of the person undergoing it, it can be justified as both consistent with that person's utility and with the deontolgical principle that (s)he should be treated as an end in him/herself. The principle of paternalism is that it can be acceptable to impose treatment in these circumstances. However, again, to do so would override the right of self-determination. In medical ethics the right of self-determination is closely interwoven with the principle of autonomy.

The term autonomy is derived from the Greek words 'autos' meaning self and 'nomos' meaning rule or law. These were initially put together to describe political self-governance in the context of the Greek city state. Political self-governance was merely the logical extension of the principle of individual self-determination into the realm of a collective system of organisation. Logically, within this system, medical practice would be consistent with self determination and forced intervention would be limited to occasions where it was a necessary defence of the rights of a third party (e.g. a paternity test), the rights of a wider section of the public (e.g. in a public health emergency) or where in a medical emergency it has been necessary to intervene before it is practicable to obtain voluntary agreement. However, the term autonomy has also been given other meanings one of which is the *personal ability to act in a self-directed manner consistent with ones own interests.*[7] In this sense a person has a degree of autonomy relative to their capabilities. A legitimate role for paternalism arises from the fact that as a common sense exercise of compassion it will sometimes be necessary to make a decision on behalf of a person in their interests if they lack the capabilities necessary to adequately determine their own interests in the matter. This lack may be connected with being a minor who is not yet mature enough to decide or

---

[7]For a description of this see S.I.Benn, Freedom, Autonomy, and the Concept of a Person, *Proceedings of the Aristotelian Society,* 1976, LXXVI, p123f.

due to such factors as mental disability and illness. An extreme example would be where a person is unconscious or in a coma.

A final principle of medical ethics that is worthy of mention is that of justice. All sorts of concepts are associated with justice such as fair treatment, equal respect, merit and so on. Essentially justice is a principle of how relations between people should rightly be organised. In healthcare there are many contexts in which justice is a central issue. For example, in relation to when a patient is cared for, Stauch, Wheat and Tingle suggest that doctors are under a perfect duty to be just in the way they decide who to treat and under only an imperfect (i.e. non-absolute) duty to provide medical treatment to everyone who requests it.[8] Justice is also relevant to the overall basis upon which healthcare, including transplantation, is distributed. Stauch et al. suggest that concepts of justice often present three models for healthcare distribution,

> First, resources may be distributed according to merit. This would mean that the most deserving persons, for example in terms of moral worth or contribution to society, would receive healthcare as a matter of priority. Secondly, resources may be distributed equally. However, this presupposes that we have a test for deciding whether the persons concerned are equal. Certainly they are entitled to equal respect and consideration, but that in itself may not be enough. This tempts us to adopt the third model, which is that resources be distributed in accordance with need.[9]

The problem with all of these approaches to distribution is that they assume society has a right to interfere with how relationships are constructed beyond protecting people from abuse. When society is doing the distributing then invariably it also obtains the goods to distribute through force - tax or compulsory insurance in the case of healthcare. Whether the approach is Marxist (each paying according to his ability, each getting according to his need) or based on some other conception of utility or deontology it necessarily presupposes that there is an ethical basis upon which to seek values from others by means of force. Contrastingly, Rand's approach is that the giving and receiving elements of any relationship are consistent with rights when they are based solely on giving

[8]Ibid.

[9]Sourcebook on Medical Law, *Cavendish*, 1998 at p45.

value for value, by free, mutual consent to mutual benefit.[10] She suggests this would lead to free market capitalism. However, in fact, one of the main objectives pursued in a free market is not to offer value for value but to maximise the value one gets irrespective of the consequences. We have obviously seen through recent history that this maximisation is often accomplished through the use of the dynamics of abuse of power where one does whatever one can get away with in relation to taking value. In essence where one profits at the expense of the environment or other humans it is 'theft'. The extent of thefts that have occurred has meant that what Marx described as the concentration of the means of production in the hands of the few has far from been accomplished solely on merit.

In healthcare terms the tensions between legitimate exchanges and the theft of value are being particularly felt in areas of biotechnology and the harvesting and distributing of body materials. Chapter 7 specifically examines exchanges in relation to organs.

Free, mutual, value-value relationships in the field of healthcare would involve people choosing to make fair contracts for health insurance and/or contracts for health services as and when needed. The responsibility for provision of healthcare of minors would rest on their parents/guardians. Contributions for the provision of healthcare for adults not capable of offering value (e.g. because of the nature of their illness) could be voluntarily given by those who were capable as an act of human solidarity and compassion.

The Legal Basis for Medical Intervention

In terms of political realities philosophers are faced with the fact that law is a tool of force. Law can be used to protect rights through imposing negative duties on persons to refrain from interfering with each other's rights of action, ownership and decision and positive duties to act in relationships of trust or responsibility such as between a medical professional and his patient. However, the nature of law is always the outcome of a struggle between interests and ethical perspectives and values. In medical law the evolution of this struggle has involved times in history where the interests or values of society were placed above the rights of the individual. An example of this is the judicial authorisation of sterilisation of certain types of mental incompetent on 'social grounds'

---

[10]See Atlas Shrugged, *Penguin Books*, 1985.

which in the US was occurring as late as 1960. It is only just over 50 years since the Nazi regime were imposing medical experiments on persons they regarded as subnormal or of inferior racial type and in 1999 itself we have had rumours of ethnic Albanians in Kosovo being forced to be a 'blood bank' for Serbian forces. If something good can be taken from atrocities it is that they have mobilised support for human rights in medicine. In Europe the Council of Europe's Convention on Human Rights and Biomedicine - Article 2 commendably states that,

> The interests and welfare of the human being shall prevail over the sole interest of society or science.

The Explanatory Report additionally comments that,

> The whole Convention, the aim of which is to protect human rights and dignity, is inspired by the principle of the primacy of the human being, and all its articles must be interpreted in this light.

Medical law in general supports the right to self-determination. Competent adults are given protection from the violation of their body through the general legal right to refuse treatment and take action for criminal assault and/or tortious battery where the medical professional makes an intervention without first obtaining consent (unless this was justified in the defence of rights of others or in an emergency). The right to refuse has been stated in various ways countless times in the case law - most famously by Justice Cordozo in the US case of Schleondorff v Society of New York Hospital (1914) 105 NE 92,

> ...every human being of adult years and sound mind has a right to determine what shall be done with his own body; and a surgeon who performs an operation without his patient's consent commits an assault.[11]

Broadly speaking, consent is the voluntary act of agreement by a person who has the competence to make that agreement. Generally it is given expressly but sometimes it can be implied.[12] The incompetent person will

[11]For statements in recent English cases see Collins v Wilcock [1984] 1 WLR 1172 and Re F (mental Patient: Sterilisation) [1990] 2 AC 1.
[12]O'Brien v Cunard SS Co (1891) 28 NE 266 (Mass Sup Jud Ct).

have consent given on his her/behalf by the person(s) legally empowered to give it. Importantly, in exercising this power, they are required to act consistently with the best interests of the incompetent. This prevents the incompetent from being used for the benefit of others unless this is consistent with his or her own best interests. However, as Ssasz has noted, their is still scope for this power to be used for authoritarian social control in the guise of genuine paternalism, such as through making decisions on behalf of people when they are actually capable of making them themselves.[13] One of the examples Ssasz cites is the labelling of political dissidents in the former Soviet Union as incompetents.[14] The more everyday dilemma is with minors who are competent to make a particular decision but are nethertheless restricted from doing so. There is a legitimate ground for some restrictions in that such minors are more vulnerable to hurting themselves than the average adult because of having less of a tendency to weigh the consequences of their decisions. This may particularly justify restrictions on certain dangerous activities (e.g. smoking, drinking, driving).

As well as being a criminal assault, an unconsented contact is a tortious battery. The medical professional cannot avoid liability for unconsented contact simply upon the basis that (s)he considered the intervention to be in the patient's best interests; Canadian[15] and English[16] authorities have established that touching need not be hostile for battery to be founded. Consent would be unreal in all situations where it has been given involuntarily, although obviously the medical professional would have to have responsibility for this involuntariness (e.g. by inducing 'agreement' by fraud or coercion) in order to incur liability. Aside from obvious uses of coercion and fraud, actions have been successfully mounted in a variety of other situations such as the patient having agreed to one procedure and a different one being performed[17] and where only a specific person's

---

[13]Ssasz, Law, Liberty and Psychiatry: An Inquiry into the Social Uses of Mental Health Practices, *Routledge and Kegan Paul*, 1974.
[14]Ibid.
[15]Malette v Schulman (1988) 47 DLR (4th) 18: A blood transfusion to a Jehovah's Witness who carried a card indicating wish not to have a blood transfusion and had not consented to it.
[16]Re F (mental Patient: Sterilisation) [1990] 2 AC 1 where Lord Goff regarded the Court of Appeals apparent endorsement of the hostility requirement in Wilson v Pringle [1987] QB 237 at 253 as incorrect.
[17]Cull v Royal Surrey County Hospital and Butler, *Br.Med.J.*,1932, 1, 1195.

touching was consented to but another person touches and this affects the quality or nature of what was done.[18]

Article 5 of the Convention on Human Rights and Biomedicine includes the statement that intervention in the health field may only be carried out after the person concerned has given free and informed consent to it. It also states that before giving consent the person shall be given appropriate information as to the purpose and nature of the intervention as well as on its consequences and risks. However, what it does not state is whether the giving of the information is just necessary before consent or actually integral to the consent itself. Philosophically speaking, the giving of consent at least implies that one knows what one is agreeing to. However, for that agreement to be real doesn't necessarily imply that one is aware of all the significant information pertaining to one's choice. Judges have naturally wanted to avoid declaring that full disclosure is integral to the consent itself because this would mean that if a medical professional failed to disclose any significant piece of information (s)he could not only be liable in tort for battery but also end up with a criminal record for assault! In Hills v Potter [1983] 3 All ER 716, Hirst J suggested this outcome would be deplorable - as did Lord Scarman in the House of Lords in Sidaway v Board of Governors of the Bethlem Royal Hospital and the Maudsley Hospital [1985] I All ER 643.

These cases came after it had already been established in Chatterton v Gerson [1981] Q.B. 432 that a patient's consent would be real, and hence no action would lie in battery, once (s)he has been informed 'in broad terms of the nature of the intervention intended'.[19] However, one of the questions that has emerged since Chatterton is whether there are certain types of intervention where disclosure is so imperative as to consider any significant omission of it as undermining the validity of consent. This issue will be examined in more detail in chapter 3 which deals with informed choice in relation to living organ donation and reception.

---

[18]Outside of private medicine consent is rarely confined to one person in operations and other medical interventions.

[19]Bristow J at 442G. Confirmed in English law by Hills v Potter [1983] 3 All ER 716, Sidaway v Board of Governors of the Bethlem Royal Hospital and the Maudsley Hospital [1985] I All ER 643 (HL) and more recently Davis v Barking, Brentwood and Havering Health Authority (1993) 2 Med LR 366. Also confirmed by the Supreme Ct of Canada in Reibl v Hughes [1980] 114 D.L.R. (3d) 646. For criticism of this approach see e.g. the Canadian cases of Koehler v Cook [1975] D.L.R. (3d) 766 and Zimmer v Ringrose [1978] 89 D.L.R. (3d) 646).

Since legal rules against unconsented contact generally do not require the patient to be given detailed information, the main legal recourse for patient complaints about disclosure has been the tort of negligence. The structure of the tort of negligence is that a legal person who owes a duty of care to another person and breaches that duty by unreasonable action or inaction can be sued where the breach causes harm. It is well established that medical professionals owe a duty of care to their patients.[20] They would also owe this duty to their medical volunteers such as living donors. This duty is breached when a medical professional's action or inaction is unreasonable, but unreasonable according to whose standards?

Generally, in negligence cases reasonableness is defined by reference to what the mythical 'common person' would consider to be reasonable and expert opinion may be brought forward from both sides to help determine what is reasonable in a particular context. Just because a practice is common does not make it reasonable and equally just because a practice is uncommon or novel does not make it unreasonable. However, when it comes to medical negligence cases judges have tended to define what is reasonable by other standards.

In English law the landmark House of Lords decision of Sidaway v Board of Governors, Bethlem Royal Hospital [1985] AC 871 concluded that a professional would be acting reasonably if doing so in accordance with a school of thought accepted as proper by a responsible body of medical opinion. This is known as the Bolam test because it is based on a declaration made in an earlier Court of Appeal case called Bolam v Friern Hospital Management Committee [1957] 2 All ER 115. It is a test which has been followed and approved in both cases of treatment[21] and diagnosis.[22]

Unless a professional has been very careless it will not be difficult to find a group of professional colleagues who consider his approach to be proper and it will not be difficult to persuade a judge that this group of professional colleagues was a competent body of medical opinion. Hence, we can conclude that the Bolam test heavily restricts liability. Is this justifiable? One of the concerns of English judges has been that to have

---

[20]Barnett v Chelsea and Kensington Hospital Management Committee [1969] 1 QB 428 [1968] 1 All ER 1068 (QBD).

[21]See Whitehouse v Jordan [1981] 1 WLR 246 (HL) particularly Lord Edmund Davies at 258.

[22]See Maynard v West Midlands Regional Health Authority [1984] 1 WLR 634 particularly Lord Scarman at 638.

expansive liability for medical negligence would have adverse effects on medical practice. 45 years ago in Hatcher v Black [1954] Times, 2 July, Lord Denning conjured up visions of Machiavelli in suggesting that expanding liability would result in the doctor or surgeon,

> ...instead of getting on with his work...forever looking over his shoulder to see if someone was coming up with a dagger.

Echoes of this are found in Lord Scarman's allusion to, 'the danger of defensive medicine developing in this country' in Sidaway and in Lord Justice Mustill's statement in the Court of Appeal in Wilsher v Essex Area Health Authority [1987] QB 730, [1986] 3 All ER 801 (CA) that,

> ...the risks which actions for professional negligence bring for the public as a whole, in the shape of an instinct on the part of the professional man to play for safety, are serious and are now well recognised.

The merits of this viewpoint can be contested. Requiring high legal standards of medical professionals can sometimes help to ensure, rather than discourage, high standards of practice. There must be some balance between protecting the medical profession and helping patients to get compensated for mistakes.

All four majority judgments in Sidaway confirmed the approach in Hatcher v Black (1954) Times, 2 July (QBD) and Bolam that the scope of reasonableness should be the same in cases involving disclosure standards as it is for cases involving use of technical skill. One could argue that there is nothing about promoting a high legal standard of disclosure that would cause defensive medicine, so why isn't reasonableness defined differently in disclosure cases? Lords Bridge and Keith in Sidaway emphasised the paramount nature of patient autonomy, making it odd for them to conclude that the Bolam test applies to disclosure cases. However, Lord Bridge did temper his support for this professional based standard,

> ...even in a case where, as here, no expert in the relevant field condemns the non-disclosure as being in conflict with accepted and responsible medical practice, I am of the opinion that the judge might in certain circumstances come to the conclusion that disclosure of a particular risk was so obviously necessary to an informed choice on the part of the patient that no reasonably prudent medical man would fail to make it.[23]

[23]Sidaway [1985] AC 871, [1985] 1 All ER 643 at 663.

In the judgment of Lord Diplock restrictive disclosure flowed more logically from his archaic and authoritarian view that it was the doctor's function to weigh and evaluate options, not the patients,

> ...all these are matters which the doctor will have to take into consideration in determining, in the exercise of his professional skill and judgement, that it is in the patient's best interests that he should take the risk involved and undergo the treatment recommended by the doctor.[24]

Lord Templeman's restrictive approach also flowed logically from his conception of the doctor-patient relationship,

> ...the doctor...must decide what information should be given to the patient and in what terms that information should be couched.[25]

Lord Scarman was the only judge to assert the view that professional perceptions should not exclusively or dominantly determine what should be disclosed. His Lordship felt,

> ...it would be strange if courts should be led to conclude that our law, which undoubtedly recognises the right of the patient to decide whether he will accept or reject the treatment proposed, should permit the doctors to determine whether and in what circumstances a duty arises, requiring the doctor to warn his patient of the risks inherent in the treatment which he proposes.[26]

One could be forgiven for thinking the majority in Sidaway had swapped their judicial robes for white coats and stethoscopes. Several cases following Sidaway interpreted it as meaning that judges had no role in defining whether the action or inaction of medical professionals in cases coming before them were reasonable or not.[27] This position has been heavily criticised by judges[28] and academics[29] and English case law has

---

[24][1985] 1 All ER 643 at 656.
[25]Ibid at 666.
[26]Ibid at 649.
[27]E.g. Gold v Haringey Health Authority [1987] 2 All ER 888(albeit in the context of alternative treatments rather than risks of treatment), Palmer v Eadie (18 May 1987, unreported), CA and Blyth v Bloomsbury HA [1993] 4 Med LR 151 CA.
[28]See Australian cases of F v R [1983] SASR 189 (Sup. Ct of Aus) and Rogers v Whittaker [1992] 175 C.L.R. 479 and the Supreme Court of Ireland in Dunner v National Maternity Hospital [1988] IR 91.

now moved some way from it. The Court of Appeal in Joyce v Merton, Sutton and Handsworth Health Authority 27 BMLR 124-157 (applying Bolam) held that only limited weight will be given to the defence of practitioners that they had followed *their* normal practice if there are witnesses and documentary evidence showing that proper practice was not followed and no other expert medical evidence in favour of the defence. The House of Lords have more equivocally moved the situation forward in Bolitho v City Hackney HA [1997] 4 All ER 771 by stating that where there are two bodies of opposing opinion the one brought forward for the defence can be rejected (even if competent) if it is not logically supportable.[30]

Despite this shift one can still make the objection that legal liability in medical negligence is mainly defined by the profession from whence the defendant came and this is bound to restrict liability severely. This is particularly likely to be the case when the complaint is about disclosure because the perception of medical professionals of what they should disclose tends to be very limited, as discussed in chapter 3. The result is that this approach does little to protect patient autonomy. As Lord Scarman put it in his minority judgement in Sidaway,

> ...where doctors are allowed to limit disclosure on the basis of their clinical judgement the patient's capacity to make decisions based upon his own value commitments and weighting of the various risks is undermined.[31]

Several jurisdictions including Eire[32] and, in general, the US[33] have broadly speaking adopted a similar approach to English law in defining what constitutes reasonable and unreasonable non-disclosure. However, jurisdictions like Canada,[34] some Australian states,[35] New Zealand,[36] South

---

[29]See e.g. M.Brazier, Patient Autonomy and Consent to Treatment: The Role of the Law? *L.S.,* 1987, 7, 169; and D.Gieson, Vindicating the Patient's Rights: A Comparative Perspective, *J of Contmpry Health Law and Policy,* 1993, 9, 273-309.
[30]P779. Lord Brown-Wilkinson, giving the judgement, stressed that this would seldom occur. He later extrajudicially stated that, 'Bolitho represents an adaptation of Bolam rather than a radical break...It will be used sparingly by the courts' (*All ER Annual Review*, 1997 at p314).
[31][1985] 1 All ER 643 at 654.
[32]Dunner v National Maternity Hospital [1988] IR 91.
[33]See Mason & McCall-Smith, Law and Medical Ethics, *Butterworths,* 1991, 245.
[34]Ibid at 245.

Africa[37] and leading civil law jurisdictions like Switzerland, Austria and Germany[38] - have rejected use of such a 'professional based standard' in favour of one based on the disclosure needs of the 'reasonable patient' in the actual patient's situation. Underlying this approach, according to the Australian High Court in Rogers v Whittaker [1993] 4 Med LR 79, is

> ...the principle that, while evidence of acceptable medical practice is a useful guide for the courts, it is for the courts to adjudicate on what is the appropriate standard of care after giving weight to 'the paramount consideration that a person is entitled to make his own decisions about his life'.[39]

Disclosure standards based around patient rights sometimes refer to the transatlantic doctrine of 'informed consent'. 'Informed consent' is a term that was first used in the US case of Salgo v Leland Stanform Jr University Board of Trustees (1957) 317 P 2d 170. In Sidaway [1985] 1 All ER 643 at 654 Lord Scarman drew heavily on an informed consent approach used in Canterbury v Spence [1972] 464 F 2d 772, US App DC; cert denied 409 US 1064. Problematically, the doctrine implies that patient informedness should be integral to the giving of consent itself but is primarily used to argue that disclosure under the tort of negligence should be expansive. Accordingly, it is better simply to look in a concrete way at the manner and extent to which law supports the making of informed choices.

Legal definitions of reasonable disclosure ought to support informed choice within the limits of what it is practicable and reasonable to expect of the professional. Clearly the professional based standards give too much emphasis to what professionals tend to disclose instead of what they should disclose. Another problem is that whatever standard for disclosure is used professionals sometimes have too much scope to use 'clinical judgement' or 'therapeutic privilege' to screen out information in the patient's 'best interests'. Indeed, some judgements requiring a high level

---

[35]See for instance the New South Wales Court of Appeal Decision of Ellis v Wallsend District Hospital [1990] 2 Med LR 103 and the decision of the Australian High Court in Rogers v Whittaker [1993] 4 Med LR 79.

[36]See particularly the New Zealand Court of Appeal decision of Smith v Auckland Hospital Board [1964] NZLR 241.

[37]See particularly Castell v De Greef (1994) Case No. A 976/92 (Sup. Ct of SA, Cape of Good Hope Provincial Division, per Ackermann J.) (not yet reported).

[38]See e.g. D.Gieson, Vindicating the Patient's Rights: A Comparative Perspective, *J of Contemporary Health Law and Policy,* 1993, 9, 273-309.

[39]At 82 citing King CJ in F v R (1983) 33 SASR 189.

of disclosure are very qualified in this by the scope they give to the professional to screen out information on this basis.[40] In the extreme case the professional is allowed to covertly manipulate the process of giving information in order to increase patient compliance with his/her wishes provided that this is done with intent to promote what is considered to be the best treatment for the patient.[41] This is where medical practice gets into the realm of social control; the patient has a right to make his/her own decision but the underlying authoritarianism allows information to be conveyed in such a way that 'the perceived value of therapy takes precedence over the patient's rights to reject it'.[42]

Having proven that a non-disclosure constituted a breach of duty the patient will also have to show that the breach through non-disclosure caused harm in order for negligence to be constituted. Generally the difficulty is not in proving legal causation but in proving factual causation, i.e. that the patient would not have made the same choice had the breach of duty through non-disclosure not occurred. In practice, whatever a patient may subjectively suggest (s)he would have done had there not been a breach, a judge is likely to examine what the reasonable patient would have done[43] in the absence of very strong evidence of what the patient would have done. This is fine for patients whose perspective of medical treatment coincides with what judges consider rational but it presents difficulties to patients who have a different conception to the judges of what medical interventions might be in their best interest.[44]

---

[40]See e.g. Lord Scarman's judgement in Sidaway [1985] 1 All ER 643 at 654.

[41]See for example the majority judgements in Sidaway, particularly Lord Diplock.

[42]McLean, A Patient's Rights to Know, *Dartmouth*, 1989 at p114.

[43]Reibl v Hughes [1980] 114 DLR (3d) 1 (Can Sup Ct) actually used an objective test for causation which is absurd because causation is a matter based on the facts of what would have happened not an abstracted notion of reasonableness. The objective test in Reibl has been rejected - see e.g. Chatterton v Gerson [1981] QB 432 and Ellis v Wallsend District Hospital [1989] 17 NSWLR 553 (NSW CA).

[44]In Poynter v Hillingdon (High Court, 23 April 1997, unreported) despite the clear evidence that parents considering treatment for their child's organ disease were very much against an reductionistic approach and had agreed to it with extreme reluctance (perhaps even coercion), Sir Maurice Drake viewed matters very much in terms of *he himself* considering the reductionistic treatment proposed to be in the best interests of the child and deriving from this a conclusion that the parents would have consented to such treatment on the child's behalf even if the relevant non-disclosed informations concerning risks had been disclosed.

A final problem to note is that although a practitioner must believe that the patient (or person acting in loco parentis) understands what the procedure is to be sure of avoiding liability for assault/battery, there has been no emphasis under the battery and negligence analyses to ensure that information given is understood. This was succinctly put in Canterbury v Spence 464 F 2d. 772 (1972) at 780,

> ...the physician discharges the duty when he makes a reasonable effort to convey sufficient information, although the patient, without fault of the physician, may not fully grasp it.

Equally, in regard to the US it has been stated that there is a strong tendency,

> ...to look to legal and regulatory approaches to informed consent for the relevant standards, but it has become progressively clear that the focus of statutory law, case law and regulatory guideline has been on disclosure and that this focus is misguided. Problems about the quality and adequacy of consent probably cannot be resolved unless conventional disclosure requirements are abandoned and a shift occurs toward quality of understanding in the subject, patient and representative. From this perspective, the central problems about informed consent are issues of communication rather than the abstract and disembodied issues about proper legal standards of disclosure that have so long dominated the subject literature.[45]

Robertson has argued that,

> ...even accepting the patient's right to self-determination dictates only that he be given a reasonable opportunity to make a rational decision as to proposed medical treatment, the extent of the patient's comprehension of the disclosed information should still be a vital issue. The opportunity given may be 'reasonable' if viewed from the standpoint of the doctor, in terms of the information which he has disclosed, but that opportunity becomes wholly unreasonable for the purpose for which it is given and completely meaningless, if viewed from the patient's standpoint, if he fails to understand the information given to him.[46]

Seeds of wisdom fallen on hard legal ground.

---

[45]T.Beauchamp, A History and Theory of Informed Consent, *Oxford University Press*, 1986.

[46]G.Robertson, Informed Consent to Medical Treatment, *LQR*, 1981, 102, 111-2.

Whilst having a general right of refusal the competent adult cannot force a medical professional into providing a particular form of treatment. The professional considers treatment both within the framework of his own ethics, his professional context and the demands of law. Legislation and public policy are playing an increasingly central role in prescribing limits and conditions on medical activity, particularly when new ethical issues arise from technological developments.

It is also true that although law generally views competent adults as 'masters of their own fate'[47] it intrudes into their right of self-determination by placing limits on harmful or risky actions. In an absolute sense a person cannot usually consent to activities that cause death, serious injury or mutilation.[48] The added factor is that intrusions are occasioned not just for reasons of paternalistic protection from harm but for reasons of 'morality'. In English law, this morality is embodied within the principle of public policy or public interest and on occasion can be the determinative factor in whether or not the harmful or risky act is considered legal; for instance, the violent consensual activity of boxing is legal[49] but sado-masochistic sexual activities are normally illegal.[50] In the medical context morality is not so much at the forefront. Lord Mustill in Airedale NHS Trust v Bland [1993] 1 All ER 821 at 889 suggested that,

> Bodily invasions in the course of proper medical treatment stand completely outside the criminal law.

However, it does seem that proper or beneficent intention is not enough and that Lord Lane in Attorney-General's Reference [No.6 of 1980][1981] 2 All E.R. 1057 was correct to say that medical interventions involving harm or risk must be reasonable.[51] One situation where a physiologically maleficent procedure can be reasonable is where it involves psychological benefit. Hence in Corbett v Corbett (otherwise Ashley) [1970] 2 All ER 33 Mr Justice Ormrod held that a sex change operation was lawful; the

---

[47]Per Lord Griffith in Re F (a mental patient: sterilisation) [1990] 2 AC1 (HL).
[48]D.Gieson, International Medical Malpractice Law, *Martinus Nijhoff*, 1988, 609.
[49]Although not where done with bare knuckles - see R v Coney [1882] 8 QBD 534.
[50]In R v Brown (Anthony) [1993] 2 All ER 75, [1994] 2 WLR 556 the House of Lords declared certain acts of sexual sado-masochism to be outside of the boundaries of law. For a critique of this judgement see E.Edwards, No Defence for a Sado-Masochistic Libido, *NLJ*, 1993, 143, 552.
[51]Confirmed in Brown on this point.

underlying rationale for this being that it is a measure freely chosen in the belief that it will improve personal well-being.[52] Contrastingly, under The Prohibition of Female Circumcision Act 1985, mutilation of the clitoris, labia etc. are illegal; such interventions are psychologically as well as physiologically harmful in that they are designed to reduce sexual pleasure. They also often take place in a context of coercion or undue influence.

Approaches to the Treatment of Organ Disease/Failure

An essential context to understanding the ethical and legal issues in LDT is to understand what the alternative approaches to addressing organ disease and organ failure are both within and outside reductionistic medicine.

The Development of Transplantation and Criticisms of it

In the 19th century the idea of transplanting organs from one living creature to another was a science fiction but early in the 20th century scientists began experimentally taking an organ out of one animal and placing it in another.[53] In Ukraine in 1933 the first kidney transplant from one human to another (allograft) was undertaken. Like the animal to animal grafts it quickly stopped functioning.[54]

Although scientists were able to develop corneal transplantation and make it routine by the 1940s[55] it is probably fair to say that most of them were disheartened about the prospects for other forms of organ transplantation. One scientist had suggested as early as 1909 that there was a 'biochemical barrier' to their success.[56] However, scientists in Boston US achieved the first long term allograft survival from a living donor transplant with the use of identical twins in 1947.[57] A few years

---

[52][1970] 2 All ER 33 at 43.

[53]Ullmann claimed the earliest attempt with kidneys in 1902 (*Ann.Surg*, 1914, 60, 195-219), Jaboulay has the first recorded attempts (*Lyon M/ed*, 1906, 107, 575-577).

[54]D.Hamilton, A History of Transplantation, in P.J.Morris (ed.), Kidney Transplantation, 1988 at p4.

[55]Anon., *New Scientist,* 1989, 25. Corneal transplantation had begun in 1905.

[56]Unger, *Berl.Klin.Wschr*, 1909, 1, 1057-60.

[57]1954, Boston. See J.Murray et al., Successful Homotransplantation Between Identical Twins, *Surg Forum*, 1955, 6, 432.

later the first non-identical twin donor-recipient pair were operated on with successful graft survival.[58] The success of these allografts in terms of graft survival was an early indication that the biochemical barrier was a natural bodily tendency to reject foreign material, which could be side-stepped where the transplant was between persons of matched genetic material. With identical matches being rare, it was obvious that a passkey to widespread use of organ transplantation was the development of a successful means of suppressing the natural immunological response.

Early attempts at immunosuppression were crude. In some cases they were ethically dubious, such as the administration of sub-lethal doses of whole body irradiation, they were highly dangerous experiments that achieved only modest benefit. However, sounder methods were gradually evolved and in 1983 there was a big leap forward with the advent of use of an immunosuppressive drug called cyclosporine. Cyclosporine, used on its own or in combination with other immunosupressants, enabled the beginning of an era where reasonably long graft survival became the norm in many forms of transplantation; renal transplants were lasting a decade by the 1990s.

In the context of reductionistic medicine, the ability to undertake large numbers of transplants with reasonable graft survival rates has been something of a revolution; for many patients it is the only reductionistic treatment that could keep them alive. For end stage renal failure patients dialysis is usually available but it is normally used as a stopgap until a kidney transplant becomes available. Renal transplantation is about a third of the cost of dialysis[59] and it has much better quality of life prospects, including better health, more convenience and more likelihood of letting one work relatively unhindered. Quality Adjusted Life Year estimates have confirmed this conclusion[60] whist cost benefit analyses by De Charro[61] and Spital[62] have specifically confirmed the general superiority of

---

[58]J.P.Merrill et al., Successful Homotransplantation of the Kidney Between Non-Identical Twins, *N.Engl.J.Med,* 1960, 262, 1251.

[59]*The Sunday Times* 1995, 30 July. There will of course be variation depending on the type of dialysis used.

[60]See commentary on A.Maynards use of the Rosser Valuation Matrix in comparing transplantation with dialysis in R.West, Organ Transplantation, *Office of Health Economics*, 1991, 26.

[61]Rotterdam Symposium (transcript held at the EUROTOLD project).

[62]R.Spital, M.Spital and A.Spital, The Donor's Decision in Renal Transplantation: A Cost Benefit Analysis, *Am J Kid Dis*, 1987, IX(5 May), 396-403.

LDT over dialysis. However, the broader question is why use reductionistic treatment of organ disease and not holistic ones or why not use both?

Reductionistic medicine has commonly been associated with a great deal of benefits but its use has also been heavily criticised. Ivan Illich, in his landmark book *Limits to Medicine: Medical Nemesis and the Expropriation of Health*, paints a picture of its use encroaching on autonomy and even producing clinical damage outweighing its benefits.[63] It has also been noted that the Newtonian-Descartes paradigm of science has been superseded by a new paradigm which, it has been argued, is inconsistent with the use of reductionism[64] and consistent with a holistic approach.[65] This point is really too broad to explore in detail in this book. However, as a context to examining reductionistic approaches to organ disease, it is important to outline the potential relevance of a holistic approach.

About 70-90% of medical practice worldwide is organised outside the reductionist paradigm of thought.[66] In Western Europe and North America reductionism has been the twentieth century medical orthodoxy but support for largely holistic alternatives to this orthodoxy has grown in the last few decades. For instance, by 1990, US inhabitants were spending $13.7 billion on alternative healthcare and were making more visits to alternative providers (425 million) than to family physicians and internists (388 million).[67] A more recent study found that about 50% of those who are family practice patients in the US still also use alternative providers.[68]

Most of the traditional systems of holistic medicine (e.g. Chinese, Tibetan and Ayurvedic medicine) and some of the more recently developed or expanded holistic approaches (e.g. homeopathy, chiropractic) are based on clearly elucidated principles and have been subject to extensive testing for efficacy. In some cases, this testing has even accorded with reductionist approaches to medical research (e.g. use of the randomised clinical trial). As far as organ disease is concerned, reductionist treatments

---

[63]Limits to Medicine, *Penguin*, 1977 at pp13-16.
[64]L.Dossey, Space, Time and Medicine, *Shambala*, 1982.
[65]Rychlak, The Psychology of Rigorous Humanism, *Wiley,* 1977 at 193.
[66]Chantilly Report, XV.
[67]David Eisenberg et al., Unconventional Medicine in the United States: Prevalence, Costs and Patterns of Use, 328:4, *N Engl J Med*, 1993, 246.
[68]N.C.Elder et al., Use of Alternative Health Care by Family, 1997 (Mar-Apr), *Arch Fam Med*, 6, 181.

do not claim to have a curative answer to most serious forms of organ disease. Even if a holistic approach only cured or delayed the need for dialysis and/or transplantation in a minority of cases it could: benefit that minority's quality of life;[69] benefit the remaining majority by reducing scarcity-pressures on transplantation and dialysis; *and*, finally, reduce health care costs.

As far as the legal aspects of treatment choice for organ disease are concerned, many legislative regimes refer to the need for transplantation to be therapeutic if it is to be used.[70] Examples of a more stringent approach include: the Russian Federation[71] and Belarus[72] where organs and tissues can only be transplanted if other medical procedures cannot safeguard life or restore health; Ecuador where transplantation can only be used where it is the sole means of prolonging or improving his life;[73] *and* Algeria where it can only be used if it is the sole means of preserving life or physical integrity.[74] It is highly unlikely that these requirements, or the duty of care of the medical professional within the tort of negligence, would be interpreted in such a way as to impose liability for failure to use a holistic treatment for organ disease or even failure to discuss holistic options. However, the medical profession might better serve its patients if it had greater knowledge and understanding of possibilities for holistic treatment.

Organ Shortages and their Significance

Technical developments in transplantation have continued to move it forward in the 1980s and 1990s. However, after the introduction of cyclosporine revolutionised graft survival rates, the main issue in many forms of organ donation has been one of procuring sufficient organs to

[69]During my investigation I was informed of a case that neatly illustrates this point. A woman in her early twenties had gone to hospital with kidney disease and been told that she would soon need to be on dialysis and then receive a transplant. Strongly disconcerted by this she went to visit a herbalist who advised her on diet and gave her a course of herbs. After taking this uncostly, and relatively uninvasive course of action, her kidney disease disappeared within a period of months and, taking care of her diet, she has remained well for many years since.

[70]E.g. Bolivia Law of 15 March 1982 at section 1, India Act No. 42 of 1994 at section 3.

[71]Law of 22 December 1992 at section 1.

[72]Section 4.

[73]Law No. 64 of 26 May 1987 at section 2.

[74]Law No. 85-05 of 16 February 1985 at section 166.

meet the demand for them.

A few second and third world countries with reductionistic systems for the treatment of organ disease have developed transplantation to a modest degree but many conduct little or no transplantation. In such cases the levels of deaths that could have been prevented by a better programme is high and there are increased possibilities of patients buying an organ on the black market with its associated health risks. Obviously some renal patients can be maintained on dialysis in the hope that a suitable organ will turn up but many of these countries have insufficiency funding to offer dialysis to all kidney patients who need it. In some cases insufficient funding can also lead to less than ideal equipment, which in the worst case scenario will compromise safety and quality.[75]

When it comes to first world countries rates of transplantation are typically far higher. However, the supply of organs has generally not been able to meet demand. As early as 1989, G.Koostra et al., found that in Western Europe less than half of those persons deemed suitable for organ transplant therapy are transplanted.[76] In the 1990s the waiting lists for almost all types of organ transplant has increased in the US and Western European countries.[77]

The main form of transplantation with living and dead donors is of kidneys and the number of people waiting for a kidney worldwide now stands at around 40,000.[78] Eire managed to reduce its waiting list by 11% from 1997-1998 having reduced it 3% in the year before. Eire has consistently kept pace with demand over a period of years as, more or less, have Austria, Norway, Portugal and Spain. However, in order to achieve this they have maintained kidney transplant rates of around 40 per million population or above. Even this level of transplantation has proven insufficient to meet demand in some countries, such as the US and Belgium. It must also be noted that more people would validly go on the

---

[75]For example, in Romania there is insufficient money to buy the machinery necessary to meet best practice in ensuring prospective living donors are in a fit and healthy state to donate. This has been a major reason behind the rare use of LDT in Romania (Statement of Professor Proca, Bucharest Centre, at a EUROTOLD meeting in 1996).

[76]*Trans Proc*, 1989, 20, 809.

[77]See Council of Europe, Transplant Newsletter, 1996.

[78]B.Miranda, R.Matesanz, International Issues in Transplantation. Setting the Scene and Flagging the Most Urgent and Controversial Issues, *Annals of New York Academy of Science,* 1998, 862, 129-143.

waiting lists in most countries were it not for the shortage demanding a more clinically selective approach. The combined procurement rate of Western Europe plus the Czech Republic, Poland, Cyprus and Hungary was 29.4 per million population in 1997. In Australia and New Zealand it was 26 per million population and in Canada 32.9.[79] The limitations of these rates are clear when one takes into account that similar rates have not been able to prevent year on year increases in waiting lists.

The problem is worse when one takes into account the progressive rates of incidence, or at least diagnosis, of end stage renal failure. The statistical projection in the United States is that the number of patients on dialysis with end stage renal disease will increase from its current level of 200,000 by a rate of 7-9% per year to more than 350,000 patients by the year 2010.[80] The message is clearly that even those countries who can currently meet demand will need to re-evaluate their approach to see if extensive increases in transplants per million population can be brought. At the same time this must not be counterproductive either in terms of accepting organs of a drastically lower quality or in breaching the requirements of ethics.

Improving Cadaveric Procurement

Eire is an example of a small close-knit country that has managed to meet the need for kidneys almost entirely through reliance on cadaveric organs. Spain is the only larger country to have done so and this is partly attributable its high levels of road traffic deaths. However, some of its success may be attributable to taking a very localised approach to transplant procurement and co-ordination.[81] There are possibilities that features of its approach could be adopted elsewhere with a beneficial impact on procurement. In the US evidence has for some years pointed toward a more localised approach to co-ordination, procurement and allocation having benefits.[82]

---

[79]ITCS World Transplant Statistics.

[80]Ad Hoc Committee on Nephrology Manpower Needs. Estimating Workforce and Training Requirements for Nephrologists Through the Year 2010, *J Am Soc Nephrol*, 1997, 8(9), 1-32.

[81]See *Lancet*, 1998, 351, 1868. For a commentary on the Spanish approach see B.Miranda et al., Integrated Ways to Improve Cadaveric Organ Donation, *Trans Proc*, 28(1), 1996, 96-97.

[82]F.Rapaport et al., July 1990 Report of the United Network for Organ Sharing, *Trans Proc*, 1991, 23, 899-900.

The BTS 1995 Working Party Report, after examining the Spanish model, concluded that,

> (d)evelopment of the UK co-ordinator network should undoubtedly be a central element in the drive to increase organ donation.[83]

Countries with low population densities tend to have lower cadaveric procurement because as the authors of the Kings Fund Research Report state,

> In general, the less densely populated a country the longer the average distance between hospitals, transplant centres, and those suffering from a cerebrovascular accident. All these factors will make it harder to reach and transport patients to ICU, and more difficult and time consuming to collect and transport organs without affecting their suitability.[84]

It may be that over time improvements in transportation can be made with some positive knock-on impact on procurement. A more immediate way in which cadaveric procurement can be improved is by ensuring sufficient availability of ICU support and beds. In the UK, for example, there have been many cases where competition for beds has led to a practitioner withdrawing or not instituting ventilatory or haemodynamic support, which can lead to potential donors failing to become actual donors.[85] Whatever the cost of making the necessary improvements in ICU beds and support it is likely to be recouped through the saving generated from lesser reliance on dialysis. Most countries do not remove organs from a deceased person without the consent of relatives (see below). Perhaps up to 10% of organs are lost by the failure to ask relatives in times.[86] This could be avoided either by making it a routine policy to ask or making it law to do so.

---

[83]BTS, 1995, p30.

[84]B.New et al., Kings Fund Research Report, 18 at p28. Comparing 17 countries, the Kings Fund Report indicated that five of the bottom six cadaver procurement nations also corresponded to the lowest population density nations. These five were Finland, Sweden, Norway, Australia and Canada with the exception being the United Kingdom.

[85]See S.M.Gore, Intensive Care Unit Funding: Survey of Staffing and Bed Occupancy in November 1989, *Care of The Critically Ill*, 1991, 8, 79-80.

[86]S.M.Gore et al., Organ Donation From Intensive Care units in England and Wales: A two year Confidential Audit of Deaths in Intensive Care, *BMJ*, 1992, 304, 349-355.

Evidence suggests that relatives refuse to allow the deceased's organs to be used in around 15-30% of cases.[87] Relatives are not always happy about the way they are approached. Cleiren's study found the following 'complaints':

- Procedure too hasty, there was no time to think it over;
- Doctor was too businesslike, showed no emotion;
- Not enough information was given;
- There was neither opportunity nor time enough to say the last 'good-bye' to the deceased;
- Consent was asked at the wrong moment (before the death was confirmed or at the same time that the family was informed of the death of the relative);
- Family felt pressured by request for organs; *and*
- After consent was given there was a second request for more organs.[88]

Obviously some people will never be happy about the way that they are asked but as well as these complaints it is evident that professionals are often uncomfortable about approaching relatives.[89] Greater training in this area might make professionals more confident and this might have a knock-on effect in increasing the numbers of positive responses. Nonetheless, it is also likely that some relatives will not offer however they are asked because they know of objection on the part of the deceased or themselves consider donation to be inappropriate. It must be remembered in this light that around 15% of people have indicated in public surveys they are against donating their own organs after death,[90] with about half of this number saying they would not even accept a transplant for themselves.[91] Some people strongly object to organ transplantation as an approach to medicine on scientific, spiritual or religious grounds.[92]

---

[87]Ibid.

[88]M.P.H.D.Cleiren, Life After Giving. A Research Into the Experience of the Next of Kin of the Organ and/or Tissue Donor, *D.S.W.O. Press,* 1992.

[89]See e.g. survey of 10% of US neurosurgeons by J.M.Prottas and H.L.Batten, Neurosurgeons and The Supply of Human Organs, *Health Affairs*, 1989, 119-131.

[90]1992 surveys by OPCS, RSGB and Gallop Poll. The combined results of these 3 major surveys indicates that around 70% of people are in favour of donating their organs at death with about half of the remainder neutral or undecided.

[91]For instance reservations about the medico-legal method of establishing death were 7% in an OPCS survey and 5% in a survey conducted by Wakeford and Stepney, *Br J Surg,* 1989, 76(5), 435-439.

[92]See Kostakis et al., *Trans Proc*, 1990, 22, 1432-1433.

The above measures could play a significant 'bit part' in dealing with organ shortages but other measures will be required to fill the major role. One of the ethically more controversial approaches would be to breach the right of living persons to have their body left inviolate upon their death. The most extreme example of this would be to conscript the organs from the body *even if* the person specifically objected to this outcome when they were alive. This only occurs in countries like Iraq and China and in these cases only for executed prisoners. The next most extreme position is to conscript the organs *unless* the person specifically objected to this outcome when they were alive. This is legally allowed and often occurs in Austria.[93] A more common approach as a matter of law[94] or practice[95] is to also ask the relatives of the person and allow them to prevent the organs being extracted or to do so if the person didn't make it clear during his life that (s)he wanted to donate, as in Belgium.[96]

These last two approaches operate according to what is often called 'presumed consent' or 'opting-out' where consent or agreement to removal is presumed in the absence of evidence to the contrary. 'Presuming consent' can result in more organs being procured than a system based on the agreement of relatives - often called 'broad opting-in'. However, if relatives are going to be asked anyway then presumption of consent is only useful in procurement terms in so far as one can automatically take the organs of people who die without having any relatives or at least any contactable relatives. In addition, given that surveys typically show that around half of the public oppose presumed consent[97] there is a danger that it would alienate a significant section of the public to introduce it and have counterproductive consequences for procurement. So far the evidence from countries with presumed consent systems does not support this conclusion but neither does it support the view that the effect of presumed

---

[93]Conference of European Health Ministers (1987), Current legislation in Council of Europe Member states and Finland and Results of European Co-operation, Council of Europe Strasbourg.

[94]Including France (see J.Hors et al., France Transplant in R.Matesanz et al. (eds.) *Transplant,* 4 - Produced with the Council of Europe, Paris) and Spain (see R.Matesanz and B.Miranda (1992) Organizacion Nacional de Transplantes, in R.Matesanz et al. (eds.), *Transplant* ibid).

[95]E.g. Greece, Italy and Spain.

[96]See P.Michelson, Effect of Transplantation Laws on Organ Procurement in J.L.Touraine (ed.), Organ Shortage the Solutions, *Kluwer*, 1995, 34-39 at 39).

[97]See Kings Fund Research Report, 18 at p43.

consent on procurement will be dramatic.[98] The International Forum for Transplant Ethics in its recent article *The Case For 'Presumed Consent' in Organ Donation* takes the approach that,

> ...the onus is on those who oppose it (opting out) to demonstrate that the benefit that flows from it is outweighed by the harm.[99]

At the time of writing, this approach of viewing the ethics of 'presumed consent' as simply a matter of determining whether it has utility appears to have led the BMA to support it. The ethical flaw of this way of thinking is that a utilitarian need for organs doesn't suddenly make it acceptable to desecrate a dead person's body and use it for transplantation simply because they have failed to object to this when they are alive. There is also no such thing as 'presumed consent' in philosophical or legal terms. One implicitly or explicitly consents or one doesn't consent at all. Consent to organ donation cannot be implied simply from absence of refusal because studies have shown that there is a large percentage of people who do not consider themselves to be organ donors. Indeed, recent studies in USA[100] and Holland[101] indicate only 36% and 38% of people respectively claim to be potential organ donors. The only ethically acceptable system is one which respects rights. Many countries broadly accept this principle by having what are called broad opting-in systems[102] but the problem with these is that relatives can agree to removal or non-removal instead of the decision being purely determined by evidence of the will of the deceased.

---

[98]The Kings Fund Research Report, 18, 58-59 states that, 'the evidence suggests that the introduction of presumed consent in Belgium had a significant impact on the availability of organs...the evidence from Singapore adds to that of Belgium as to the efficacy of presumed consent legislation'. However, John Fabre of the British Transplant Society persuasively shows how the increases in CDT in Belgium merely equate roughly to those in the UK and Eire when differences in road traffic death rates have been factored in (See Organ Donation and Presumed Consent, *The Lancet*, 1998, 352 (July 11) at 150).

[99]*The Lancet*, 1998, 351(May 30), 1650-1652, 1650.

[100]D.S.Kittur et al. Incentives for Organ Donation, *The Lancet, 1991,* 338, 1441-1443.

[101]W.Kokkedee, Kidney Procurement Policies In the Eurotransplant Region: 'Opting in' Versus 'Opting Out', *Social Science and Medicine,* 1992, 35(2), 177-182.

[102]Countries with broad opting-in include the UK, Eire, United States, Holland, Germany, Canada, New Zealand and Australia.

An alternative approach to 'presumed consent' is to force people to express a view. Under the 'confirmed opinion and forced commitment' system devised by G.Pennings[103] all persons would have to register their wishes regarding disposal of their body after death, but as well as registering 'yes' or 'no' they could register 'cannot answer the question'. This system might increase numbers of people registering as donors. Within it, the will of the deceased could be treated as final because,

> ...allowing the next-of-kin to object to a donation would come down to treating a person's altruistic desires as suspect, as something which has to be corroborated by others'.[104]

Treating the deceased will as final would turn increased registration into increased harvesting. However, if relatives continued to have 'the last say', the system might still turn increased registration into increased harvesting in that relative refusal would be less likely in the event of the deceased will to donate having been clearly registered.

Pennings' system, involves the deontological notion that people have a social duty to undertake a certain act, in this case registration in relation to transplantation. Rather like systems of compulsory electoral registration, it involves compelling people to undertake this 'duty'. However, utility is treated as the overarching principle just as it is in 'opting out' systems, albeit here the infringement of rights is more minor. The contention might be rightly made that one should perform certain duties to others within society if one is to reap the benefits but the action consistent with rights that follows this is not to force an act but to withdraw the benefits of organ transplantation from those competent adults who do not make a positive choice to bequeath organs within a reasonable period of time.

99% of cadaveric kidneys come from donors whose hearts are beating but are brain dead.[105] However, similar graft survival results can be obtained from using donors whose hearts have stopped but who have not yet reached brain stem death.[106] Some transplant centres are utilising non-

---

[103]Ch22 in Organ and Tissue Transplantation in the European Union: Management of Difficulties and Health Risks Linked to Donors, Y.Englert (ed), *Martinus Nijhoff,* 1995, Ch22.

[104]See note 103.

[105]Cho et al., Transplantation of Kidneys From Donors Whose Hearts Have Stopped Beating, *New Engl J Med*, 1998, 338(4), 221-225.

[106]Ibid.

heart beating donors (NHBDs) extensively with the effect of increasing their cadaveric procurement by between 25 and 40%[107] and occasionally upwards of this.[108] However, there are serious ethical and legal concerns about using such donors.[109]

One method for using NHBDs involves inserting a catheter tube through the groin area of the deceased into the cadaver, by which means the kidney can be chilled in situ as a stop-gap measure to maintain the organ until relatives are available to offer consent (or refusal) to removal of organs. Another is the University of Pittsburgh Medical Center protocol. Under the protocol, where consent is given, patients with profound brain damage are removed from ventilatory support after 2 minutes of 'irreversible' loss of cardiac function and after they die their organs are removed.

Both methods treat the patient as a means to an end unless their is clear evidence (such as in a living will) that they accord with his/her will. The consent of relatives is both ethically and legally insufficient in such cases since neither procedure can be described in the patients best interests. As far as the Pittsburgh protocol is concerned, in most countries the law doesn't recognise a person as dead until brain stem criteria are met. Without the patients consent, removing ventilatory support for expedient purposes before brain stem death would probably be construed as unlawful killing. It has been suggested that the removal of ventilatory support is acceptable under the Pittsburgh protocol because the patient is for all practical purposes dead or about to die. However, against this, it can be argued that 2 minutes of loss of cardiac function is not proof of irreversibility. Changing, or making exceptions to, legal criteria for death simply in order to harvest more organs cannot be defended. Hence, unless

---

[107] R.Schlumpf et al., Transplantation of Kidneys From Non-Heart-Beating Donors: Protocol, Cardiac Death Diagnosis and Results, *Trans Proc*, 1996, 28(1), 107-100; G.Kootstra et al., Twenty Per Cent More Kidneys Through a Non-Heart Beating Programme, *Trans Proc,* 1991, 23, 910-911 and Daeman et al.'s more recent study at Koostra's Maastricht centre which indicated that a non-heart beating programme contributes 40% (J.H.C.Daeman, Non Heart-Beating Donor Program Contributes 40% of Kidneys For Transplantation, *Trans Proc*, 1996, 28(1), 105-106).

[108] Cho et al., Transplantation of Kidneys From Donors Whose Hearts Have Stopped Beating, *New Engl J Med*, 1998, 338(4), 221-225.

[109] For analysis see F.Th.De Charro et al., Donor Recruitment in Europe, in F.Th.De Charro et al., Systems of Donor Recruitment, *Kluwer,* 1992, 5 *and* DPT Price, Organ Transplant Initiatives: The Twilight Zone, *J Med Eth*, 1997, 23, 170-175.

the debate is clearly resolved in favour of two minutes loss of cardiac function constituting death *and* this resolution is reflected in reformed law, the Protocol should only be used with patient consent. For present purposes this consent would constitute an agreement to allow one's death to take place more hastily than it would have done had ventilatory support continued. However, this should not fall foul of restrictions on euthanasia since it is simply the exercise of the ethical and legal right to refuse life-sustaining treatment.

Another method of increasing cadaveric procurement that raises ethical issues is elective ventilation. The Royal Devon and Exeter Hospital was the first British hospital to develop an elective ventilation protocol.[110] This involved, with relatives' consent, transferring patients in deep irreversible coma and believed to be dying imminently of intracranial haemorrhage to intensive care, so that artificial ventilation could be commenced immediately respiratory arrest occurred and until brain stem death tests could be satisfied. The organ procurement result was evaluated as a 50% increase in organs over a four year period.[111] The number of donors used was not statistically significant[112] but it is fair to say that,

> Elective ventilation has provided initial evidence of a substantial impact on donation rates; implementation of this procedure is recommended if legal and ethical questions relating to the interests of the potential donor can be resolved.[113]

Ethical objections to EV include the possibility that it might increase the number of patients in a persistent vegetative state (PVS), the view that prolonging death is unacceptable[114] and the view that scouting around an ICU unit for organs offends the dignity of the dying process.[115] These objections are exacerbated or diminished depending on whether or not the patient has given advance agreement to EV. Advance agreement removes the *ethical* objection to the fact that the procedure is not in the patients best

---

[110]T.Feest et al., Protocol for Increasing Organ Donation After Cerebrovascular Deaths in a District General Hospital, *Lancet,* 1990, 335, 1133-1135.

[111]B.New et al., Kings Fund Research Report, 18 at p55.

[112]G.Routh, Elective Ventilation For Organ Donation - The Case Against, *Care of The Critically Ill,* 1992, 8, 60-61.

[113]B.New et al., Kings Fund Research Report, 18 at p8.

[114]G.R.Park et al., Organ donation (letter) *BMJ,* 1993, 306, 145.

[115]See D.Bihari's quote in the Kings Funds Research Report, 18 at p65.

interests but whether it removes the *legal* objection is a different matter. In jurisdictions where such advance agreements do not constitute legal consent practitioners must act in the best interests of the incompetent patient. EV simply to facilitate the successful removal of the patient's organs would be against the patient's best interests and constitute battery as noted by the Health Departments of England and Wales in guidelines of October 1994.[116] As yet there is no sign that the government will take up the BTS's call for legalisation.[117]

Artificial Organs, Cloning and Xenotransplantation

One strategy for addressing organ shortages is to wait until developing supply technologies such as artificial organs, cloning and xenotransplantation come into use. The problem with such an approach as regards artificial organs is that technical development is being plagued with problems.[118] The technology is likely to take several years to develop as is the development of a cloned complex solid organ.[119] It is xenotransplantation upon which most of the hopes of the near future have been pinned. Transplantations with organs from 'mutagenic/transgenic' pigs and from higher primates have already been conducted in experimental fashion between animal species.[120] Technical developments in this area are happening with remarkable speed. The potential use of xenotransplantation has been the subject of two major recent reports in the UK which have taken a broadly positive approach to it.[121] However, with

---

[116]A.Somerville, Medical Ethics Today: Its Practice and Philosophy, *BMA*, 1993). PIVOT (the potential of elective ventilation for organ transplantation) study was proposed to examine issues in EV but was abandoned due to the questionable legality of EV (See B.New et al., Kings Fund Research Report, 18 at 56).

[117]Report of the BTS Working Party on Organ Transplantation, *BTS*, 1995 at p32.

[118]R.A.Rettig, Artificial Kidneys and Artificial Hearts, *Southern California Law Review*, 1991, 65, 503-28.

[119]For a debate on the legal and ethical issues see *New Engl J Med*, 1998, 339(2) at 119-136. Transplantation of a cloned hand occurred for the first time in 1998.

[120]Studies have suggested that non-human primate kidneys could function normally in a human and sustain life for as long as 9 months (see e.g. D.K.C.Cooper et al. (eds.), Xenotransplantation: The Transplantation of Organs Between Species, *Springer Verlag*, 1991.

[121]Animal-to-Human Transplants: The Ethics of Xenotransplantation, *Nuffield Council on Bioethics*, 1996; *and* A Report by the Advisory Group on the Ethics of Xenotransplantation, *Department of Health*, 1997.

the continued problem in overcoming immunological rejection, it is by no means certain when, or even if, animal-human transplants would achieve reasonable graft survival rates. In addition, xenotransplantation raises serious ethical concerns, some of which are doubtless reflected in the generally negative public perception of it.[122]

One public health concern is that there is the real risk of pathogens being transmitted, such as those capable of infecting foetuses congenitally or transmitted in the germline.[123] However, much more serious than this is the possibility of cross species transmission of endogenous retroviruses.[124] Stoye has illustrated that a long chain of events would have to take place for these viruses to pose a public health threat. He notes that some evidence points towards the viruses having a low level of infectivity but also points out that some people will oppose clinical trials because if infection in humans were to occur the risk would be unacceptably large.[125] Indeed the worst case scenario would be a pandemic and there are perhaps lessons to be learned from the recent fiascoes in the farming industry (particularly BSE) about the dangers of insufficiently protecting consumers. Calls for immediate experimental trials of animal to human transplants must in the light of public health concerns alone be considered excessively risky or even foolhardy.

Beyond public health concerns, xenotransplantation also raises the fundamental ethical issue of whether it is acceptable to control and end an animal life in order to benefit a human one. Fox and McHale[126] have rightly argued that this issue was underplayed in the Nuffield and Department of Health Reports. They note the bias that can stem from conceptualising the issue of xenotransplantation primarily within the terms of the organ shortage. Western reductionistic medicine is biased towards using animals towards human medical ends, being distinct from most holistic traditions which use animals to such ends much more scarcely and in some systems not at all. Xenotransplantation itself, obviously only

[122]Dr Ben Mepham, Centre for Applied Bioethics, University of Nottingham has noted that only 36% of Europeans thought xenotransplantation was morally acceptable according to a Eurobarometer survey.
[123]Jonathon Stoye, No Clear Answers on safety of pigs as tissue donor source, *The Lancet*, 1998, 352, Aug 29, 666-667 at 666.
[124]Ibid at 667.
[125]Ibid.
[126]Xenotransplantation: The Ethical and Legal Ramifications, *Medical Law Review*, 1998, Spring (6), 42-61 at 44.

exists relative to the use of reductionistic medicine and a rational approach would be to examine holistic medicine as a means of organ disease cure and prevention if only to accomplish a minimisation of the interference with life that xenotransplantation involves both in terms of mutagenics and killing. Irrespective of the relevancy of a holistic approach to organ disease, it has been cogently argued that animals have rights as ends in themselves.[127] To suggest that xenotransplantation is unjustifiable one does not have to accept that these rights are equal to those of humans but merely that they are sufficient to warrant non-interference or simply that they are sufficient to warrant other methods of meeting the organ shortfall, such as increased use of consenting living donors, being more acceptable.

LDT

From the supply perspective clearly some improvements can be generated from making cadaveric procurement more efficient and by using NHBD by catheter insertion where there is the prior evidenced agreement of the potential donor. However, in most countries these improvements would be unlikely to stem the growth of waiting lists let alone diminish them so we are left with the possibility of expanding upon the current use of LDT.

Current use of LDT varies markedly between countries and even between individual centres. Countries like Eire, Portugal and Spain typically have an annual rate of LDT of less than 1 per million population as do most of the countries of the former Central and Eastern European Bloc. Western European countries like Belgium, Germany, France, Italy, Austria and the UK have moderate rates of under 5 per million population.

Only a few countries in the world have higher rates. In 1997 The Netherlands did 5.8 LDTs per million population (p.m.p.), Australia and New Zealand did 6.2 p.m.p., Switzerland 7.6 p.m.p., Greece 7.8 p.m.p., Denmark 8.7 p.m.p., Canada 9.5 p.m.p., USA 13.2 p.m.p., Sweden 13.8 p.m.p. and, as usual, Norway topped the list with 15.5 LDTs per million population.[128] Norway has achieved an annual rate of LDT in excess of 15 p.m.p. for many years. The obvious possibility is that countries which are

---

[127]For a discussion of this in the Xenotransplantation context see A.Hutchinson and P.Singer, 'Xenotransplantation: is it ethically defensible?', *Xeno*, 1995, 3, 58 at 59. For a favourable view of the ethics of xenotransplantation see A.L.Caplan, Is Xenografting Wrong?, *Trans Proc,* 1992, 24(2), 722-727.

[128]ITCS World Transplant Statistics.

not keeping pace with the demand for kidneys might practicably be able to lift their LDTs to a similar level if necessary. One of the main tasks of chapter 2 will be to examine the ethical and legal implications of using LDT in different contexts. Before this, it is important to examine the more fundamental question of whether LDT use in general can be acceptable from an ethical and legal standpoint

A basic fact about LDT is that is causes physiologically maleficence to the donor. The fact that organ removal constitutes grievous bodily harm has been used historically to contend that it might be unlawful unless done for therapeutic reasons.[129] Removal for the purposes of donation, whilst it can be a psychologically beneficial experience, is not a treatment. A clear distinction must be made between interventions which are therapeutic because psychological benefit is direct, as in the case of a sex change operation, and interventions which are non-therapeutic because they are designed for the benefit of other(s) and one's own psychological benefit can only stem vicariously from that fact. Non-therapeutic research falls into this latter category as well as living donation. However, in legal terms maleficent, non-therapeutic interventions can be perfectly acceptable under the general law. Whilst if someone is giving consent on behalf of the donor the donation must be in his own best interests, in cases where the donor has given his own consent it will be within the limits of what can be consented to for the purposes of the general law if it is 'reasonable'.

The test of reasonableness will obviously exclude certain types of organ donation as too maleficent (e.g. donating a whole vital organ). However, donation of some organs - such as kidney, liver segment and even lung lobe - is generally not too maleficent. The focus of reasonableness in donations that are not too maleficent is on their being sufficient rationale for the removal under the specific circumstances.

General law has long accepted that there can be sufficient rationale for wanting to assist or rescue another person even if it subjects one to a certain amount of harm and/or jeopardy. In some contexts judges have gone out of their way to praise rescuers and offer them legal protection.[130]

---

[129]See Bar Council Report of Organ Transplants, *BMJ,* 1971 (September), 716.

[130]See for instance Haynes v Harwood [1935] 1 KB 146 (CA) duty of care owed to the rescuer by person being rescued where rescue might reasonably have been foreseen. Videan v British Transport Commission [1963] 2 QB 650, [1963] 2 All ER 860 (CA) duty of care owed to a stationmaster rescuing his small son who had been trespassing on the lines.

The former law of former Czechoslovakia stated that donors should receive a badge and some food for their efforts! No law before or since has been quite so eloquent in recognising the value of living donation but equally neither has its general value ever been legally questioned. Instead, for the purposes of ethics and legality, the focus is on ensuring that acts of donation are limited to justifiable circumstances. Normally this will mean that the donation should be justified and better than any other options bearing in mind the prospective detriment of donating and the benefit of receiving. Living kidney donation generally involves a low level of maleficence to the donor and can have significant benefits to the recipient. It can be reasonable to use it in preference to CDT under certain circumstances because graft survival can be sufficiently superior to offset the maleficence to the donor. Under conditions of organ shortage it will often be easy to justify using it in preference to the prospective recipient having to wait on dialysis for a suitable cadaver to turn up. Firstly, there is the deterioration of quality of life and health that can be expected whilst waiting on dialysis, at least if over a significant period. Secondly, there is the possibility that a suitable CDT might not turn up in time, which has led clinicians like Weiland et al., to say they,

> ...would continue to use living-related donors even if the results of cadaveric and LRD transplantation were equivalent, otherwise, ESRD patients would be denied transplantation. [131]

As we shall see in the next chapter, there are also circumstances where living donation of liver segment and lung lobe can be justified.

Michielson's objection to LDT is based on his suggestion that informed consent is impossible because of the difficulty in assessing its risks.[132] However, in legal terms lack of certainty of risk is not per se a bar to valid consent.[133] In ethical terms the venture of rescuing often involves this kind of uncertainty but this does not make the rescuing act unacceptable.

---

[131]Information on 628 Living-Related Kidney Donors at Single Institution With Long Term Follow-Up in 472 Cases, *Trans Proc,* 1984, 16, 5-7.

[132]P.Michielson, Medical Risk and Benefit in Renal Donors: The Use of Living Donation Reconsidered, in W.Land and J.Dossetor (eds.), Organ Replacement Therapy: Ethics, Justice and Commerce, 1990, Springer-Verlag, 32-39.

[133]The Voluntarism and Informedness of Living Donors in Price and Akveld (eds.), Living Organ Donation in The Nineties: European Medico-Legal Perspectives, *EUROTOLD*, 1996, 98-115 at 99.

The other main objection that has been made to the use of LDT per se comes from Kreis who feels LDT should be avoided because hospitals can use it as a means of avoiding making a full effort to maintain and increase a cadaveric programme.[134] One can add that in countries with no CDT programme motivation to develop one could be reduced if LDT is being used. However, if this is a problem the appropriate response would seem to be to address lack of organisational motivation to reduce waiting lists rather than stop LDT.[135]

Kreis has also argued that the need for organs should be met from cadaveric donors because commercial trading in living donor organs is inescapable in countries promoting living donation.[136] The limitation with this argument is that even if one views trafficking as unacceptable there must be some balancing of the objective of stopping it with the objective of preserving all legitimate forms of donation.

The prima facie case at this point is that LDT can be ethically and legally acceptable. Consequently the remainder of the book is mainly focused on ethical and legal issues and preconditions concerning its use.

---

[134]Ibid at 1513. He quotes a study of Bart et al. (*Transplantation*, 1981, 31, 379) which discovered that potentially US kidney procurement could reach 110 p.m.p.

[135]Sometimes a demotivating factor can be the fact that the financial rewards in countries with private dialysis facilities are great. On this and broader questions of motivation see a comparison and analysis of Norwegian and French practices (with particular regard to LDT), Hilde Lorentzen and Florence Paterson, The Use of Living Donors For Kidney Transplants: Second Order and Third Order Decision Making, copy available from OSC, FNSP CNRS, 49 Rue de L'Universite 75007 Paris.

[136]*Trans Proc*, 1987, 27, 1510-1514 at 1513.

2 Beneficence and Maleficence

Introduction

This chapter looks at the maleficence (i.e. harm and jeopardy) involved in renal and other forms of living organ donation and the beneficence (i.e. benefits). It then moves to a consideration of when LDT use is ethically and legally legitimate in terms of maleficence and beneficence and in the light of alternative choices.

Beneficence of LDT to the Recipient

We have already established in chapter 1 that transplantation is in most cases preferable to dialysis, but when is LDT a better option than CDT for the recipient? As examined in chapter 4, the EUROTOLD recipient interview/questionnaires found 3 out 84 recipients who would not go through the whole process again and some recipients were concerned about issues like heavy side effects from drugs. However, concerns of these type tend to be also present in equal measure in the case of cadaveric donation. The big issue for the recipient is generally not a comparison of the downsides of different forms of transplantation but of the benefits.

Recipient Benefits from Renal LDT Versus Renal CDT

Extensive study by D.E.R.Sutherland et al., in the US, suggests that LDT produces considerably better results than cadaveric[137] and this conclusion is supported by research in Norway[138] and indeed by most clinicians.[139]

---

[137]*Trans Proc* 1985, 17, 1503 and *Trans Proc* 1985, 17, 110.

[138]A.Jakobsen, Living Renal Donors - The Norwegian Experience.

[139]See e.g. A.Jacobsen (ibid); Spital et al., The Living Kidney Donor: Alive and Well, *Arch Intern Med,* 1986, 146 at 1993; W.Bay and L.Herbert, The Living Donor in Kidney Transplantation, *Annals Intern Med,* 1987, 106, 719; H.Wilms, Indication for Living Donation in Kidney Transplants, *Trans Proc,* 1988, 20, 797; *and* V.Bonomini, Ethical Aspects of Living Donation, *Trans Proc,* 1991, 23, 2497.

One 1990 study was typical in finding that after 10 years 77% of grafts from LDTs were functioning as against 58% from CDTs.[140]

Graft survival rates can be affected by a number of factors, perhaps the most critical of which is the level of HLA match.[141] The degree of HLA match with CDTs is down to both any minimum requirement laid down by law or guidelines and to what organ(s) happen to turn up. Most LDTs are between nuclear genetic relatives and therefore have some HLA match. The largest source of living donors is parents who will have a 50% HLA match to their genetic offspring. The other main source is siblings who will be at least 25% matched. A 25% living donor match is likely to provide a better graft survival result than the average CDT in use today.

Figure 1: EUROTOLD's European Transplant Centre Questionnaire - HLA Match Policies

46% of responding centres with an LDT programme (when weighted by catchment population) had a centre policy of requiring a minimum HLA match. 80% - 81% (when weighted by catchment population) tissue type and cross-match all prospective donors that have an ABO blood match.

It is also possible for LDTs between unrelated persons (usually spouses) to have good graft survival rates.[142] Such LDTs are a significant

---

[140]R.Gabriel, A Patient's Guide to Dialysis and Transplantation, 4th Ed, 1990.

[141]Another factor is health which will often relate to age. Most transplant centres have a maximum age for transplantation between 60 and 80. However, from a clinical standpoint it is more rational to take the approach of the Oslo transplant centre of not having maximum age criteria and simply screening out patients who aren't sufficiently healthy. 20% of respondents to EUROTOLD's Transplant Centre Questionnaire had an age matching policy; some evidence suggests closeness of donor and recipient age helps graft survival - see P.K.Donnelly et al., Matching For Age in Renal Transplantation, *New Engl J Med*, 1990, 322(12), 851-852. For a contrasting view see Kostakis et al., *Trans Proc*, 1990, 22, 1432-1433).

[142]B.A.Elick et al., *Trans Proc,* 1990, 22, 343-344; P.Berloco et al.'s, *Trans Proc,* 1991, 23, 912-913; R.J.Ploeg et al., Living Unrelated Kidney Donation: An Under-utilised Resource?, *Trans Proc,* 1993, 25(1), 1532-4 at 1533; P.I.Terasaki et al., High Survival rates of Kidney Transplants From Spousal and Living Unrelated Donors, *New Eng J Med,* 1995, 333(6), 333-336; Alfani et al., Living Unrelated Kidney Transplantation: A 12-Year Single Centre Experience, *Trans Proc*, 1997, 29, 191-194 at 193.

minority of the total LDTs used since the 1960s.[143] Living unrelated may or may not be matched and just as with cadaveric donation it is possible by law or guidelines to impose a minimum standard.

If one compared CDTs with equally HLA matched LDTs the LDTs would probably produce significantly better graft survival results. This is due to a number of factors such as:

1. The fact that with LDT one can better plan and work-up the operation for the recipient and one can immunise him/her with the future donor's blood;
2. The fact that the future donor's kidney is likely to be in better general condition than that of a deceased person; *and*
3. Conducting a transplantation prior to dialysis has quality of life benefits and will optimise graft survival.[144] Conducting a transplantation shortly after dialysis has started has these benefits over conducting it much later.[145] Using LDT means one can exploit these advantages much better than one can if one is at the mercy of waiting for a suitable cadaveric organ to turn up. The longer the average waiting time for a cadaveric organ the more pronounced the superiority of LDT in this sense.

In practice many centres are more selective in terms of HLA match when using LDT than when using CDT.[146] On the one hand this makes statistical comparisons difficult but on the other if a centre chooses to be more selective with LDT it serves to amplify its graft superiority when used. In turn this makes its use more easily justifiable in the face of the fact that it will cause the donor some harm and jeopardy. However, if there is a

---

[143]H.H.Sadler et al., *Semin,* 1971, 3, 86.

[144]See P.K.Donnelly, Pre-Dialysis Living Donor Renal Transplantation - Is it Still the Gold Standard for Cost, Convenience and Graft Survival?, *Trans Proc*, 1995, 27(1).

[145]E.R.Maher et al., Mortality and Morbidity of Long Term Haemodialysis, *Lancet*, 1987, i, 452-453 and N.G.Kutner et al., End Stage Renal Disease Treatment Modality and Patient Quality of Life, *Am J Nephrol,* 1986, 6, 396-402.

[146]The number of centres attaching strong importance to HLA is clearly increasing while the number attaching no or little importance is decreasing and is now a fairly small minority (F.P.Brunner et al., Combined Report on Regular Dialysis and Transplantation in Europe, 1988, *Nephrol Dial Transplant,* 1989, 4 (supp 4), 5-29).

waiting list for cadaveric transplantation the benefits of a more immediate living donation might cancel out the rationale for requiring LDT to have superior HLA match. If the waiting period is likely to be significant there is a clear rationale to simply use the best living donor available, even if mismatched, if that accords with the wishes of the prospective donor and recipient. This is exactly what Norway has done and the results it has with mismatched LDTs are no worse to its average for CDTs as a whole.[147] In any case, most countries have massive scope for the expansion of their LDT programmes without even resorting to mismatched LDTs. Equally, if waiting lists are short there is still a justification for doing LDT selectivity where the prospective graft survival is considerably superior to that expected from an average CDT. If there is sufficiency of kidneys from cadaveric procurement, LDT ought still to be used in instances where there is a full house HLA match because the graft survival expectancy will be around 37 years which is 4 times that expected from the average CDT.

Recipient Benefits in Non-renal LDT's Versus Non-Renal CDTs

Preliminary evidence indicate that liver segment LDT has similar results to liver CDT. The justification for using it is founded more on clinical need than results; there is a chronic shortage of transplantable livers.[148] It is particularly difficult to find cadaveric livers small enough for patients who are young children and consequently these patients will often receive a lobe of liver from a living parent or other adult. Long term risks to the child of this procedure are not known but it is clear that there is some danger in the short/medium term of the lobe not growing proportionally to his/her own growth.

There is even less data concerning living donor lung lobe donation than there is for liver segment. However, results have been reasonable so far with graft survival rates in one study being 65% for one year and 53% at 3

[147] D.Albrechtsen et al., *Trans Proc*, 1990, 22, 1435; *and* A.Jakobsen, Living Donor Practices and Processes in Europe, in D.Price and H.Akveld (eds.), Living Organ Donation in the Nineties: European Medico-Legal Perspectives, *EUROTOLD*, 1996, 1-12. See also Cecka and Terasaki, Living Donor Kidney Transplants: Superior Success Rates Despite Histoincompatibilities, *Trans Proc*, 1997, 29, 203.

[148] See, for example, C.E.Broelsch et al., Liver Transplantation Including the Concept of Reduced Size Liver Transplants in Children, *Ann Surg,* 1988, 208(4), 410-420; S.Raja et al., Liver Transplant From Live Donors, *Lancet,* 1989, ii, 497.

years.[149]

LDT small-bowel segment donation is experimental and so is its cadaveric counterpart. Graft survival for both modalities is not yet clear. Living donor pancreas segment donation is extremely rare, partly due to the fact that there is no shortage of available cadaveric pancreases, and also because of the serious risks involved. Results are not very good so far.

Maleficence to the Donor

Renal Living Donation

Aside from a small amount of inevitable harm (such as pain and scarring to the wound site) living donor kidney transplantation has a number of risks to the donor including risks of having an operation in itself (e.g. approximately 1/4000 risk of death[150]) and risks related to nephrectomy and living with one kidney. The risks can be grouped into risks of mortality, risks of morbidity and long term complications and risks.

In terms of mortality it is not always easy to discern whether deaths are caused by donation or by other independent factors. Additionally, not all donor deaths are reported. Estimations of mortality must suffice. Spital et al.'s mid nineteen eighties study of US transplant centres had 79 out of 83 responding centres answering a question about donor mortality, 94% of which had not experienced a donor death.[151] Some of the major centres for LDT in the world have reported that they have experienced no fatalities from donations, such as Oslo Transplant Centre (over 500 donors at point of report)[152] and the University of Wisconsin Medical School (681 donors at point of report).[153] However, deaths from donation do occasionally

---

[149]L.R.Shaw et al., *The Lancet,* 1991, 338, 678-681. ULTRA allowed a friend living lung lobe donation in 1996.

[150]R.A.Sells, Voluntarism and Informed Consent in De Charro et al. (eds.), Systems of Donor Recruitment, *Kluwer,* 1992, 87.

[151]A.Spital et al., The Living Kidney Donor, *Arch Intern Med,* 1986, 1993. See also a study of 9 US Centres with 536 donors over 12 years by M.D.Smith et al., *Am J Kid Dis,* 1986, 8(4), 223-233.

[152]A.Jakobsen, personal communication 1996.

[153]M.J.Waples et al., Living Donor Nephrectomy: A 20 Year Experience, *Urology,* 1995, 45(2), 207-210.

happen. Bay reviewed 16 studies from around the world and identified 3 deaths from 2495 donors.[154] This points toward a mortality rate of just over 0.1%.

However, the figure that is probably a fairer indication of the risk is 0.03% which Najarian et al. derived from the largest scale study yet of 19368 living related donor nephrectomies between January 1980 and January 1991 obtained from a survey of all members of the American Society of Transplant Surgeons. In total the study discovered 17 postoperative deaths over a period of 20 years in the USA and Canada, the major cause of the deaths being pulmonary emboli.[155] Centres less experienced with LDTs might be predicted to have more difficulties because donor nephrectomy is a complex procedure. Nonetheless, Najarian et al.'s, assessment that the risk of mortality is low seems justifiable.[156]

In terms of risks of morbidity, serious postoperative incidence has been assessed at 17% in one study[157] and 7% in another.[158] However, most of the evidence points toward its being in the range of 1-3%.[159] The incidence of simple complications (e.g. infection of the wound site) in a 1974 University of Minnesota study by R.Simmons was reported as 28.2%[160]

---

[154]See W.J.Bay et al., The Living Donor in Kidney Transplantation, *Ann Intern Med,* 1987, 106, 719-727. See also Bonomini et al., Is Living Donation Still Justifiable, *Neph Dial Trans,* 1990, 5, 407-409 and Williams et al., *Ann Intern Med,* 1986, 105, 1; Talseth et al., *Kidney Int,* 1986, 29, 1072.

[155]J.S.Najarian et al., 20 Years or More of Follow-up of Living Kidney Donors, *The Lancet,* 1992, 340 at 807.

[156]Ibid.

[157]M.J.Waples et al., Living Donor Nephrectomy: A 20 Year Experience, *Urology,* 1995, 45(2), 207-210.

[158]J.F.Dunn, Living Related Kidney Donors: A 14 Year Experience, *Ann Surg,* 1986, 203, 637-643.

[159]See e.g. R.M.R.Taylor et al., Renal Transplantation in the United Kingdom and Ireland - The Centre Effect, *The Lancet,* 1985, i, 798-802; T.Sherwood et al., Renal Angiography Problems in Live Donors, *Br J Radiol* 1978, 51, 99-105; Levey et al., Kidney Transplantation From Unrelated Living Donors, *New Eng J Med,* 1986, 314, 914; and D.A.Ogden, Consequences of Renal Donation in Man, *Am J Kidney Dis,* 1983, 2, 501-511. For a lower rate see e.g. T.Yasamura et al., Experience with 246 Living Related Donor Nephrectomy Cases at a Single Institution in Japan, *Jpn J Surg,* 1988, 18, 252-258.

[160]*Trans Proc,* 1977, 9, 143.

and in a 1984 updated study at the University by Weiland et al., as 17%. Most studies have reported simple complications to be within the range of 15-30%.[161]

Taking minor and major complications over a range of studies Tilney and Kirkman have found complications rates within the range of 15-47%.[162] Wide variations in rates of complication between different studies may partly be due to different ideas about what constitutes a complication. It is also influenced by the degree of rigour applied to follow-up; many studies focus on the more immediate postoperative period but complications like depression, pain and discomfort at the wound site, chronic urinary infection and incisional hernia may not become apparent until later. While patients are likely to come back to the transplant centre in the event of a serious complication they may be commonly failing to do so in the event of more minor complications, which would therefore be under-reported.

Possible longer term risks of donation include hypertension, proteinuria and progressive failure of the remaining kidney. Some studies have found that kidney donation poses no risk with regard to these conditions.[163] Other studies have identified one or more of these conditions as material risks in donation.[164] However, the presence of risk factors may not correlate with decreased renal function. For instance, increases in hypertension tend only to match those occurring in the general population and increases in proteinuria tend not to result in glomerulosclerosis at least in the medium term. Some reports show LDT does not have serious clinical effects on the donor after 20 years[165] and even 25 years or more.[166] Najarian's recent study involving follow-up from 21-29 years (average 23) concludes that,

---

[161]See e.g. Sollinger et al., *Transplantation,* 1984, 38, 664-668; M.Hoette et al., *Kidney Int,* 1986, 29, 430; and P.Berloco, *Trans Proc,* 1985, 17(2), 13-17.

[162]Consideration of Kidney Donation Using Living Related Sources, *Transplantation and Clinical Immunology,* 1985, 16, 207-213.

[163]For a review of these studies see B.L.Kasiske et al., Long-Term Effects of Reduced Renal Mass in Humans, *Kidney Int,* 1995, 48, 814-819.

[164]See ibid.

[165]Such as Vincenti et al., *Transplantation,* 1983, 36, 626; R.M.Hakim et al., *Kidney Int,* 1984, 25, 930; *and* J.A.Velosa et al., *Trans Proc,* 1985, 17, 100.

[166]See e.g. W.J.Bay et al., Prognosis After Donor Nephrectomy: An Update, *Int J Art Org,* 1987, 10, 9-13 and J.S.Najarian et al., 20 Years or More of Follow-up of Living Kidney Donors, *The Lancet,* 1992, 340, 807-810.

'renal transplant donors are not at increased risk for development of renal failure' and that other risks are low.[167] Most importantly, Kasiske et al. have conducted a substantial review of 48 studies with 3124 patients and 1703 controls using multiple linear regression to combine studies and adjust for differences in the duration of follow-up, the reason for reduced renal mass, the type of controls, age and gender.[168] The authors pointed out that differences in the results of previous studies may have been due to,

> ...differences in the amount of renal mass removed, age at the time of renal mass reduction, unsuspected renal damage to the remaining kidney, or other factors. In addition the relatively small numbers of patients in most studies and the use of different controls have made the interpretation of results difficult.[169]

To address this they carried out a meta-analysis; testing if reduction in renal mass leads to progressive changes in any of proteinuria, hypertension and/or renal function in humans. The conclusion was that the reductions in renal mass did not have any of these consequences. Some increases of proteinuria were detected following uninephrectomy but these did not progress during the period of follow-up while increases in blood pressure were sufficiently low not to cause an increased incidence in hypertension. The considerable weight of this study in combination with other recent results is probably enough to assert that mid to long-term risks of nephrectomy are minimal.

There are no donor studies on 30-40 year risks. However, De Charro et al. note that,

> ...animal experiments have demonstrated that adverse outcomes resulted after nephrectomy in rats after 40% of normal life span, which would point to adverse outcomes in humans after approximately 30 years.[170]

---

[167]Ibid at 809.
[168]B.L.Kasiske et al., Long-Term Effects of Reduced Renal Mass in Humans, *Kidney Int,* 1995, 48, 814-819.
[169]Ibid at p814.
[170]F.Th.De Charro et al., Donor Recruitment in Europe, in De Charro et al. (ed), Systems of Donor Recruitment, *Kluwer*, 1992 at 10. See also A.Chanutin et al., Experimental Renal Insufficiency Produced By Partial Nephrectomy, *Arch Intern Med,* 1982, 49, 767-787 *and* T.H.Hostetter et al., Hyperfiltration in Remnant Nephrons: A Potentially Adverse Response to Renal Ablation, *Am J Physiol,* 1981, 241, F85-F93.

D.M.Narkun-Burgess et al.,[171] comparing 62 US soldiers who lost one kidney during the Second World War and were followed up for 45 years after uninephrectomy with 620 controls, found they showed no increases in mortality, prevalence of hypertension and renal dysfunction which could be related to the previous loss of a kidney. However, this study may contain inherent bias in so far as the soldiers are likely to have been a more healthy sub-group than the control sample. More data is needed to firmly assess very long term risks in donation.

Liver Living Donation

Experience of liver LDT is very limited, both in terms of the numbers of such transplants and the fact that the procedure only started to be utilised in the late 1980s.[172] Obviously, there is no donor data relating to long term risks. There is experience of livers being reduced in people with problematical liver conditions and this suggests that risk to a living liver segment donor should be low. Some early studies suggested comparable risks to those involved in donating a kidney[173] and some recent studies report no serious complications from donation.[174] However, R.W.Busuttil pointed out higher risks were consistent with the complexity of the segment removal procedure.[175] He found that complications include bile leak, incidental splenectomy, subphrenic collection and wound infection.[176]

Lung Lobe Living Donation

The 30-day surgical mortality rate for lobectomy in lung cancer patients who are under 60 years old is 1.3%.[177] However, where long lobe is removed for donation purposes this risk is likely to be closer to 1% because

[171]Forty-five Year Follow-up After Uninephrectomy, *Kidney Int,* 1993, 43, 1110-1115.
[172]S.Raia et al., *Lancet,* 1989, 26, 497.
[173]E.g. P.A.Singer et al., *New Engl J Med,* 1990, 321, 620.
[174]E.g. M.Haberal et al., Living Donor Transplantation: Single Centre Experience, *Trans Proc,* 1996, 28(1), 65-7).
[175]Living Related Liver Donation: CON, *Trans Proc,* 1991, 23(1), 43-5.
[176]Ibid.
[177]E.g. R.J.Ginsberg et al., Modern Thirty Day Operative Mortality for Surgical Resections in Lung Cancer, *J Thorac Cardiovascul Surg,* 1983, 86, 654-658.

the living donor would enter the removal procedure in good health.[178] Experience is so limited that it is difficult to assess other risks and harms at this stage. Reduction of lung capacity by 25% will affect the performance on lung capacity related activities (e.g. opera singing and vigorous physical exercise) and may prove to significantly adversely affect quality of life and longevity by increasing vulnerability to respiratory conditions.

Living Donation of Other Organs

Actual harms and risks involved in small bowel segment donation appear to be limited and acceptable.[179] Living donation of pancreatic vessel length is widely viewed as unacceptable. Its risks include splenectomy, infection and loss of endocrine and exocrine function.[180] Heart and cornea could only be legally donated incidentally to a therapeutically necessary removal.

Psychological Benefits for the Donor and Their Significance

Questionnaire and interview studies conducted with living donors support the common assertion that people tend to derive psychological benefit from being a living donor. Fellner and Marshall's 12 donor study found that donation had a consistently positive long lasting impact on the donor's life.[181] Similarly, R.G.Simmons, S.D.Klein and R.L.Simmons found in a one year follow-up study of living donors that donation was typically an exceedingly positive experience for the donors.[182] This result was

---

178 L.R.Shaw et al., Ethics of Lung Transplantation with Live Donors, *The Lancet,* 1991, 338, 678-681.

179 E.Deltz, Medical Risk and Benefit in Small-Bowel Segment Donors, in W.Land and J.Dossetor (eds.), Organ Replacement Therapy: Ethics, Justice and Commerce, *Springer Verlag* at 110-116.

180 See D.E.R.Sutherland et al., Medical Risks and Benefit of Pancreas Transplants From Living Related Donors, in W.Land and J.Dossetor, ibid at 92-101.

181 C.H.Fellner, J.R.Marshall, Twelve Kidney Donors, *J.Am.Med.Assoc,* 1968, 206, 2703-2707 and Kidney Donors Revisited, *Am J Psychiatry,* 1977, 134, 575-576.

182 R.G.Simmons et al., The Gift of Life: The Social and Psychological Impact of Organ Transplantation, *John Wiley & Sons*, 1977. This was confirmed in a later follow-up - see R.G.Simmons and C.R.Anderson, Social-Psychological Problems in Living Donor Transplantation, in J.L.Touraine et al. (eds.), Transplantation and Clinical Immunology XVI, *Elsevier Science Publishers*, 1983, 47-57.

confirmed in a 5-9 years post-transplant study by Simmons and Anderson which found donors had higher self-esteem, positive changes in depressive affect and increased family closeness.[183] Eisendrath's study also concluded that donation tends to have a positive impact on the lives of donors.[184] Bunzendahl et al., found a neutral evaluation by 83 donors of their general quality of life after donation, but with positive improvements in self-esteem for the majority of donors.[185] Similar results were found by Sadler's study.[186]

Westlie et al.'s quality of life study of 494 Norwegian donors, questioned up to 19 years post-donation, found that they scored better than controls on 13 out of 19 quality of life indicators and specifically in 6 out of the 10 of these indicators that were psychological.[187] The EUROTOLD donor interview/questionnaires given to Polish, Slovenian and Slovakian donors asked if they felt more highly of themselves after donation. Most felt the same, one felt worse and 11 out of 48 felt more highly of themselves. Interestingly, the recipients tended to share the perspective of the donors that the donors had themselves.

Asking the donors if they felt 'more highly' of themselves was methodologically biased. The phrase 'more highly' may have been associated with arrogance by some donors and consequently they may not have marked that they felt this way in spite of experiencing self-esteem increases. It would have been better to ask donors if they felt 'better' about themselves. There can be a positive growth in the donor's relationship with the recipient from donating. Donors in the EUROTOLD donor interview/questionnaires generally felt close with the recipient before the donation. However, 12 out of 76 positively expressed that they felt even closer afterwards and only three felt less close. One Norwegian donor expressed a result that might be expected to be fairly common that

---

[183]Ibid.

[184]R.M.Eisendrath, Psychologic Considerations in the Selection of Kidney Transplant Donors, *Surg Gynec Obstet*, 1969, 129, 243-248 *and* The Role of Grief and Fear in The Death of Kidney Transplant Patients, *Am J Psych,* 1969, 126, 381.

[185]Retrospective Evaluation of Psychosocial Factors in Former Living Related Kidney Donors in Land and Dossetor (eds.), Organ Replacement Therapy: Ethics, Justice and Commerce, *Springer Verlag,* 1991 at p57.

[186]See Sadler et al. in The Gift of Life: The Social and Psychological Impact of Organ Transplantation, *John Wiley & Sons*, 1977, p502.

[187]Quality of Life in Norwegian Kidney Donors, *Nephrol Dial Trans*, 1993, 8, 1146-1150.

he talked 'more about feelings now' with the recipient.

The above studies paint a positive picture of donation, but there can be problems. R.G.Simmons et al.'s study found that,

> (d)espite this benign picture for the majority of donors, at all points in time there appeared to be a small group of donors who were extremely ambivalent or regretful of their decision (5% - 8%).[188]

Similar results were found in the EUROTOLD project donor questionnaire/interviews where approximately 5% of donors (3 out of 76) said they would not go through the whole process again if the clock were turned back. However, the average is probably lower than this when we take into account that the largest living donor attitudes study (n=474) by Westlie et al., found only 1.4% of donors who felt that they would not donate if the clock were turned back and a very high 94% positively expressed that they would probably or definitely donate if the clock were turned back.[189]

Findings of psychological/psychiatric trauma from donating are apparently more common than feelings of regret. Morris et al. evaluated the quality of life of 12 donors 9 - 23 months after donation. The main questionnaire focused on both the donor's relationship with the recipient and the experience of donation. A general health questionnaire was also used.[190] In 4 out of 12 donors significant psychiatric morbidity was found. Hirvas et al. conducted a study of 68 donors 6 months and then 6 years after donation.[191] The donors were interviewed by a psychiatrist and a Rorschach test was performed. 24 donors experienced mild trauma while a further 12 had experienced moderate to severe trauma.

There has been specific analysis of depression in some studies. In a 1966 study, Kemph found unconscious resentment by donors to recipients and moderate depression in all the donors studied.[192] Kemph's view that

[188]The Gift of Life: The Social and Psychological Impact of Organ Transplantation, *John Wiley & Sons*, 1977 at 431-3.

[189]L.Westlie et al., Quality of life in Norwegian Kidney Donors, *Nephrol Dial Transplant*, 1993, 8, 1146-1150.

[190]P.Morris, B.St George et al., Psychosocial Complications in Living Related Kidney Donors: An Australian Experience, *Trans Proc,* 1987, 19, 2840-2844.

[191]J.Hirvas, M.Enckell et al., Psychological and Social Problems Encountered in Active Treatment of Chronic Uraemia, *Acta Med Scand,* 1976, 200, 17-20.

[192]See J.P.Kemph, Renal Failure, Artificial Kidney and Kidney Transplant, *Am J Psychiatry*, 1966, 122, 1270-4.

donors might be predisposed to post-operative depression because they are giving 'something for nothing' was supported by W.Cramond et al. in this early period.[193] However, later studies have not found incidence of depression higher than in the general population. Indeed, in 1985, Simmons and Anderson analysed the combined effect of large scale donor studies (N=1460, 1501, 2460) and their controls, finding that they had similar pre-donation measures of depressive effect but that the donors had considerably 'better' (less depressed) measures both 1 year and 5-9 years after donation.[194] In addition, Simmons and Bernstein have found depression to be rare in adolescent kidney donors.[195]

The conclusion at this stage must be that whilst donating isn't necessarily going to be a life turning event or one that pulls a person out of depression neither is it an event that will normally bring on depression, and overall the tendency is for it to have at least some psychological benefit. However, not surprisingly, it appears that donors cannot always separate the experience of donating in its own right from the outcome achieved and this can leave them more vulnerable to feeling dissatisfaction with having donated in cases where the graft outcome is poor.

Simmons and Karnstra-Hennen studied 147 living related donors between 1970-1973 who received survey interviews pre-transplant.[196] At the time the article was written 47 of the donors had corresponding recipients who had 'lost' the donated kidney. The authors were able to interview a sample of 30 of these donors of which 17% indicated feelings of regret about donating compared to 3% of the group whose recipients still had functioning grafts.[197] In Westlie et al.'s study, the 94% of donors who would probably or definitely donate again was compared to 89.2% in the sub-group of donors whose recipients had died, with higher numbers in the second cohort definitely not wanting to donate again (4.3% as against 1.4%). However, Westlie et al.'s study also indicated that the sub group of

---

[193]See W.Cramond et al., Psychological Screening of Potential Donors in a Renal Homotransplantation Programme, *Brit J of Psychiatry*, 1967, 113, 1213-1221.

[194]60% and 49% of donors respectively at these two times having better results than the controls.

[195]The Adolescent Kidney Donor: The Right to Give, *Am J Psychiat*, 1974, 131, 1338.

[196]The Living-Related Kidney Donor: Psychological Reactions When the Kidney Fails, *Dialysis and Transplantation,* 8(6), June 1979.

[197]16 corresponding recipients were dead, 6 on dialysis and 6 had new functioning grafts.

donors whose recipients grafts had failed still scored as highly as the control group on quality of life factors.[198] Bunzendahl et al.'s study of 83 donors in Hannover, Germany, found that 89.7% of donors with successful recipient grafting would donate again if the clock were turned back as against 84% for those without successful recipient graft survival.[199]

When is Living Organ Donation Ethical and Legal in Terms of Maleficence and Beneficence?

Clearly, like many forms of rescuing behaviour, living donation of an organ is often experienced as a positive thing. However, the rescue needs to be a common sense one in terms of the other harms and benefits in order for it to be ethical. For instance, at the one extreme it would be absurd to suggest that it would be ethical for someone to cause serious harm and jeopardy to themselves in order for a very small benefit to accrue to another. On the other hand if a rescuing act is of low harm and jeopardy to them for significant benefit to another then we would describe it as an ethically sensible expression of the rescuing act and consider any psychological benefit to them as a bonus.

Ensuring Maleficence to the Donor is Within Reasonable Limits

One of the donor-recipient interviews I conducted involved a father whose two sons both needed a kidney transplant. They agreed amongst themselves that he would give his kidney to the son who at that time most needed to come off dialysis. Unfortunately, after the donation had taken place, the condition of the son who remained on dialysis worsened considerably. The father then offered to donate his single remaining kidney as highlighted in the television documentary, 'The Decision: Whose

[198]L.Westlie et al., Quality of life in Norwegian Kidney Donors, *Nephrol Dial Transplant*, 1993, 8, 1146-1150.

[199]Retrospective Evaluation of Psychosocial Factors in Former Living Related Kidney Donors, in Organ Replacement Therapy: Ethics, Justice and Commerce, Land and Dossetor (ed.), *Springer Verlag*, 1991, 57.

Kidney Is It Anyway?'[200]

Nys has argued that donation of any organ essential to unassisted continuance of life (unless incidental to a therapeutic removal)[201] should be prohibited out of respect for the primum non nocere principle.[202] Certainly, the father's rationale for wanting to donate in the above case was that he felt there would be a net benefit; he regarded the prospect of his son being enabled to live a fruitful life to be worth the consequence of him giving up unassisted life since he was old and could probably live much of the rest of his life on dialysis. However, the obiter dicta statement in Urbanski v Patel [1978] 84 DLR 3d 650 that removal of the remaining vital organ of a pair is outside the limits of what can be consented to (in this case removal of the second of two kidneys), is surely good law. Indeed, removal for the purposes of donation of any organ essential to the maintenance of unassisted life would surely be regarded as a battery and assault in legal terms. So would removals, for the purpose of donation, that cause excessive levels of harm and/or jeopardy either by their nature, such as removal of a cornea,[203] or because of the donor having the type of medical condition that makes him/her unusually vulnerable.

Most jurisdictions use transplant legislation to prohibit donations that would involve excessive harm and/or jeopardy to the donor irrespective of whether the donor agrees to the removal.[204] A few jurisdictions use legislation simply to prohibit the removal of organs essential to the donor's unassisted life (e.g. Tunisia[205]) or whose removal would jeopardise the

---

[200]Tuesday 20 February 1996 at 9pm on Channel 4 in the United Kingdom.

[201]Both heart and cornea transplantation can occur incidentally to a therapeutically necessary removal. 3 cornea and 26 hearts were live donated in 1991 in the UK on this basis (*UKTSSA*, Annual Report, 1991).

[202]Of course this should not preclude removal of these organs for therapeutic purposes and living donation as a merely incidental fact to this (e.g. domino heart procedure). See Nys, Desirable Characteristics of Living Donation Transplant Legislation, in D.Price and H.Akveld (eds.), Living Organ Donation in the Nineties: European Medico-Legal Perspective, *EUROTOLD*, 1996, 116-125.

[203]K.Norrie, Human Tissue Transplants: Legal Liability in Different Jurisdictions, *I.C.L.Q.*, 1985, 42, 442 at 447.

[204]A notable exception is France (see *IDHL*, 1994, 45(4), 473-482). Section 5(4)c(ii) of Hong Kong's Ordinance (No. 16 of 1995) only regulates limits to harm / risk for donations requiring special authorisation, i.e. those defined as not between genetic relatives or spouses of 3 or more years standing. UK law is similar (HOTA only regulates limits for donations not defined as between genetic relatives).

[205]Law No. 91-22 of 25 March 1991 at section 4.

donor's life (e.g. Peru,[206] Romania,[207] Algeria[208] and Turkey[209]). More commonly, legislation goes beyond protecting life to protecting health.

Some provisions protect health through limiting removals to those that do not cause excessive levels of harm. For example, Argentina's law states that LDT cannot be used where it will cause serious harm to the health of the donor[210] and Belarus draft law states that only a paired organ, part of an organ, or a tissue whose absence does not entail irreversible damage to health may be withdrawn from a living donor for transplantation purposes.[211] Spanish legislation states that the organ concerned must be one whose removal is not just compatible with the donor's survival but also does not seriously diminish his functional capacities'.[212] The word 'functional' would seem to imply physical functioning but also the ability to work, maintain relationships, etc. Commenting on these restrictions Casabona states that,

> ...single vital organs may not be removed nor may single remaining organs from pairs...Limbs are also excluded as are any parts of the body the removal of which would involve diminished bodily functions. The removal of paired or double organs is permissible when the remaining organ can act as a functional substitute. The same is true of regenerable tissue (blood, medulla, bones, cartilage, etc.). It is therefore necessary to carry out a full medical examination of the donor so as to determine whether or not his/her current health would result in his/her being seriously affected by the removal of the organ. If the donor's physical and mental health is good enough for the removal to go ahead, a medical practitioner other than those who will perform the operation must make a statement to that effect.[213]

---

[206]Supreme Decree No. 014-88-SA of 19 May 1988 at section 14 - see *IDHL*,1994, 45(1), 36-7 at p37.
[207]Article 4(1) of 1996 Law.
[208]States that the removal of organs or tissues must not endanger the life of the donor (Law No. 85-05 of 16 February 1985 at section 162).
[209]Law No. 2238 of 29 May 1979 at section 8.
[210]Law No. 24193 of 24 March 1993 at section 14. Section 15 creates regulations which determine the list of organs which are acceptable for living donation.
[211]Section 6.
[212]Crown Decree No.426 of 22 February 1980 at section 2(b). The law also states the obvious that the donor must be, '(i)n a state of health compatible with the removal procedure' (section 2(a)).
[213]Casabona, The Living Donor in Spanish Law, Copy Held at EUROTOLD.

A reform of general Spanish law in 1983 explicitly recognises living donation as an exception to the rule that intrusions on bodily integrity are illegal.[214] Bolivian law requires that the removal not be one that will seriously damage the donor's health.[215] Paraguay's law which states that the donation must not adversely affect the donor's ability to live.[216] Some legislative provisions require that harm be medically certified as below a certain level. For instance, Hungary's law states that three physicians from the medical establishment not involved in the removal and transplantation procedures must determine that the donor will not suffer irremediable injury.[217] Russian Federation law states that a living donor may only donate organs or tissue where, according to the findings of a committee of medical specialists, his health will suffer no significant damage.[218]

Many legislative provisions require removals to cause neither excessive harm nor excessive jeopardy to health. Germany's law is quite stringent here. It states that there must be 'no foreseeable risk' to the donor 'beyond that of the operation'. This is a criterion which, at best, only the donation of kidneys, out of all the potential forms of living organ donation, can fulfill. The law also states that the donor must not be 'likely to suffer any serious damage to his or her health other than the direct results of the organ removal'. If anything, the first requirement is so strict as to make this second one superfluous.[219] Ecuador's law regulates against excessively harmful donations by prohibiting removal of single vital organs and regulates against excessive jeopardy by prohibiting removal involving a reasonably foreseeable risk of death or total or permanent incapacity of the donor, a threat to the life of the donor or of a significant deterioration of his health.[220] As with Germany's law, we run into problems of interpretation - the problem in this case being how to interpret living organ donations as acceptable because all threaten the life and health of the donor up to a certain point. Possibly one could interpret the requirement as applying to more than de minimus threats in which case at least donation of a kidney would be acceptable.

In the light of these concerns of interpretation, Finnish legislation is a

---

[214]Ibid.

[215]Regulations of 15 March 1982 at section 2 and 3(b).

[216]Law No. 836180 of 15 December 1980.

[217]Ordinance No. 18 of 4 November 1972 at section 1(3).

[218]Law of 22 December 1992 at section 1.

[219]Act of 5th Nov 1997 at section 8(1)c.

[220]Law No. 64 of 26 May 1987 at section 2.

little better drafted. It states that,

> (t)he intervention shall not entail a serious risk to, or harm the health of, the donor...the transplant (must) not involve any reasonably foreseeable risk of death or total permanent incapacity of the donor.[221]

One could presume that 'reasonably foreseeable risk' of death or total permanent incapacity would exclude de minimus risk of such an outcome. Polish law is even more straightforward, it simply requires that a medical check-up prior to donation ascertains that the risk does not surpass the permissible anticipated limits for such medical operations and does not seriously in an adverse manner affect the health condition of a donor.[222]

Sometimes a legislative provision focuses exclusively on preventing particular types of jeopardy and not actual harms. For example, Kuwait's law prohibits removals liable to bring about death and those liable to prevent the donor 'carrying out his activities'.[223] Cypriot law states that there must be *no* serious and manifest risk to the life (or health) of the donor, other than that resulting from the removal itself. Portugal's law states that donations shall not be permitted if,

> ...there is a strong probability of serious and permanent impairment of the physical integrity and health of the donor.

Under ordinary circumstances kidney LDT would be legally acceptable because the risk of serious and permanent impairment of the physical integrity and health of the donor is minimal.[224] Lebanon's law states that tissues or organs can't be removed from a person whose, 'state of health precludes such removal or if there is a risk or serious danger to the health of the donor'.[225] Slovakian law prohibits donations which it is anticipated will seriously jeopardise the donor's state of health.[226] Slovenian law has the very basic requirement that the donation must be a reasonable risk for the donor and recipient and have a strong possibility of success.[227]

---

[221]Law No. 355 of 26 April 1985 at section 3.
[222]Law of 26 October 1995 at Article 9(1) point 4.
[223]Decree-Law No. 55 of 20 December at section 3.
[224]Law No. 12 of 22 April 1993 at section 6(4).
[225]Decree No. 109 of 16 September 1983 at section 1.
[226]Law of 24 August 1994 at section 46(2).
[227]1996 law at Article 2.

Norway's law would benefit from redrafting in respect of the fact that it seems to unrealistically exclude any jeopardy by stating that,

> (t)he operation may be performed only if *no* direct danger to the donor's life or health results therefrom.[228] (ital. added)

Similarly Denmark's law states that,

> ...the intervention may only be performed if, taking into account it's nature and the state of health of the person giving consent, it may be undertaken without *any* immediate danger to that person.[229]

Some provisions require medical certification that risks are below a certain level. For example, Bolivian law states that at least two physicians must certify that removal of the organ will not seriously damage the donor's health or chances of survival.[230] Greek law states that there must not, in the opinion of the responsible physicians in the treatment unit where the removal is to be performed, be 'any manifest serious risk to the life or health of the donor'.[231] Canada's model law states that non-regenerative material must be transplanted only after an independent assessment which will take into account whether the removal will create a substantial health or other risk to the donor.[232] In Hong Kong proposed distant genetically related and emotionally related living donations (apart from spouses of 3 years standing) must seek validation from the Board set up under the law. The Board will simply note the risk involved in the procedure at issue as one of the factors bearing on its determination.[233]

Some jurisdictions limit harm and jeopardy via specific limits on what organs can be donated. In most cases this limitation will just apply to incompetent adults or minors. However, occasionally it also applies to competent adults. For instance, Slovenia's law only allows donation of liver segment and donation of a single kidney.[234]

Occasionally provisions fall out of line with medical advances. For

[228]Law No. 6 of 1973 at section 1.
[229]Section 13(4) Law No. 402 of 13 June.
[230]Regulations of 15 March 1982 at section 3(b).
[231]Law No. 1383 of 2 August 1983 at section 5(c).
[232]The Uniform Human Tissue Donation Act 1990 at section 7(6).
[233]Under Ordinance No. 16 of 1995 at section 5(4)c(ii).
[234]Article 8 ibid.

instance, in Hungary the donation of parts of a single organ (such as liver segment and lung lobe) is contradicted by the provision that organs can *only* be donated if they are one of a pair.[235] In Romania harvesting of unique organs such as heart, liver, pancreas etc. can only be performed from brain-dead persons.[236] A clinically indicated domino heart procedure might be precluded - although it might be contended that donation would be acceptable in such a case because it is merely incidental to therapy.

Ensuring that Maleficence to the Donor is Outweighed by Benefit to the Recipient and that the Living Donation is the Best Choice Available

The majority of kidney LDTs cause a low level of harm and jeopardy to the donor and have high anticipated benefits for the recipient. They produce better graft survival for the recipient in most cases than CDT. Nethertheless, where CDT is available it generally ought to be preferred because it doesn't involve maleficence to a donor. Exceptional situations do exist such as where an LDT has prospects of multiply superior graft survival to the use of an average CDT (e.g. where there is an identical HLA match) or where for some clinical reason CDT is not a viable option for the recipient. However, it is really when there is a waiting list for CDT that the significant use of LDT comes into its own right.

When there is a waiting list the likely time that the recipient will have to wait for a CDT needs to be factored into the equation. Or rather the lower quality of life and health consequences of the extra wait on dialysis need to be factored in. Under some circumstances it may be that the maleficent consequences of waiting outweigh the maleficent consequences of living donation for the donor and accordingly LDT could be preferable if its graft survival were equal or even slightly inferior to that of the average CDT.

In the case of liver LDT some evidence suggests that graft survival is not as good as with its cadaveric counterpart.[237] Since liver LDT also causes greater maleficence to the donor than renal LDT we ought to be very careful about its use. Interestingly, the Council of Europe's Committee of Ministers of Member States has provisionally produced Recommendation No. R (97) 16 On Liver Transplantation From Living Related Donors. Point i) of the Appendix states that on current evidence it should only be used for liver transplantation into children. It also states

[235]Ordinance No. 18 of 4 November 1972 at section 1(3).
[236]Article 9(3) of 1996 law.
[237]R.W.Busutill, Living Related Liver Donation: CON, *Trans Proc,* 1991, 23, 43-5.

that it should only be considered when there is a shortage of cadaveric organs (i.e. when alternatives that do not carry the risks incurred by a living donor have been exhausted). Point ii) explains that potential recipients should have been previously assessed for suitability for CDT and that if the potential recipient is considered suitable for LDT (s)he should be kept on the cadaveric list in case a suitable cadaveric liver becomes available. The potential recipient is to be informed of the possibility of LDT if it seems unlikely that a suitable cadaveric organ will become available in the required timescale. These principles are similar to those used by centres who are doing liver LDT already.[238] An interesting additional feature in the Appendix is the requirement that liver LDT should only be performed with the approval of an appropriate transplant regulatory body with the procedures used being registered with the authority and the results being monitored by a recognised method of peer review (until such time as the results are acceptable).

Shaw et al. have suggested that in order to justify living lung lobe donation the only recipients that should be used are those for whom a cadaveric organ is unlikely to become available, are likely to deteriorate without transplant but are sufficiently healthy to go ahead and agree to participate in rehabilitation programmes and to refrain from smoking.[239] However, lung lobe LDT is probably less than half as successful as kidney LDT in terms of graft survival[240] and much more jeopardising to the donor. Are the benefits of doing it so marginal that it might be better to just accept death and spend the money on another form of healthcare?

One situation where living donor pancreas segment donation is sometimes considered is where cadaveric donation cannot easily be used, for instance with highly sensitised diabetics. However, Koene simply concludes that living donation of pancreas segment is not justifiable because it has high risk to the donor and equivocal benefits.[241] Certainly, it is much harder to justify than the previously discussed forms of organ LDT

---

[238]M.Haberal et al., Living Related Liver Transplantation in an Adult and A Child, in W.Land and J.Dossetor (eds.), Organ Replacement Therapy: Ethics, Justice, Commerce, *Springer Verlag*, 1991, 83-91.

[239]L.R.Shaw et al., Ethics of Lung Transplantation with Live Donors, *The Lancet,* 1991, 338, 678-681.

[240]Ibid.

[241]R.Koene, Long term Clinical and Ethical Issues in Living Organ Donation, in D.Price and H.Akveld (eds.), Living Organ Donation in the Nineties: European Medico-Legal Perspectives, *EUROTOLD*, 1996, 33-41 at 40.

and its use has not surprisingly been extremely rare.

Under general principles of law, for a living donation to be within the limits of what can be consented to, requires not just the maleficence to the donor to be within absolute limits but also reasonable in the light of the levels of benefits the LDT will offer over and above other therapeutic options available to the recipient. Gieson suggests that it,

> ...would seem that both donor and recipient have the right to expect that the surgeon has made sure that the transplant is absolutely necessary and is only performed after all other methods have failed.[242]

This view seems far too absolute. It is particularly too absolute in kidney donation where there is generally a clinical superiority of LDT over the average expected CDT of a sufficient nature to warrant a professional taking the view that if the LDT will only cause a small amount of harm and jeopardy it is justified. In addition, it must be noted that in many situations LDT is the only readily available therapeutic option and it seems entirely consistent with the professional's duty of care to recommend it if it averts the possibility of the recipient having to wait a significant time on dialysis having to bear health deterioration and a lower quality of life. Skegg seems to be more on the mark in suggesting that under conditions of kidney shortage judges would largely defer to a medical judgement that it was better to get a kidney from a living donor than to wait,

> ...a court is unlikely to inquire closely into whether there are good reasons for a particular intervention. There is no danger of a court attempting to decide whether there are good reasons for removing a kidney from a living donor, instead of keeping the patient on dialysis in the hope that a suitable cadaver kidney would become available.[243]

However, if there were no waiting list or if the particular removal involved greater than average harm and/or jeopardy judicial scrutiny would doubtless be closer than it would be for removal of other types of organs. The law would pay particular attention to prospective LDTs which were in some way innovative. One requirement is that new forms of treatment

---

[242]International Medical Malpractice Law, *J.C.B. Mohr (Paul Siebeck) and Martinus Nijhoff*, 1988, 608.

[243]Law, Ethics and Medicine: Studies in Medical Law, *Clarendon Press*, 1988, 36.

must be likely to be better than the old ones.[244] The burden of proving a choice was the best practice lies with the defendant in many jurisdictions.[245] However, this must be taken within the overall context that the intention is not to discourage innovative treatment since,

> ...every innovation has to be performed for a first time. That something has not been done before is not proof that it ought not be done.[246]

Transplant legislation sometimes directly requires a rationale for preferring LDT. Canadian model law requires those undertaking the authorisation process to take into account whether LDT is the treatment of choice[247] and Colombian law requires LDT to be for a therapeutically indispensable transplantation.[248] Argentina's law states that LDT can be used where,

> ...other means have been exhausted or are insufficient, or if they do not constitute an appropriate therapeutic solution for a particular patient.[249]

Ecuador requires positive histocompatibility results between the donor and recipient,[250] which would seem to exclude the possibility of using mismatched donors. Some other jurisdictions have a requirement that there must be toleration of materials (e.g. Mexico and Cyprus[251]). This does not significantly restrict the use of LDT because it allows HLA mismatched donors. On the other hand some approaches restrict the use of LDT by placing its use within the context of a bias towards the use of CDT.

---

[244]See Civil Liability of Physicians for New Methods of Treatment and Experimentation: A Comparative Examination, *Med Law Review*, 1995 (Spring), 3, 22-52 at 29-30.

[245]See e.g. Anderson v Chasney and Sisters of St Joseph [1949] 57 Man R 343; Crits v Slyvester [1956] O.R. 132 (Ont C.A. per Schroeder J.A. at 148); G.Memeteau, Le Droit Medical, Litec, 1985, 307-308.

[246]Per Hurtley JA in Qidway v Brown [1984] 1 N.S.W.L.R 100.

[247]Uniform Human Tissue Donation Act 1990 section 5(3) and section 7(6).

[248]Decree No. 1172 of 6 June 1989 at section 24.

[249]Law No. 24193 of 24 March 1993 at section 2 (taken from *IDHL*, 1994, 45(1), 35-36). Additionally where living donation is specifically proposed it must, 'offer the likelihood of success with regard to preserving the life or improving the health of the recipient' (section 14).

[250]Law No. 64 of 26 May 1987 at section 2.

[251]Law No. 97 of 1987 at section 7.

Guiding Principle 1 of the WHO Guiding Principles on Transplantation suggests that organs should preferably come from deceased persons and similarly Article 19(1) of the Convention on Human Rights and Biomedicine states that organs and tissue can only be taken from a living person where there is not a suitable one available from a deceased person and there is no alternative therapeutic method of comparable effectiveness. Swedish law states that the use of living donors should be limited as much as possible.[252] Belgian law states that,

> ...if the removal of organs or tissues from living persons may affect the donor, or if such organs are non-regenerable, it may only be performed if the recipient's life is in danger and if the transplantation of organs or tissues from a deceased person could not produce an equally satisfactory result.[253]

It is likely that judges would take the fact of renal failure as danger to the prospective recipient's life even if the danger is not immediate. However, the general tenor of the Belgian law is discouraging of LDT as is the fact that there is ambiguity surrounding exactly when CDT could not produce an exactly satisfactory result,

> Should this requirement be understood 'in abstracto,' which means that transplantation with a cadaveric does not offer, as a rule, similar results as transplantation with a living donated organ, or 'in concreto', which means that if no cadaveric organ is available in a given case the condition is fulfilled. But what is the meaning of 'not available'? In the region? The country? Europe? Worldwide?[254]

It is a sad, but not entirely surprising, result that EUROTOLD's Professional Attitudes Questionnaire found a number of Belgian transplant professionals thinking that LDT was *illegal* in their country! The problems for professionals wanting to use LDT are exacerbated further in Mexican law which states that LDT may only occur when organs or tissues from

---

[252]Explanatory Memorandum to the new Act of 8 June 1995 On Transplantation etc. See Linda Nielson, Living Organ Donors: Legal Perspectives From Western Europe, in D.Price and H.Akveld (eds.), Living Organ Donation in the Nineties: European Medico-Legal Perspectives, *EUROTOLD*, 1996, 58-71.
[253]Law No. 32 of 13 June 1986 at section 6.
[254]Ibid.

cadavers *cannot* be used.[255] Strictly defined, this would limit use of LDT to emergencies where CDT was not available and situations where the recipient cannot take CDT for medical reasons. Creative judicial interpretation would be needed to allow LDT where CDT cannot be used because the recipient is low down on a waiting list. Slovenian law states that a living person can only donate liver segment and single kidney[256] and this must be to a recipient who is genetically or familially linked where it is not possible to get a cadaver within a reasonable time and use of LDT 'assures much better possibilities of medical treatment'.[257] Ethical committee approval must be given.[258]

Conclusion

Why should highly harmful and/or jeopardising donations be viewed as outside the limits of what can be validly consented to? One argument is that a person couldn't possibly mean to consent to such activities. However, this is patently untrue in some cases - such as the Leicester donor who wanted to give his second kidney for reasons that to him were perfectly legitimate. Another argument advanced is that prospective donors are in a pressurised situation where it is difficult to turn down donation even if it is very risky and harmful. Carl Elliot poses the question,

> ...what would we think of a person who would take advantage of a donor's willingness to take life-threatening risks? [259]

The problem with this view is that some donors may want to be exploited in this way. They would not be alone in this. Indeed some people choose

---

[255]The General Law on Health 26 December 1983 at section 322. Mexican law also requires the recipient to be suffering from an ailment which can be effectively treated by means of the transplant and is not suffering from other diseases which could foreseeable jeopardise the success of the transplant (Federal Regulation of 16 August 1976 at section 35).

[256]Article 8 of 1996 law.

[257]It is unclear what the ambit of family and genetic links is under the law.

[258]Article 8 of 1996 law.

[259]C.Elliot, Doing Harm: Living Organ Donors, Clinical Research and The Tenth Man, *J Med Eth,* 1995, 21, 91-96.

professions, such as being a fireperson, where when a life-threatening situation arises they want to be called upon to perform a rescue, even at some risk to their own lives. We could also say that it is preferable in ethical terms for someone to undertake a harmful and risky activity that, like living donation, has a purpose of rescue than to undertake a harmful and risky activity that, like boxing, is for entertainment. It is doubtful whether it is really acceptable from a rights perspective to use law to try and protect competent adults from their own voluntary assumptions of risk and harm even where we view these assumptions as excessive. However, there probably is a legitimate basis on which to restrict donation.

Elliot states that when someone chooses to risk themselves they also risk harming others and these effects should be taken into account, 'any system of practices in which people are likely to be harmed should be set up in ways that minimize this possibility'.[260] The justification for law stepping in is not to prevent people voluntarily assuming risk but to prevent others from using the fact that a person has consented as a basis for mutilating them. In the medical context the law acts to ensure that medical professionals act within the limits of ethical and this must mean that it is justifiable to put a ceiling on the absolute levels of harm and jeopardy that professionals may expose those in their care to. Ensuring that harm and jeopardy are proportional to benefits is also justifiable. Not only will these limits serve to protect the medical profession as a whole from unethical activity of specific members but it means that if tax or medical insurance payers foot the bill for healthcare their money is more likely to be put to effective use. The critical question is where the limits ought to be placed.

One view is that too much has been made of harm and jeopardy in living donation and not enough of the benefits of preferring LDT. Living donation will generally be the best way of meeting the combined interests of a prospective kidney recipient and donor under conditions of significant organ shortage and sometimes the best option where there is no shortage. One of the reasons LDT is not often widely used even in the context of organ shortages is that patients and their families are not always pro-actively informed that it is a possibility. Medical professionals often push LDT to the background, presumably mostly because of concerns about maleficence, and guidelines and legislation often overly restrict the

[260]His view is also that in order to minimise risks it would be better to have a system of living organ transplantation in which nobody is able to make a financial profit from the procedure. For further consideration profit issues see chapter 7.

freedom to use it.

A new approach in legislation and guidance to practitioners needs to avoid cultivating a general bias or preference for CDT. Providing harm and jeopardy to the donor is within reasonable limits (i.e. at least generally as it is in kidney, liver segment and lung lobe donation) the concern should focus on whether LDT is the best option in terms of the collective interests of the donor and recipient as a pair in the light particularly of the likely waiting time for CDT and the consequences of this. Guidance should recognise that the results of even mismatched LDTs are in any case as good as the average CDT and accordingly a relaxed approach to LDT HLA match requirements wherever expected waiting times are of a level likely to have a significant quality of life and / or health impact on the prospective recipient. Provided that LDT is a reasonable clinical choice the key thing for the practitioner is really to give the prospective donor(s) and recipient enough information/evaluation about the options, in a balanced fashion, to make their own judgements and there should be nothing to preclude them from even preferring LDT partly on the grounds that it will help the transplant community by taking a person off the waiting list.

One final point concerns persons who have consent given on their behalf. In considering such a person as a donor one cannot legally take into account the interests of him/her and the recipient collectively. One can only take into account his/her own interests which means that the prospective psychological advantages of gifting have to outweigh the prospective physiological harm and jeopardy. This is discussed in more detail in chapters 5 and 6.

3 Informed Choice

Introduction

What is an Informed Choice?

In a typical model of rational decision-making a decision-maker would:

1. Canvass a wide range of alternative courses of action;
2. survey the full range of objectives to be fulfilled;
3. carefully weigh whatever is known about the costs and risks of negative and positive consequences flowing from each alternative;
4. intensively search new information relevant to further evaluation of the alternatives;
5. correctly assimilate and take into account any new information or expert judgement to which the individual is exposed;
6. re-examine the consequences of all alternatives before making a final choice; *and*
7. make detailed provisions for the implementation or execution of the chosen course of action, with special attention to contingency plans that might be required if various known risks were to materialise.[261]

It can be argued that some people know what is best for themselves intuitively. However, information, and analysis of it, can often be an aid to the effective use of intuition and for most people is essential in more serious decision making in order to avoid heightening the risk of making a decision which is contrary to their best interests.

The Role of Medical Professionals in Supporting Informed Patient Choice

Patients usually rely heavily on practitioners to help them make decisions about medical interventions. Barnard's model of negotiation emphasises a broad role for the practitioner as facilitator as well as medical expert,

[261] I.Janis and L.Mann, Decision Making: A Psychological Analysis of Conflict, Choice and Commitment, *The Free Press*, 1977 at 11.

> ...patients possess a positive potential for growth and health. Medical interventions and knowledge, in this perspective, are only one among many determinants of personal health. A major role of the physician is to assist the patient to reclaim or renew his or her own strengths and tendencies toward growth. In certain circumstances this may entail the application of technical modes of healing. In all cases, however, it will require the effort of helping the patient to clarify personal needs and goals, and to select, with the help of the physician, plans and actions consistent with and supportive of personal values.[262]

However, he adds that in practice use of the reductionistic biomedical model tends to result in an approach where the practitioner determines the course of action and the patient follows it:

> The physician diagnoses and recommends; the patient answers questions accurately and follows advice.[263]

This perspective is echoed in the comments of Sheila McLean who suggests that this form of medicine functions primarily along the lines that a medical professional can 'solve' problems in the same way that a mechanic might fix a malfunctioning car.[264] It is not entirely surprising in the light of these comments that empirical studies cannot support the view that practitioners are effectively facilitating informed choice by patients. Faden and Beauchamp note a study in which US physicians were asked, 'what does the term informed consent mean to you?' Only 26% of physicians indicated that informed consent had anything to do with patients' giving permission, consenting, or agreeing to treatment; only 9% indicated that it involved patients' making a choice or stating a preference about his or her treatment, and recognition by the patient of what is taking place.[265]

---

[262]Barnard, The Personal Meaning of Illness, in J.Shlien (ed.), Client-Centred Dimensions of Medicine and Health Care, *Client-Centred Therapy*, 337-351 at 350-351.
[263]Ibid at 339.
[264]S.McLean, A Patients Right to Know, *Dartmouth*, 1989 at p4.
[265]Faden and Beauchamp, A History and Theory of Informed Consent, *Oxford University Press*, 1986. See also Lidz and Meisel, Informed Consent and the Structure of Medical Care, in President's Commission for the Study of Ethical Problems in Medicine and Biomedical and Behavioural Research, Making Health Care Decisions, *Washington D.C.,Government Printing Office,* 1982, 333-340.

Study of Informed Choice in LDT

Fellner and Marshall found that living donors were tending to make,

> ...an immediate major decision, before even inquiring into the possible consequences for themselves, or seeking reassurance as to the eventual benefits for the recipient.[266]

This led them to conclude that informed consent in living donation is a myth.[267] Simmons et al. reported findings that donors considered donating as soon as they found out about the need in 88% of cases.[268] 61% followed a non-deliberative model of decision-making and only 25% reported having a period of deliberation with a conscious choice.[269]

EUROTOLD's interview/questionnaires (see Table 1) confirm that most donors adopt a non-deliberative model of decision-making. In the typical scenario, disclosure by medical professionals was not ideal but significant. However, this disclosure tended not to translate into the donors being aware of risks at the time of deciding or even at the time of donating. Indeed, EUROTOLD found cases where donors admitted interrupting or not listening to disclosures. Generally this was because they felt they didn't need the information because they had already decided but in one case it was also a defence against the possibility that information about risks might be off-putting. More commonly, donors were reifying their decisions or helping persuade themselves to donate by adopting the misconception that there is no risk in donation.

Table 1: Donor Informed Choice - EUROTOLD Interview/Questionnaire Results

Issue	
Decided without thinking it over	36/48
Not aware of risks at time of donation	31/48
Couldn't remember what risks told about	11/24
Felt donating had no risk	19/26

---

[266] Twelve Kidney Donors, *J Am Med Assoc,* 1968, 206, 2703-2707 at 2706.

[267] Kidney Donors - The Myth of Informed Consent, *Am J Psych*, 1970, 126, 1245-1251.

[268] Gift of Life, *Wiley and Sons*, 1977 at 242.

[269] Ibid at 244.

Some donors received information from more than one source. Most donors received information from a nephrologist and a considerable number received information from a transplant co-ordinator. Other sources included surgeon, nurse, transplant co-ordinator, boyfriend, family doctor. A few donors sought out some information on their own, the most typical sources being mass media (TV and Press) and ex-donors and occasional sources being medical books and GPs.

Qualitative feedback from semi-structured interview/questionnaires with samples in Oslo, Leicester and Dublin did actually present a more satisfactory level of awareness in a significant number of donors. The Oslo sample were generally quite aware, with one donor saying, 'I knew I might have pain afterwards, that I might feel sick, ..about the possibility of narcosis' and another commenting on the risks being well explained and adding that he knew the success rate of living donation to be around 90-92% because of good statistics given to him and that he knew the wait for a cadaver kidney was one year or more with possible deterioration on dialysis. Most of the donors in these samples were satisfied with disclosure with such comments as 'very good information,' 'I felt the doctors told me everything' and 'they went to a great deal of trouble to ensure that I knew what was going to happen'. A few donors expressed negative overall picture of disclosure and several expressed specific concerns such as not being informed about the possibility of sepsis at the incision site, that information concerning 'whether or not I would be O.K. on one kidney could have been better' and that they could have been told more about the possible impact of the donation on their sex life.

Westlie et al.'s study asked 474 Norwegian donors about the quantity and quality of information provided and who provided it.[270] In terms of quantity of information, most donors felt they had received enough information but some were unsure or felt they had insufficient information on a number of subjects (see Table 2 on page 69). In particular, this was the case for longer term information about post-operative recovery. Around half of the donors expressed positive views about the quality of information provided and a further 35.9% said it was 'acceptable'. However, improvement was needed at the lower end of satisfaction; 13.7% of donors found quality less than acceptable and this included 1.8% who found it was not helpful at all. Nephrologists at the recipient's hospital and

[270]L.Westlie, P.Fauchald et al., Quality of Life in Norwegian Kidney Donors, *Nephrol Dial Transplant,* 1993, 8, 1146-1150.

doctors and nurses at the National hospital were the main information providers for the donor. Other sources, such as previous donors, were relied on to a much lesser extent. Most donors (90.3%) responded that they would go to nephrologists at the recipient's hospital if they needed information on kidney donation and transplantation. This pattern of informational reliance on one person could be problematical in terms of getting the full range of information and perspectives on transplantation. Where dialysis is privately run,[271] self-interest (in other words financial profitability from keeping people on dialysis) could sometimes be a distorting factor in information disclosure by nephrologists.

Table 2: Norwegian Donor Perceptions on Whether They Received Enough Information (Westlie et al.'s study)

Percentage receiving enough information on	yes	yes & no	no
How you were selected as a donor?	83.1	10.2	6.7
What surgery would be like?	70.6	20.3	9.1
What post surgery hospitalisation would be like?	51.7	26.5	21.7
What your recovery at home would be like?	45.3	23.5	31.2
What chances of success for recipient were?	71.8	18.8	9.4

EUROTOLD questionnaires/interviews were unusual in that they also examined informed choice in relation to recipients. The position was not particularly satisfactory (see Table 3). Recipients seemed to be generally more able to describe the benefits of LDT than to describe the potential risks. However, as an overall assessment they, it can be said that they seemed to be making more of an informed choice than donors.

Although levels of satisfaction with disclosure were not specifically tested, some qualitative data was obtained on this from the Leicester, Oslo and Dublin samples on this matter. Most of the recipients felt disclosure was adequate or good but there were some complaints. The worst case was a recipient who felt 'left in the dark... there was no real information' and stated that he was not informed of a possible deleterious impact on his sex life from the operation and that his brother, the donor, had been treated like 'a piece of meat'. Other concerns included feeling uninformed about drug

[271]E.g. Germany.

side effects (including 'moon face'), a recipient not being informed about the possibility that her eyesight would deteriorate after the operation (she was diabetic) and a recipient feeling the doctors seemed to have no time to answer questions and in most cases talked down to her. A few Oslo recipients felt disclosure was insufficient, including one who felt that she could have been informed more about the medicines she would have to take and their side effects and another who felt that 'sometimes the doctors forgot they were dealing with people'.

Table 3: Recipient Informed Choice - EUROTOLD Interview/Questionnaire Results

Issue	Total
Decided without thinking it over	18/54
Reconsidered	6/19
Not aware of risks to self at donation	29/52
Not aware of risks to donor at donation	16/52
Felt donating has no risk	5/30
Aware of effect on donor's health	22/50
Aware of match advantage of LDT	28/50
Aware of pre planned operation advantage of LDT	17/50
Aware of earlier transplantation advantage of LDT	21/50
Felt receiving has no risk	9/30

Recipients sometimes obtained information from more than one source. Generally they obtained information from nephrologists. Sources used by a few recipients included medical literature, transplant co-ordinator, psychologist, surgeon, nurses and previously transplanted patients.

Introducing the Legal Issues

We have seen in chapter 1 that general principles of law support informed choice to a certain degree but are there any special considerations when it comes to the living donor and recipient? In terms of disclosure Gieson's rule of thumb is that research experiments require higher standards of disclosure than therapeutic experiments (i.e. innovative therapy[272] or

[272] Zimmer v Ringrose [1981] 28 A.R. 69, (1981), [1981] 4 W.W.R. 75 (C.A.).

therapeutic research) which in turn require higher standards than therapeutic treatments.[273] Gieson states extensive and detailed information must be given to prospective living donors.[274] The ground for this is that for the purposes of disclosure living donation is akin to a research experiment in so much as both are elective, designed for someone else's benefit and expose the subject to harm and jeopardy.

For the purposes of Gieson's classification, receiving a liver segment or lung lobe from a living donor would probably be considered a therapeutically innovative or therapeutically experimental procedure - not so much in terms of the transplantation into the recipient him/herself but in terms of the possible impact of removal on the donor - data pertaining to which is scant and non-existent in relation to long term impact.

Receiving a kidney from a living donor is normally a therapeutic treatment, i.e. involving normal and approved (or orthodox) procedures. Gieson seems to bracket it together with such treatments for the purposes of disclosure[275] and McK Norrie states that there would be a much higher standard applied to the donor.[276] However, even the recipient undergoing a therapeutic treatment ought to be given special consideration for disclosure purposes because of his/her interdependence with the donor. The regular patient is given information pertaining to the impact of an intervention and its alternatives upon him/herself. Contrastingly, both the prospective donor and recipient must receive not just this information but also the information pertaining to the impact of the intervention and its alternatives upon each other. Without such information it is impossible to make a reasoned choice. However, focusing on the recipient it can also be argued that his/her interdependence with the donor should influence not just the range of what is disclosed but the overall standard. It can be stated that the prospective recipient has a duty to only use LDT where justified because of the harm and jeopardy it will cause to the donor if used. In order to carry out this duty effectively the prospective recipient would need a high standard of disclosure. It could be argued that this should be reflected in

---

[273]D.Gieson, Civil Liability of Physicians For New Methods of Treatment and Experimentation: A Comparative Examination, *Med Law Review*, 1995 (Spring), 3, 22-52 at 25.
[274]D.Gieson, International Medical Malpractice Law, *J.C.B. Mohr (Paul Siebeck) and Martinus Nijhoff*, 1988.
[275]Ibid at 608.
[276]K.McK Norrie, Human Tissue Transplants: Legal Liability in Different Jurisdictions, *ICLQ*, 1985, 34, 442.

the legal standard of disclosure to the recipient which, if not as high as that given to the donor, should be higher than that applied to the typical patient.[277]

The application of the tort of battery and the tort of negligence to the living donor and recipient will be examined in the next sections as will legislative disclosure requirements which typically exist in relation to the donor[278] and occasionally also the recipient. As we shall see some provisions not only obligate the professional to disclose certain information but to communicate what is disclosed in a particular manner and even make efforts to ensure that what is disclosed has been understood.

The Relationship of Informed Choice to Obtaining Consent to LDT

As discussed in chapter 1, the professional must generally obtain consent to undertake an intervention in order to avoid committing a criminal assault and tortious battery. We have seen that under the tort of battery the patient *generally* only needs to be informed in broad terms of the nature of the procedure intended in order for consent to be real.[279] However, as Gieson has suggested, non-therapeutic interventions performed for research purposes have been treated as requiring the highest standard of disclosure. Hall JA giving the judgement of the Canadian Court of Appeal in Halushka v University of Saskatchewan [1965] 53 DLR (2d) 436 concluded that in considering such an intervention a person,

> ...is entitled to a full and frank disclosure of the facts, probabilities and opinions which a reasonable man might be expected to consider before giving his consent.

---

[277]This would help ensure 'moral' decision-making - see Schwartz's three necessary and sufficient conditions for moral decision-making in Elicitation of Moral Obligation and Self-Sacrificing Behaviour, *J Pers & Soc Psych*, 1970, 15(4), 283-293.

[278]Occasionally only to particular kinds of donor. E.g. UK law only imposes a duty in relation to donors not legislatively classed as genetically related to the recipient (see HOTA 1989 section 2(3)), Hong Kong law only regulates disclosure where the donor is not legislatively classed as genetically related to the recipient and not the recipient's spouse of 3 or more years standing (Ordinance No 16 of 1995). Indian law has a similar provision (see Act No. 42 of 1994, *IDHL*, 1995, 46(1), 34-38).

[279]Chatterton v Gerson [1981] QB 432, [1981] 1 All ER 257 (QBD).

Halushka was approved in Zimmer v Ringrose [1981] 28 A.R. 69, (1981), [1981] 4 W.W.R. 75 (C.A) and in Weiss v Solomon (1989) 48 CCLT 280 (Qu Sup Ct) it was stated that the highest possible standard of disclosure was required in cases involving non-therapeutic research.[280] The most interesting feature about Halushka was that it considered full disclosure to be integral to actually obtaining consent and hence *required to avoid liability in battery* in cases of non-therapeutic research. This position would probably also be taken in jurisdictions which are dominated by a restrictive approach to liability for disclosure failures, i.e. those based around the Bolam test.

It has already been emphasised that the living donor's position is akin to that of the non-therapeutic research volunteer for disclosure purposes.[281] Hence, the argument can be clearly made that the full disclosure to the donor should occur under the head of battery despite the fact that an organ would be donated for treatment of the recipient rather than as part of a non-therapeutic research experiment. From the donor's perspective the clear advantage of full disclosure being required under the head of battery is that it properly protects his *right* to know by making significant non-disclosures actionable per se. If liability were only under the head of negligence the donor would probably have little problem proving that a significant non-disclosure was unreasonable but would also have the more difficult task of proving that the unreasonable non-disclosure caused him to decide in a manner he would not have decided if reasonable disclosure had taken place.

The issue that has not been fully explored in the literature is whether the recipient should be entitled to full disclosure under the head of battery as well. I have earlier argued the grounds for the recipient to be treated differently to the typical patient and it seems likely judges would give this argument some credence, but it is probable that this would only result in a higher standard being applied under the tort of negligence. Gieson suggests that where LDTs are experimental therapy recipients should 'be fully informed about all the risks associated with them before their consent is obtained'.[282] This might hint towards disclosure in such cases being

[280]See B.Freedman and K.Glass, *Law, Medicine and Health Care*, 1990, 18 at 395.
[281]See Gieson, Civil Liability of Physicians for New Methods of Treatment: A Comparative Examination, *Med Law Review,* 1995 (Spring), 3, 22-52 at 33.
[282]International Medical Malpractice Law, *J.C.B. Mohr (Paul Siebeck) and Martinus Nijhoff,* 1988, 608.

considered under the tort of battery but it seems unlikely that this would happen in practice.

Questions about the applicability of the battery analysis to the donor and recipient are not explicitly resolved within transplant legislation. Such legislation will normally impose obligations on practitioners in relation to donors, and sometimes recipients, consenting and being informed. However, legislation rarely explicitly states what liability will arise upon breach of these obligations. In the absence of a legislative remedy for breach of legislative obligations it must be assumed that the legislative obligations are intended to confirm or redefine the scope of practitioners' obligations under the general law. Exactly how this will be done in individual cases will, unsatisfactorily, often be a matter of semantic interpretation.

In some cases legislation imposes a duty to *disclose* but apparently *not as a function of obtaining valid consent.* For instance, in Germany,[283] Finland[284] and the Russian Federation[285] the duty to obtain the donor's consent and the duty to disclose to the donor are separate and unconnected requirements. Similarly in Costa Rica a person can only act as a living donor 'after they have been informed of the risks and possible consequences of the surgery entailed by donation'[286] but there is no requirement that they get this information before consenting. Russian Federation law also speaks of the duty to obtain recipient consent and 'in addition' the need to inform.[287] In cases such as these the judge will continue to have the role of interpreting whether disclosures required under legislation should be integral to obtaining consent and hence actionable under the head of battery where breached *or* not integral to obtaining consent and hence actionable only under negligence. The judge could use the semantics of the legislation to argue that the latter position is the correct one.

---

[283]Act of 5 Nov 1997 at section 8(1)(1)b.
[284]Section 2(3) of ordinance No. 724 of 23 August 1985.
[285]Law of 22 December 1992 at section 12.
[286]Law No. 5560 of 20 August 1974 at section 15. Some other examples are Cyprus (Law No. 97 of 1987 at section 4), Colombia (Decree No. 1172 of 6 June 1989 at section 35 c and e), Kuwait (Decree Law No. 55 of 20 December 1987 at section 3 and 4), Lebanon (Decree No. 109 of 1983), Mexico (Federal Regulations of 16 August 1976 at section 31V and V1) and Panama (Law No. 10 of 11 July 1983 at section 6 and 21).
[287]Law of 22 December 1992 at section 6.

In some cases legislation imposes an obligation to disclose and even ensure understanding of this disclosure before consent is obtained. For example, Algerian Law states that the donor 'may only express his consent after he has been informed by the physician of any medical risks which the removal may entail.'[288] Norwegian law goes further in requiring that before giving his consent the donor must be provided with disclosure and the physician ensure that this disclosure and its significance is understood.[289] In such cases, the implication might be that consent would not be valid unless the legislative disclosure/understanding obligation was first fulfilled. If this is the case, breach of the legislative disclosure/understanding obligation would lead to liability in battery. An alternative construction would be that consent could be obtained irrespective of whether the legislative disclosure/understanding obligation has been fulfilled but that failure to fulfill it before obtaining consent would in itself constitute a breach of duty under the tort of negligence and would thus potentially be actionable as negligent.

Informed Choice in Relation to the Tort of Negligence

As already stated, once informed in broad terms of the nature of the procedure intended, the recipient will probably only have negligence available as a course of action for non-disclosures. To prove negligence, the recipient will have to show that there was an unreasonable non-disclosure causing him/her to take a course of action (s)he would not otherwise have taken.

Reasonableness of Disclosure

We have seen that the recipient has a case for a higher standard of disclosure than the typical patient, what might this mean in concrete terms?

Under a professional based standard of disclosure, a professional would probably be required to give the recipient disclosure of significant harms, risks and benefits in donating and receiving and information to compare

[288] Law No. 85-05 of 16 February 1985 at section 162.

[289] Law No. 6 of 9 February 1973 at section 1. See also Argentina (Section 11 of Law No. 21541), Denmark (Law No. 402 of 13 June 1990 at section 13(3)), Hungary (Ordinance 18 of 4 November 1972 section 2(1)-2(3).

the alternative options including CDT. As to risk disclosure, Lord Bridge in Sidaway said certain risks would have to be disclosed irrespective of medical opinion.[290] He suggested that substantial risks of grave adverse consequences (such as 10% chance of a stroke) must be disclosed.[291] Under this test the recipient might be able to expect information about several types of risk to him/herself such as risk of rejection, the possibility of very serious cumulative side effects from drugs and the possibility of sexual dysfunction (such as impotence) plus any other serious risks applying in reception of a specific type of organ (e.g. lung lobe). The recipient could not necessarily expect disclosure of risks to the donor in kidney donation since there are no substantial risks of grave adverse consequences. However, in other forms of organ donation there might be required disclosures of risk to the donor, e.g. incidental splenectomy in liver segment donation and lobectomy in lung lobe donation.[292]

Lord Bridge's view might be considered too restrictive in the LDT context; one might think that reasonable disclosure would include those donation risks that were not substantial but significant and related to adverse consequences that were not grave but simply significant (e.g. risk of septicaemia to the donor's wound-site, which is usually less than a 5% risk, risk of donor serious injury and/or death in the more novel risky forms of living organ donation - i.e. lung lobe and pancreas vessel length donation). Lord Templeman in Sidaway took a different approach. He felt that general dangers inherent in an operation did not have to be disclosed[293] but 'special' dangers particular to it would have to be disclosed. Presumably this meant special dangers of a significant nature which in renal LDT might include the types of risks discussed above plus such things as risk to the donor of temporary restricted physical capacity after removal, wound-site septicaemia and any special risks associated with the particularities of the participants (e.g. poor health condition). Were the LDT to involve a different organ there would probably be additional disclosures.

Under a reasonable patient based test the recipient would receive a higher standard of disclosure. One would expect the recipient to receive disclosure of all harms to him/herself and the donor that were more than de minimus. One would also expect disclosure of all *the significant risks of*

[290][1985] 1 All ER 643 at 663.
[291]Ibid.
[292]See chapter 2 for further discussion of risks in particular forms of LDT.
[293][1985] 1 All ER 643.

significant harm, such as risk of the graft being lost and of the recipient dying.

How far broader social and economic concerns in LDT would have to be disclosed to the recipient is debatable. Lord Scarman noted that the problem in requiring disclosure of 'non-medically oriented' factors that bear on the patient's decision, 'for example, his family, business or social responsibilities'[294] is that the doctor may not be aware of them. In Arato v Avedon (1993) 858 P.2d 598 a failure to disclose prognosis information that had a knock-on effect to the patient's business interests was held not to be a breach of duty.

It seems, from the standpoint of a professional based test at least, a competent body of medical opinion could probably be brought forward to support non-disclosure of non-medically oriented factors. However, if these factors were obvious to the doctor and of obvious importance to a patient they would certainly have to be disclosed under a reasonable patient based test and would possibly have to be disclosed under a professional based test irrespective of medical opinion. Were a procedure non-therapeutic they would probably be considered part of the full disclosure expected under the tort of battery. Certainly disclosure to a donor within either the tort of battery or negligence ought to include information pertaining to such things as the significant financial implications of donating and the major ways in which (s)he can be defrayed or reimbursed for expenses/lost earnings. Obviously it would be useful if the recipient were also given such information but it may not be required by law.

We have seen that the donor would probably be entitled to full disclosure under the tort of battery but Lloyd LJ in Gold v Haringey Health Authority [1987] 2 All ER 88 seemed to suggest that non-therapeutic procedures should be considered under the tort of negligence and that overall making a legal distinction between them and therapeutic procedures would go against the whole thrust of the House of Lords decision in Sidaway.[295] Some writers have considered a donor's position in relation to the tort of negligence and concluded that even under a professional based test judges would require a high standard of disclosure irrespective of whether a competent body of medical opinion was urging a lower standard

---

[294]Sidaway [1985] 1 All ER 643.

[295]Giving the judgement of the Court of Appeal (Watkins and Stephen Brown LJJ agreed) reversing the view of the trial court.

to be applied. As Skegg puts it,

> ...if a doctor involved in renal transplantation failed to disclose the risks of nephrectomy to a potential living donor, before obtaining his consent to the removal of one of his kidneys a judge would be virtually certain to hold that the doctor was in breach of his duty of care to the donor, even if (which is not the case) the doctor could adduce evidence that his conduct was in accord with a common and professionally approved practice.[296]

Factual Causation

Proving factual causation can often be a problem in establishing negligence as we saw in chapter 1. However, when it comes to the prospective recipient and donor there is typically a decision to be made between LDT or CDT and, in particular, non-disclosure of significant information that pertains to determining which option is preferable could result in the prospective recipient undertaking the option that (s)he would not have taken if non-disclosure had not occurred. In this respect a professional not disclosing to the prospective recipient and donor on such questions as when CDT is likely to become available and the significant harms, risks and prospective benefits of CDT and of LDT, runs the risk of being successfully sued in negligence.

Disclosure in LDT Under Transplant Legislation

The Donor

A few jurisdictions specify the depth of disclosure that is required. For example, the information that must be disclosed under legislation in Romania,[297] Slovakia,[298] Mexico[299] and Bolivia[300] must be disclosed fully and in Belgium it must be disclosed completely.[301] One can probably read into these requirements the presumption that information of de minimus

[296]Skegg, Law, Ethics and Medicine, *Oxford University Press*, 1984, 85.
[297]Law of 1996 at Article 4(2)
[298]Law of 24 August 1994 at section 46(3).
[299]Federal Regulations of 16 August 1976 at section 29.
[300]Regulations of 15 March 1982 at section 10.
[301]Law No.32 of 1986 at section 9.

significance would not have to be disclosed. Perhaps Hungary[302] and Poland[303] have a better approach in requiring that the specified disclosure is in detail. Slovenian law requires it to be 'appropriate'[304] which might take into account the specific needs of the donor but isn't necessarily a guarantee that it will be detailed. All in all these terms are a little vague and might usefully be supplemented by guidelines providing something of a model of what information should be disclosed.

There are considerable legislative variations as to the range of information that must be disclosed to the donor. Many legislative provisions are narrowly drawn around disclosure of risks and consequences arising directly out of the procedure. For example, Mexican law provides that the donor must have been,

> ...fully informed of the risks to himself of the operation and the consequences to himself of the removal of the organ, and the degree of probability of a successful transplant.[305]

Hungary's law states that the donor must be informed,

> ...in a thorough and detailed manner, of the necessity for the operation, the risks it entails, and the sequelae which may occur subsequently.[306]

Poland's law states that the donor must,

> ...be informed in detail about the intervention, the risk connected with it and any possible typical consequences for his health condition.[307]

Slovenian law requires an

> ...appropriate explanation about the nature, purpose and course of the operation, probability of its success and usual risks.[308]

In Finland a physician, not being the physician who is caring for the

---

[302]Section 2(1) of Ordinance No.18 of 4 November 1972.
[303]Law of October 26, 1995 at Article 9(1) pt. 5.
[304]The Law of 1996 at Article 10.
[305]Federal Regulations of 16 August 1976 at section 29.
[306]Section 2(1) of Ordinance No.18 of 4 November 1972.
[307]Law of October 26, 1995 at Article 9(1) pt. 5.
[308]The Law of 1996 at Article 10.

recipient, shall explain to the donor what is entailed by the procedure and its effects for the donor himself and for the recipient.[309] Cypriot law requires disclosure of the medical consequences of removal.[310] Kuwait's law only requires disclosure of the effects to the donor's health that may result from the removal[311] and Sweden's law only the nature of intervention and the risks entailed.[312] Sri Lanka[313] and several Australian laws[314] simply require the physician to explain the nature and effect of the removal and several laws only require disclosure of risk.[315]

The Third Conference of European Health Ministers in Paris (16-17 November 1987) suggests that the donor should be given,

> ...appropriate information before the removal about it's possible consequences, in particular the medical, social and psychological effects, as well as about the implications of the donation for the recipient.[316]

Some jurisdictions do take a similar expansive approach to the range of what should be disclosed to the donor. Spanish law states that the living donor as well as being informed about the foreseeable physical, mental and psychological consequences of donation must also be informed about the possible effects of the donation on the donor's personal, family and professional life and the benefits which it is hoped the recipient will derive from the transplant.[317] In Belgium the physician who is to carry out the removal must provide clear and complete information to the donor and any

---

309 A statement must be included in the application to the National Board of Health that this information has been given to the donor (Law No.355 of 26 April 1985 at section 2 - see also Ordinance No. 724 of 23 August 1985).

310 Law No. 97 of 1987 at section 7(3).

311 Decree No. 55 of 20 December 1987 at section 4.

312 Law No. 831 of 8 June 1995 at section 10 (see *IDHL*, 1996, 47(1), 28-30 at 29).

313 Act, No. 48 of 1987 at section 8(3).

314 Northern Territory Act No. 121 of 1979 at section 10(b), Tasmania The Human Tissue Act 1985 at section 9(b) and Western Australia Act No. 116 of 1982 at section 8(1)(c).

315 For example: Algerian Law No. 85-05 of 16 February 1985 at section 162; Bolivian Regulations of 15 March 1982 at section 10; Bulgaria's 1996 law; Slovakia Law of 24 August 1994 at section 46(3).

316 Adopted as para 11. of The Council of Europe Recommendation No.R (79) of The Committee of Ministers to the Member States. Reprinted in WHO, Legislative Responses To Organ Transplantation, *Martinus Nijhoff*, 1994, Appendix 1.

317 Crown Decree No. 426 of 22 February 1980 at section 3.

person whose consent is required on the physical, mental, family, and social effects of the removal procedure.[318] In Colombia the donor must be given,

> ...prior information on the consequences of his decision to the extent they are foreseeable from the somatic, mental and psychological standpoint, and on the possible repercussions that the donation may have for his personal, family and professional life, as well as on the anticipated benefits of the transplantation for the recipient.[319]

In Romania the law states that the donor can only give consent after being

> ...fully informed by the doctors about the possible physical, psychical, family and professional risks and consequences following the act of harvesting.[320]

Tunisian law requires the donor to be informed of the possible consequences of his decision including all the foreseeable physical and mental consequences of organ removal, and the possible repercussions of removal on the donor's personal, family and professional life and all the results that the recipient can anticipate as a result of the transplantation.[321] Turkey has a similar provision with the unique addition that the donor's spouse is also to be informed.[322]

The recent Netherlands law states that disclosure must include information on,

> ...the nature and object of the removal, and also the foreseeable risks for his health and the conditions affecting his life.[323]

The Netherlands transplant law is unique in expressly stating that the donor must be given information on the provisions of the law itself concerning the reimbursement of expenses.[324] It also has the very thoughtful feature of requiring the information to be presented in different formats; it must be

[318]Law No.32 of 1986 at section 9.
[319]Decree No.1172 of 6 June 1989 at section 35.
[320]Law of 1996 at Article 4(2).
[321]Law No. 91-22 of 25 March 1991 at section 7.
[322]Law No. 2238 of 29 May 1979 at section 7(a).
[323]Ibid.
[324]Law of 1996, section 3(2).

presented, 'orally and in writing and, where appropriate, with the aid of audiovisual means'. This approach will particularly aid persons with certain types of disability (e.g. reading, hearing difficulties).

Germany's law is mainly focused on the medical aspects of the procedure in it's statement that the donor must,

> ...be informed by a physician about the type of intervention, its scope and the possible, also indirect, repercussions and delayed sequalae of the intended organ removal for his or her health, the organ transplant's expected chances of succeeding.[325]

However, this sentence goes on to add that the donor is to be given 'other facts which are evidently of importance to him or her with respect to organ donation.'[326] This suggests that specific broader information must be given by the physician either if he should reasonably know that the donor would want it or if the donor asks him for it.

Recipients

There is little discussion of the depth of disclosure to recipients under transplant legislation although India's 1994 law requires the medical practitioner to explain all possible effects, complications and hazards; 'all' presumably meaning all that are beyond the de minimus level. A number of jurisdictions address the range of information that must be disclosed. Most of them take a similar approach to Indian law.

Argentinean law states that the recipient must be informed of the likely risks and benefits of the procedure.[327] Similarly, Panama's law requires that physicians who undertake a transplant inform the recipient of the risks and consequences of the procedure.[328] Greek law requires physicians responsible for the removal to provide the recipient with information relating to the possible consequences of the removal and transplant.[329] More narrowly, Russian Federation law only requires the recipient to be informed of possible complications.[330]

---

[325]Act of 5 Nov 1997 at section 8(4)2.

[326]Ibid.

[327]Transplantation Law No. 24193 of 24 March 1993 at section 13.

[328]Law No. 10 of 11 July 1983 at section 6.

[329]Section 5-6 of Law No. 1383 of 2 August 1983.

[330]Law of 22 Dec 1992 at section 6.

Bolivian law includes two very specific statements that the recipient is to be informed as to whether the organ came form a living person or a dead one and is to get information,

> ...regarding the results of tissue compatibility tests between the organs or tissues of the donor and of the recipient as well as the potential immunological risks and reactions (this information is to be provided in writing).[331]

All of these jurisdictions would allow for disclosure of more significant physiological and psychological consequences and potential consequences but what about other issues such as potential economic impact or impact on the family? Such issues are potential effects or consequences arising from the LDT but not in the strictest sense arising directly out of the procedure itself.

Requirements as to Ensuring Understanding of Disclosure Under Transplant Legislation

In order to obtain consent to an intervention a practitioner has to communicate certain information and must believe that the patient has understood the information or at least understood the nature and purpose of the intervention intended. However, some transplant legislation appears to place a more definite obligation on the practitioner to ensure that what is disclosed is understood.

The Donor

Some jurisdictions have provisions which leave one uncertain as to whether they are implying that the disclosure and/or other information must be understood by the donor. For instance, Romanian law states that consent must be given in a deliberate manner;[332] which could mean a conscious intent based on a certain understanding of what is involved is required. Belgium's legislation requires donation to occur knowingly,[333] which presumably means there must be a certain awareness of what is

[331]Decree No. 55 of 1987 at sections 9 and 10.
[332]Law of 1996 at Article 4(1).
[333]Law of 13 June 1986 at section 8(1).

involved. More definitively, The Netherlands law requires the person removing the organ to ensure that the donor has given consent with full knowledge of the consequences.[334] The Council of Europe's Draft Protocol on Organ Transplantation[335] and several jurisdictions such as the Russian Federation[336] and Portugal[337] may obligate the professional to ensure a certain level of understanding is held by the donor through stipulating that donor consent must be informed. Legislative provisions that refer to the need for donor consent to be deliberate or knowing or informed might be interpreted as requiring understanding of significant psychological and physiological aspects and also interpreted in the light of any specific disclosure requirement within the relevant legislation. Oddly, Italian law may reflect different cultural priorities and mitigate against the requirement for informed understanding by requiring donation to occur spontaneously!![338]

Several jurisdictions follow a specification of what must be disclosed with an obligation on the practitioner to ensure that disclosure is understood. For instance, Norway's law states that before giving his consent the donor must have been provided by a physician with information on the nature of the operation and its possible consequences and that this physician has an obligation to ensure that the donor has understood the information provided to him and its significance.[339] Lebanon's law requires the physician to inform the donor of the consequences and risks of the intervention and satisfy himself that the donor has properly understood.[340] South Australian law requires the practitioner to ensure the donor has understood, in the light of medical evidence furnished him, 'the nature and effect of the removal and the nature of the transplantation'.[341] Similarly, Danish law requires the physician to ensure donor understanding of disclosure of the nature of the procedure, its consequences, and the risks.[342]

---

[334]Law of 24 May 1996 at section 3(2). See *IDHL*, 1996, 47(4), 469-475.
[335]Steering Committee on Bioethics (CDBI) (97)5, Article 7.
[336]Law of 22 Dec 1992 at section 11.
[337]Law No. 12 of 22 April 1993 at section 8(1).
[338]Law No. 458 of 26 June 1967 applying only to kidney donation.
[339]Section 1 of Law No. 6 of 9 February 1973.
[340]Decree No. 109 of 16 September 1983 at section 1(2)).
[341]Section 9(2) of the Transplantation and Anatomy Act 1983.
[342]Section 13(3) of Law No. 402 of 13 June 1990.

In the UK, donors that are defined as non-genetically related to the recipient under HOTA[343] are required to give consent under regulation 3(2)b of The Human Organ Transplants (Unrelated Persons) Regulations 1989.[344] Regulation 3(2)e adds that the donor and recipient must both have been interviewed by a person who appears to the ULTRA to have been suitably qualified to conduct such interviews. This person then reports to the Authority that certain conditions are satisfied and refers to any difficulties of communication experienced and how these difficulties were overcome.[345] One of factors ULTRA must be satisfied of[346] is that a registered medical practitioner has given the donor an explanation of the nature of the medical procedure for, and the risk involved in, the removal of the organ in question.[347] Additionally, under regulation 3(2)b the authority must be satisfied that the donor *understands* the nature of the *medical procedure and the risks* as explained by the registered medical practitioner, and consents to the removal of the organ in question.[348] Similarly, in Hong Kong in the case of donations *not* between genetic relatives or spouses of 3 or more years standing there must be authorisation by the body set up to deal with such donations under the law and amongst other things the body must be satisfied that the donor understands the nature and consequences of the removal.[349]

Some legislation leaves the matter of what must be understood to interpretation. For instance, Slovenian law simply requires that the donation be based on the appropriate information. This would presumably require at least the understanding of the significant physiological and psychological issues involved and specifically definite consequences and

---

[343]Including distant relatives, spouses and persons who are only related emotionally (HOTA section 2).

[344]SI No. 2480 passed by the Secretary of State pursuant to HOTA section 2(3).

[345]The Human Organ Transplants (Unrelated Persons) Regulations 1989 (SI No. 2480). Regulation 3(2)e.

[346]Regulation 3(1)c ibid. An exception is donations that are subsidiary to medical treatment (e.g. therapeutically necessary heart or cornea removal).

[347]Regulation 3(2)a ibid.

[348]Presumably a decision by ULTRA on donation could be subject to judicial review for incorrect application of the regulations. However, section 2(3) of HOTA only requires that the Authority is *subjectively* satisfied that the requirements under the regulations have been met so for successful review there would probably have to be *very strong objective evidence* that the Authority couldn't have been satisfied.

[349]Section 5(4)c of Ordinance No. 16 of 1995.

potential risks and benefits of a significant nature.

The Recipient

The only jurisdictions which require actual understanding by the recipient of information communicated are Hong Kong (for donations which are *not* between genetic relatives or spouses of 3 or more years standing[350]) and Portugal.[351]

Therapeutic Privilege and Informed Choice

The notion of therapeutic privilege is particularly in line with the idea that it is for the medical practitioner to determine what disclosure is reasonable in the circumstances. Hence, whilst concealment offends the principle of self-determination and can actually compromise the independence of decision-making, it is widely applied under the professional based test.

Clearly for the donor and recipient, as any patient,[352] disclosure would normally be expected in relation to specific questions asked. The grounds for non-disclosure to a recipient should not include the possibility of refusal per se because this would undermine the recipients ability to exercise his/her ethical duty to consider whether living donation is justifiable. Non-disclosure to the recipient might in some cases be justified (even where there is a reasonable patient test in operation) if disclosure would be likely to cause significant harm in the light of mental attributes the recipient is clearly known to have. Rogers v Whittaker [1993] 4 Med LR 79 at 83 noted the possibility of non-disclosure in cases where the patient is nervous, disturbed or volatile.

In the context of the tort of battery it was stated in Halushka that there were no grounds to allow 'therapeutic privilege' to justify non-disclosure in relation to non-therapeutic research interventions. Gieson has noted the wider logic that therapeutic privilege should not apply to any intervention

[350]Section 5(4)c of Ordinance No. 16 of 1995.

[351]Law No. 12 of 22 April 1993 at sections 7 and 8(1).

[352]See Blyth v Bloomsbury Health Authority [1993] 4 Med LR 151 and for further discussion see Kennedy and Grubb, Medical Law: Text With Materials, *Butterworths*, 1994, 205-211.

where therapy is not intended, including living donation.[353]

Even if disclosure to the donor was primarily a matter for the tort of negligence it is difficult to see therapeutic privilege being a valid consideration. Skegg, considering the worst scenario of the professional-based disclosure test, concludes that even if there was an established practice of non-disclosure in non-therapeutic cases (which there is not),

> ...it is highly unlikely that judges would accept that evidence of such a practice conclusively established that a doctor was not in breach of the duty he owed to the patient.[354]

It would be hard to justify concealment from the living donor and Edmund Davies LJ has even extra-judicially stated that disclosure must take place where the donor does not wish it,

> ...however eager the donor is to play out his self sacrificial role, the surgeon is under a legal duty to make clear to him the risks involved. He may not want the truth, but in this case the truth must be forced upon him.[355]

The Impact of Innovation on Disclosure in LDT

Innovative treatment in the field of transplantation could be said to include new forms of LDT which are not established as normal treatments. This would probably be the case with lung lobe, bowel segment and pancreas section transplantation using living donors and might even still be the case with respect to living donor liver segment donation.

Where there are unknown factors, including the possibility of unknown risks materialising, frank disclosure/explanation of this would be expected under general principles of law.[356] However, disclosure is unlikely to be affected by the fact of innovation per se. It would be influenced if the innovation is of a nature or degree that makes the intervention more unpredictable, in terms of its levels of benefit and harm, than a standard

[353]D.Gieson, International Medical Malpractice Law, *J.C.B. Mohr (Paul Siebeck) and Martinus Nijhoff*, 1988, 608.
[354]Skegg, Law Ethics and Medicine, *Oxford University Press,* 1984, 84.
[355]The Patients Right to Know the Truth, *Proc Roy Soc Med,* 1973, 533 at 535.
[356]Several authorities are presented for this view in D.Gieson, Civil Liability of Physicians for New Methods of Treatment and Experimentation: A Comparative Examination, *Med Law Review*, 1995 (Spring), 3, 22-52 at 35.

treatment. Some forms of living organ donation can be more unpredictable than standard treatment in terms of their impact for the recipient but at the same time more like a standard treatment in terms of their impact on the donor. I am thinking here of forms of organ donation where the removal has been done historically for medical reasons outside the donation context. For instance, in chapter 2 we saw that lung lobe removal has reasonably estimable risks and harms from the start because of previous clinical experience of it outside the LDT context, e.g. in lung cancer cases.

The only specific consideration of innovative treatment within transplant legislation is Colombia's transplant law which states that the donor and recipient must have been warned in advance of the impossibility of knowing with certainty all the risks that the procedure may entail, on account of the possibility of unforeseen situations.[357]

Conclusions

Liability for inadequate disclosure can clearly *benefit* medicine by providing an impetus for practitioners to fully respect and support patients to make informed, autonomous decisions. Yet we have seen that legal principles are designed in such a way as to make it difficult for a patient to make a successful claim. The problems with general principles of law will be less significant for a donor if, as may be possible, (s)he can claim under the head of battery rather than negligence. The recipient is probably in much the same position as the average patient although perhaps entitled to a slightly higher standard of disclosure.

Whilst legislation has commonly addressed the position of donor, and sometimes recipient, with regard to disclosure the relationship between legislative requirements and the torts of negligence and battery is not always clear. In addition, the way legislation is constructed and general principles are elucidated pays insufficient attention to the need to ensure effective communication and understanding of disclosures made.

Legislation ought to routinely specify what should be disclosed to both the donor and the recipient, being specific about what range of information is to be disclosed and, with non-clinical factors, requiring at least disclosure of economic consequences to the donor. Practitioners should be required to make reasonable efforts to adjust the manner of disclosure to fit

[357]Decree No. 1173 of 6 June 1989 at section 35.

the circumstances - in particular the general intellectual capabilities, language, disabilities and special learning needs of the donor or recipient. It should also specify the depth of disclosure - such as by requiring disclosure of all significant benefits and harms and of risks of both minor harms that have a significant chance of materialising and more significant harms that have more than a de minimus chance of materialising.

Legislation should also require the practitioner to take reasonable measures to ensure that the donor and recipient have a reasonable understanding of what has been disclosed. These measures might simply involve verbal questioning and interaction or could involve more formal psychological evaluation. There is a case for all breaches of the above requirements to give rise to a single civil form of action developed especially under the legislation and providing remedies such as compensation at a level that is appropriate and equitable as between the parties. Action for criminal assault could be left open in cases where the practitioner had not obtained consent but using Chatterton v Gerson as the basis for holding that consent is real once the person is informed in broad terms of the nature and purpose of the intervention intended.

The above provisions may seem stringent but if they are laid out clearly will not be too difficult for a practitioner to follow. Guidelines for informing donors and recipients within codes of practice and centre protocols would usefully supplement legislative provision.

The issues of what donors and recipients do with information having received it are explored in detail in the next chapter. However, at this point it is important to resolve the question of what practitioners should do where prospective donors and recipients make a decision to take up LDT before being given information or, where information has already been given, before it has been checked that they have understood it. Legislation could require practitioners to specify that they will not accept a decision until after disclosure and checks of understanding. Any 'choice' made by a prospective donor or recipient before this point would be treated as merely a preliminary view. Equally, if someone was saying that they did not want information their is a strong argument to say they should be given it anyway. There is a case for saying that the practitioner should only be able to use a defence of therapeutic privilege to justify withholding specific pieces of information and here only if withholding was a therapeutic necessity (e.g. with a serious phobia) and it was ensured that that the donor and recipient still had a balanced view of the merits and demerits of the respective options.

Any testing of prospective donors should be done with an awareness that it may increase the chances that the donor will feel locked into donating. It should only be done where the prospective donor has expressed a clear interest in the possibility of becoming a donor and (s)he should be routinely offered a way out of donating 'without losing face'.

4 Motivation and Voluntariness

Introduction

The medical professional has a legitimate role to identify what option might be in the patient's best interests and to advise, suggest or encourage the patient to take this option. However, this must always take place within the context of the patient's right to self-determination being paramount. Once a professional views self-determination as secondary to securing a particular course of treatment, communication will become a means to the end of securing compliance.

The most clear examples of the patient's rights not being treated as an end in themselves are the use of physical force, coercion and the use of overt persuasion and manipulation with the intent to break down the patient's true will. However, as The Presidents Commission in its 1982 Report 'Making Health Care Decisions' noted, such crude methods are of little concern in medical professional-patient relationships because it is easy to elicit compliance through more subtle means. The context of the decision can be set-up in such a way as to increase the chances of compliance. This can be either more innocent or deliberate but the crucial concern is the impact it has on the ability of a person to make a decision that is voluntary in the sense of being the decision they would have made had the decisional context not been distorted. The position of living donor, and even recipient, is interesting because family members can be as prominent as medical professionals in exerting a distorting influence. Inducing someone to donate is rather like inducing someone to undertake non-therapeutic research. It is worse than inducing someone to undergo a procedure designed for their own best interests.

We saw in chapter 1 that under general principles of law competent adults are generally protected from having to undergo a medical intervention against their will. A competent adult would never be required to donate against their will or to undertake acts preparatory to donation. If this proposition needed support it gets it from McFall v Shimp [1978] 10 Pa D&C (3d) 90 (Ct Comm Pl, Pa). In McFall the plaintiff had a rare bone marrow disease and he brought an action seeking a direction that his adult cousin, the only suitable prospective donor of bone marrow in the family, be required to submit to procedures for the extraction of bone marrow for transplantation into the plaintiff despite his unwillingness to do so. Justice Flaherty, in denying the plaintiff's claim, stated that,

> (f)or our law to compel the defendant to submit to an intrusion of his body would change every concept and principle upon which our society is founded. To do so would defeat the sanctity of the individual, and would impose a rule which would know no limits, and one could not imagine where the line would be drawn.

It was remarkable that this case was even brought given that the competent adult's right to refuse medical treatment is so well embedded in law.

A practitioner forcing an intervention or undertaking one knowing that consent was involuntary (and therefore invalid) could be criminally sanctioned for assault and sued for battery. To avoid these outcomes consent must be obtained and consent is treated as unreal both in cases where intervention is brought about by coercion and in cases where it is induced by an outside influence which has overborne the independence of the decision. Whilst LDT legislation does not usually consider recipient voluntariness it generally considers donor voluntariness, supporting the requirement for it in both a direct sense and in a more indirect sense by laying down requirements as to motivation in donation, how consent can be withdrawn, procedural formalities that must be complied with in informing the donor and obtaining consent and by placing restrictions in relation to donor status (e.g. prisoners) or relationship with the recipient.

Voluntariness in Practice

Motivation in LDT

The starting point of specific concerns about voluntariness in LDT, and an issue in its own right, is donor and recipient motivation. We saw in the last chapter that most people make medical decisions, including decisions about LDT, without much deliberation. The problem is that if people are not deliberating on their decisions they will tend to be less aware of the existence and significance of influences bearing down on them from the outside.

Lack of deliberation can be an unconscious defence mechanism to avoid awareness of one's true feelings on a matter. For instance, a desire to avoid guilt or a desire to be redeemed for past wrongs could lead someone to donate without deliberation. The Minnesota study of R.G.Simmons et al. found that a quarter of 114 donors agreed with the statement that donation was one way to 'make up for the wrongs we may have done to others in our lives'.[358] In another study, 46% of the public anticipated that they would feel intense guilt or self-criticism if they were asked to donate but refused.[359] Fellner and Marshall have pointed to definite cases where non-deliberative decisions to donate were the unconscious product of wanting to avoid inner conflict in making the decision.[360] They observed that some prospective donors passively let the selection process decide for them.[361] This point was confirmed in the Minnesota study which found 5% of donors didn't make a conscious choice about whether to donate or not but simply took a succession of steps locking them into the process of donation.[362]

In some cases agreement to donate, whether occurring passively or positively, may occur in the context of ambivalent feelings. In the Minnesota study 21% of donors, pre-transplant, agreed a little with the statement 'I sometimes feel unsure about donating' and a further 5% agreed with this statement a lot. A number had fears surrounding donation: 20% agreed a lot that surgery frightens them and a further 31% agreed a little. One third were concerned about their future with only one kidney and between 10 and 20% were concerned about the length of their recovery period, the timing of the operation, the financial sacrifice involved and conflicts between their obligation to their immediate family and to the recipient. Whilst ambivalence is to be expected as a feature of any decision-making context there is always the danger of a person playing it down as a factor and even suppressing it in order to avoid discomfort. Since people can suppress ambivalence even from their own awareness, it is difficult to quantify the extent to which it is present. However, there are instances where it will be self-admitted but hidden from others and the

---

358 29% agreed that they 'had done something major in their life that their family did not approve of' (Gift of Life, *Wiley and Sons*, 1977, 162).

359 Written questionnaire completed by 116 adults in a Midwestern US City concerning attitudes to donation - presented in C.H.Fellner and S.H.Schwartz, Altruism in Disrepute: Medical Versus Public Attitudes Toward The Living Organ Donor, *The New Eng J Med*, 1971 (March 18), 582-585 at 584.

360 Twelve Kidney Donors, *J Am Med Assoc,* 1968, 206, 2703-2707 at 2706.

361 Ibid.

362 R.G.Simmons et al., Gift of Life, *Transaction Books*, 1987 at 245.

ultimate example of this in the living donation situation is where a person is secretly wishing that they are found unsuitable as donors. In the Minnesota study 12% of prospective donors felt they would be relieved if they were not able to donate. A further 1% felt they would be very relieved.[363] However, a good proportion of these people probably do not end up being donors. Typically studies find only between 3 and 8% of people who having actually donated would not go through the process again if the 'clock was turned back.'[364] Many donors are actually very positive about their experience. The EUROTOLD interview/questionnaire found this was especially the case within, the admittedly hand-picked, Norwegian sample where attitudes included:

- disappointment that the kidney had failed but feeling the right decision had still been made;
- 'I can recommend it' seeing the recipient recover was 'the best happening in my life...I never had such an experience in my life';
- 'it was a normal thing to do'; it was 'very natural...I'm very satisfied';
- 'a natural process';
- a donor who felt fear about the process living with this through the recognition that her deeper feelings were in favour of donation; *and*
- a further donor fearing hospitals but wanting to help out her sister.

My view is that the Oslo centre seemed to be getting most things right when it came to donors and had contributed to the generally positive attitude of Norwegian society to living donation.

The EUROTOLD recipient questionnaire/interviews present a similar picture for receiving. Only 3 recipients stated they would not go through the whole process again; one in Leicester who had had severe health problems and 2 in Slovenia, one of whom simply stated a preference for cadaveric donation while the other was concerned about graft failure (the reason for this latter concern was not expressed although it was clear that the recipient had had a number of failed grafts). There were only 3 recipients who had reconsidered before finally agreeing to receive (2 Slovakian recipients who did not say why and 1 Polish recipient who was

---

363 Gift of Life, *Wiley and Sons*, 1977 at 154-155.

364 For example, EUROTOLD found only 3 out of the 76 donors administered its interview/questionnaire felt this way. One had regret because of it affecting income, another because of having to wait a long time for it to happen and the third because of realising that the graft would not function for a lifetime.

worried for the health of the donor) although 23 recipients found it quite or very difficult to receive, with only 16 finding it easy or not difficult.

Figure 2: EUROTOLD Donor and Recipient Questionnaire/Interview Results on Why LDT is Preferred

In the Slovenian sample the recipients stated in 17 out of 22 instances that there was more than one person offering to give them a kidney, with the final decision almost always being stated as having been taken on medical grounds. The donors had a slightly different perception of the situation with 15 out of 24 saying someone else had also offered. The final decision was invariably grounded in medical reasons, but in 1 case it was classified as 'psychological' and in another the alternative donor was in a greater state of fear about the donation. In 2 out of 3 Slovakian cases donors said they were the only person offering and were finally chosen for medical reasons which all 3 recipients said had been the basis for their decision.

In the Leicester sample reasons given by donors for donating included that: 'It was a natural thing to do/the recipient's brother couldn't (because of insurance) or wouldn't (due to being arrogant/hypochondriac)'; 'basically thought that it was a good idea'; had not liked to see her brother ill; *and* chose but thought other options not considered/'recipients mother would not have been able to cope with being a donor'. In two further cases the decision to use living donation may have been heavily influenced by the fact that the recipients were minors in considerable distress on dialysis.

In the Oslo interviews 7 donor-recipient pairs indicated a specific preference for LDT over cadaver with reason including: the fact that cadaver donation had a long waiting list; LDT offers the chance to prepare for the operation and be in control of timing more; a lesser rate of rejection/better success rate; LDT offers the chance for someone else to have a cadaver instead; and one donor rather surprisingly said that he simply hadn't considered cadaver as a possible first option! One recipient had a genetic family whose members were precluded from donating by the nature of the kidney problem. His spouse donated because she 'hoped to help my husband...I had seen so much...after I had seen his illness I wanted to do something'. Two recipients had rejection crises but the donors were more concerned for them than the fact that what they had donated might not last.

Quality HLA matches (95% and 100%) were mentioned as a basis for preferring LDT in two Dublin interviews. In a further interview it was clear that the decision to use LDT was influenced by the recipient's quality of life deteriorating on dialysis rapidly. In Romania in 4 out of 5 instances the recipient stated that the particular donor was chosen for 'medical reasons'.

Human motivation is often like an iceberg in that a large part of it lies beneath the surface of conscious awareness. Some prospective donors insulate themselves from information which challenges their initial decision (reification).[365] Since donation is a rescuing type activity it can also be uncertain whether the feeling of 'duty' to donate stems from internalised social programming (social morality) or from a deeper sense of it being the right thing to do. The following extract of a EUROTOLD interview with a Norwegian donor and recipient illustrates this point,

> Donor: ...it was just a matter of course. That's how it is.
> Interviewer: Somehow then, er just sort of...the right thing to do?
> Donor: Oh yes...there's a problem that you have no other choice but er... you were very glad also that you were accepted as a donor (laughing).
> Recipient to Interviewer: ....But may I ask a question? Although you are doing the questioning!
> Recipient to Donor: You say you had no choice and I think that I understand what I mean but isn't that sort of contrary to what the situation should be. I mean when, isn't it supposed to be that before people become living donors ...shouldn't he have a choice...I mean you felt compelled to do this - or what do you mean by 'had no choice'?
> Donor: I think that first of all of course you have a responsibility as a father, you have to live up to that and you have to do the best for your own child...that's one thing and er...if I had been asked and given the possibility to say yes or no I would feel like there's no question of yes or no in a situation like ours...this was, as I tried to put it, as a matter of course and on that point there was no question of a choice. We had never thought of doing anything...I was I would say very blessed that I was able to do this sort of thing. It generated great happiness. One could say beforehand that we should do it together, we should fix it, and then the situation was clear, there were no obstacles, it was go ahead.
> Interviewer: (later): ...when you say you have no choice that can be taken in two ways and I take it one way but some people would say they have no choice and this meant they were like forced or pressured.
> Donor: Yes but I didn't mean it that way.
> Interviewer: Yes, like this was a different kind of feeling of no choice...you know that this was just the right thing.
> Donor: Yes at this stage it (the choice) did not exist and that way I was not given the choice in a positive way.
> Interviewer: Umm (listening).

---

[365]Kidney Donors, in J.Macauley and L.Berkowitz (eds.), Altruism and Helping Behaviour, *Academic Press*, 1970, 279.

Recipient: I have been thinking a bit about that - both my parents have a terrible sense of duty - you know a sense of duty to life in general.. and er er.. I saw that particularly right before we had the surgery... and you know I knew that things could go wrong and I thought that would be absolutely awful - I couldn't live with that but then I sort of remembered the situation at the summerhouse. I was sitting on the terrace over breakfast and I sort of put this question sort of timidly and I just remembered they both jumped in their chairs and said, 'please I want to do this'. This spontaneous reaction was my proof that this was really something they wanted to do and not something they felt they should do from any kind of negative duty...so I sort of cling to that (laughing). That was very important to me.

Decisional Context Distortion in LDT

Saks has stated that in US medical practice some features of the process used by physicians to obtain informed consent from patients,

> ...bear a troubling resemblance to the procedures used by police to obtain confessions from suspects: demand characteristics of the situation, perceptual and judgmental distortions, social relations distortions, and semantic and verbal distortions.[366]

He suggests that prospective donors are vulnerable to pressure to donate.[367] Studies show that a significant minority of donors are aware of experiencing pressure. Simmons et al. noted overt pressure in 11% of cases[368] while Westlie et al.'s study of Quality of Life in Norwegian donors[369] indicates that 15.7% of donors experienced pressure in the process, 9.3% of this being to donate and 6.4% not to donate. The sources of this pressure were friends, family and medical personnel. As only 4.9% of donors experienced family conflict over the donation it may be that pressure was exerted as much, or more so, by friends and medical personnel as the by family itself.

Interestingly, EUROTOLD donor questionnaire/interviews found no

---

[366]Social Psychological Contributions to a Legislative Subcommittee on Organ and Tissue Transplants, *American Psychologist,* 1978 (July), 680-690 at 685.
[367]Ibid.
[368]Gift of Life, *Wiley and Sons*, 1977, 158. Most of the donors who were openly pressured were ambivalent about donation - see next section.
[369]*Nephrol Dial Trans*, 1993, 8, 1146-1150.

evidence that donors were pressured to donate. One donor had married the recipient knowing that she had kidney problems which might get worse but there was no sign that the donation was in exchange for the marriage or money. In one instance a man had donated to his brother in law (who had the same rare blood group type), there being no evidence of dubious motivation in this case. Pressure *not to donate* was reported by 5 out of 21 donors in the Slovenian sample. In the recipient questionnaire/interviews 5 out of 48 recipients felt pressure to receive including 1 in the Slovenian sample who felt pressure from the donor, 1 in the Slovakian sample who felt pressure from the donor and from parents and 3 in the Polish sample, two of whom felt pressure from medical staff. 3 recipients felt pressure not to receive from a living donor.

It must be stated that EUROTOLD did not use a family systems based analysis of pressure in relation to LDT and only examined experience post donation. There is a need for European based studies that will track and uncover donor, recipient, medical and family actions and motivations before, during and after the act of donation.

Family conflict could be linked to pressure in some cases. Westlie et al.'s study indicated that 95.1% of donors said the donation had not led to any conflicts in relation to their family. The remainder said it had led to 'some' conflict (3.7%) or 'severe' conflict (1.2%), this mainly being with a spouse. R.G.Simmons et al. pointed to increased family cohesiveness consequent upon donation. They found that the donor search led to family conflict in 25% of cases but suggest that these were families who were more likely to have had a history of significant family conflict.[370] Donor-recipient dependency might also lend itself to pressure. Westlie et al.'s study found 68.3% of donors were able to categorically state there was no dependency between them and the donor.[371] Some of the remaining cases may have involved some dependency, which may have resulted in some decisions being partly based on donors feeling pressure inside of themselves to donate or from the recipient. However, dependency could have started post-donation in some instances.

The problem of asking donors if they experienced or complied through pressure is that most influences are of a subtle and often hard to detect nature rather than being more overt attempts at manipulation or coercion. These subtle pressures can take many forms.

---

[370]Gift of Life, *Wiley & Sons* 1977 at 435.

[371]*Nephrol Dial Trans*, 1993, 8, 1146-1150.

General psychological literature shows that one can increase the likelihood of someone performing a 'target behaviour' by using what is called the 'Foot in the Door Technique' of getting the person to undertake preliminary behaviours.[372] Generally speaking, the more preliminary behaviours that are induced the greater the probability that the person will perform the target behaviour.[373] This type of activity is most common among salespeople who are often concerned above all else to have you reach a particular outcome that accords to their interests and may unconsciously or quite deliberately distort communication to that end. However, the same situation could arise in LDT. Where getting someone to offer to be a living donor is unconsciously or consciously the target behaviour, induced action taking encouraging 'compliance' would include getting subjects to discuss the position, go for a blood test and get a check of tissue compatibility and health suitability. Typically after undertaking such acts the subject would find it psychologically more difficult to withdraw from becoming a person who offers to donate. Schwarz's experimental study of volunteering to be a bone marrow donor found evidence that action taking was being induced prior to a person being asked whether or not they want to donate[374] and the same is likely to frequently occur in organ donation.

Clearly what should be happening is that as soon as LDT has been raised as a possibility with prospective donors they should be given all the significant information pertaining to evaluating it alongside the alternatives. Then the professional should check that the key issues have been comprehended. At this point the prospective donors can be entered into tests with their agreement on the basis of the understanding that this is to see who, if anyone, is suitable. Prospective donors ought not to be tested unless they feel that they might want to go on to be an actual donor. Equally the stance taken towards them should not assume that they will want to donate if they are found medically suitable. Indeed, centres should give them a way out without losing face. This is standard practice at the Oslo centre where the transplant professionals are quite prepared to use the

---

[372]J.L.Freedman and S.C.Fraser, Compliance Without Pressure: The Foot in The Door Technique, *J of Personality and Soc Psych,* 1966, 4, 195-202.

[373]A.Bandura, Principles of Behaviour Modification, *Holt, Reinhart and Winston,* 1969.

[374]S.H.Schwartz, Elicitation of Moral Obligation and Self sacrificing Behaviour: An Experimental Study of Volunteering to Be a Bone Marrow Donor, *J of Personality and Soc Psych*, 1970, 15, 283-293.

truth creatively by telling the relatives of the prospective donor that (s)he was medically unsuitable. However, EUROTOLD found that this is not routine practice in all European centres.

Figure 3: Should Donors be Approached Pro-actively and, if so, by Whom?

The British Transplantation Society in its recent survey of UK transplant centres found that 15 out of 31 active in LDT took a pro-active approach to potential donors.[375] EUROTOLD's Transplant Centre Questionnaire found that in European Transplant Centres there was often more than one way in which donors were approached. In 72% of responding centres with an LDT programme there were cases of the patient approaching his/her family about the possibility of LDT, in 39% there were cases of the spouse or parent of the patient approaching the potential donor, in 12% there were cases of the transplant co-ordinator making the approach and in 46% of cases there were cases of nephrology staff making the approach. The EUROTOLD donor questionnaires/interviews found that most donors were pro-actively *informed* of the recipient's need for a transplant[376] and roughly half were pro-actively *asked* to donate. This included 12 of 24 Slovenian donors (6 asked by the recipient, 4 by the nephrologist, once both and once unstated),[377] 2 out of 3 Slovakian donors (1 was asked by the recipient and 1 by a nephrologist), at least 3 out of 5 Romanian (by the recipient) and 11 out of 21 Polish donors (4 by the recipient and 7 by others).

A pro-active approach to *informing* potential donors and to asking them seems acceptable provided that medical professionals do all that is practicable to encourage prospective donors to feel that they can refuse to donate if they want to (including offering them a way out without losing face). In principle it is not unacceptable for the recipient or a relative of the recipient to inform and ask the prospective donor but in many ways it would be better if the medical staff did this because the prospective donor is more likely to feel able to say no to a member of medical staff. The medical staff can also more easily conform to requirements concerning the way that prospective donors are informed and asked, which would usefully be laid down under a code of practice or protocol.

---

[375]See P.S.Veitch, Recent Initiatives From the British Transplant Society, in D.Price and H.Akveld (eds.), Living Organ Donation in the Nineties: European Medico-Legal Perspectives, *EUROTOLD*, 1996, 19-23.

[376]Half of the 24 Slovenian donors first found out that the recipient needed a transplant from the recipient him/herself and most of the others had first been told by other medical staff. In the Polish sample the recipient explained the need in 2 cases, a sister-in-law in one case and a member of the medical staff in 14 cases. Of the 3 Slovakian donors 1 had first been made aware by the recipient the other 2 by medical staff.

[377]10 donors agreed explicitly that they donated without being asked.

Other facets of induced compliance discussed in the psychological literature include the fact that a person is more likely to undertake the 'target behaviour' if they are exposed to influences in favour of undertaking that behaviour. This effect is amplified where the persons favouring that behaviour are considered to be *experts*.[378] Interestingly in LDT, the prospective donor and recipient are likely to be exposed to influences that at least advocate transplantation and in some cases LDT. The key influences are generally experts (e.g. in nephrology, transplant surgery). However, prospective donors and recipients can also be encouraged by modelling[379] and social comparison[380] to accept LDT where past donors and recipients speak to them about the experience. In the case of prospective recipients, sometimes waiting for a cadaveric organ might be a target behaviour because this is viewed as the best option or because the professional/organisation has an incentive to keep a person waiting (e.g. a dialysis unit with an economic incentive to draw out time on dialysis).

The influence on the donor of medical experts advocating transplantation can increase after the initial blood test in that they become the main source for information about the courses of action.[381] The prospective donor is being asked to make a big sacrifice but the need to pass tests exerts an influence in favour of donating by redefining the situation as one where the donor is lucky to have the opportunity to donate. Tests also add credibility to the expert views of the physicians, helping to obfuscate any ambivalence the potential donor is experiencing.[382] The

---

[378]For this effect of expert power generally see J.R.P.French and B.Raven, The Bases of Social Power, in D.Cartwright and A.Zander (eds.), Group Dynamics, *Harper and Row,* 1968. For the impact of unanimity on decision making in general see S.E.Asch, Effects of Group Pressure Upon The Modification and Distortion of Judgements, in H.Guetzkow (ed.), Groups, Leadership and Men, *Carnegie Press*, 1951.

[379]Bandura, Principles of Behaviour Modification, *Holt, Reinhart and Winston,* 1969.

[380]L.Festinger, A Theory of Social Comparison Progress, *Human Relations,* 1954, 2, 117-140.

[381]The Minnesota study of Simmons et al. found that, 'after the blood test most donors directed their information seeking toward the transplant physicians rather than towards an outside source,' Gift of Life, *Wiley and Sons*, 1977 at 257.

[382]D.J.Bem, Self Perception: An Alternative Interpretation of Cognitive Dissonance Phenomena, *Psychological Review*, 1974, 81, 506-520.

expectations of others can build as the process progresses, leaving it increasingly difficult for the donor to withdraw.[383] The process of giving information can be consciously or unconsciously adjusted to encourage taking up the target behaviour. This might manifest in a different way of presenting and evaluating risks and benefits and even the withholding of certain information that would tend to reduce the likelihood of compliance.

Clearly, the above issues should be born in mind by professionals when examining LDT. There is no real sign that large numbers of prospective donors and recipients are being manipulated but it will probably be possible for improvements in the process to be made in most cases and it is useful for professionals to be aware of the pitfalls.

The Basic Legal Requirement for Voluntariness

Whilst the requirement of voluntariness is legally obvious but, at least as far as the donor is concerned, most transplant legislation makes explicit reference to the need for it or embodies the requirement for it within a statement of the need for consent.[384] Typically, a legislative provision literally will just simply state that consent must be given voluntarily.[385] Variations on this include requiring it to be given: freely;[386] freely and voluntarily;[387] in accordance with the donor's will;[388] without coercion;[389]

---

[383]Gift of Life, *Wiley and Sons* 1977 at p260.

[384]E.g. Algeria, Bulgaria, Cyprus, Denmark, Ecuador, Kuwait, Norway, Panama, Slovakia, Sth Africa, Sth Australia, Vietnam, Western Australia and Zimbabwe.

[385]E.g. Finland (Law No. 355 of 26 April 1985 at section 3) and Iraq (Resolution No. 776 of 9 June 1981 at section 1(a) and 1(b).

[386]E.g. Greece Law No. 1383 of 2 Aug 1983 at section 5, Northern Territory Law No. 121 of 1979 at section 10(iii), Poland Law of 26 Oct 1995, Article 9(1) at point 7, Portugal Law No. 12 of 22 Apr 1993 at section 8(1), Paraguay Law No. 836180 of 15 Dec 1980 at section 276, Sri Lanka Act No. 48 of 1987 at sections 7 and 8), Lebanon Decree No. 109 of 16 Sept 1983 at section 1(3), Syrian Arab Republic Law No.31 of 23 Aug 1972 at section 2(3), Queensland The Transplantation and Anatomy Act 1979-1984 at section 12(b)(iii), The Netherlands Law of 24 May 1996 section 3, Tasmania The Human Tissue Act 1985 at section 9(c)(iii), Tunisia Law No. 91-22 of 25 March 1991 at section 2. This approach is also adopted in the Council of Europe's Resolution 78(29) at Article 3 and its Draft Protocol on Organ Transplantation Steering Committee on Bioethics (CDBI) (97)5 Article 7 which also states that consent must be informed, express and specific.

[387]Colombia (Decree No. 1172 of 6 June 1989 at section 32(c)).

and knowingly.[390] These requirements appear to be very similar. However, the term knowingly might refer to knowing all the relevant information for making an informed choice rather than just being about making a voluntary choice in the sense of knowing that the purpose of removal is for implantation into a recipient. Interpretational problems also arise with Romania's law which states that consent must be given in a deliberate manner[391] as well as freely. A 'deliberate manner' may imply that the decision must be made with aforethought rather than impulsively or it may simply mean that consent must be express rather than implied.

Motivation is an additional factor that transplant legislation can regulate, and not just in terms of the reason for donating being non-commercial. Mexican law, amongst other things, requires the donor to give his consent freely, without moral coercion, unambiguously and voluntarily![392] Under Cuban law donation must be, 'a free and expressly voluntary act of the donor or of his representative, performed for humanitarian reasons'.[393] Humanitarianism is a requirement also found it Turkish[394] law where practitioners have a duty to refuse organs not given out of humane aspirations. The problem in practice is that it is difficult enough to detect donations that are pathologically or commercially motivated let alone make a distinction between who is giving out of 'egotism' rather than as an act of human service to another.

The requirement for consent makes donations that are the product of coercion legally unacceptable. However, some legislation precludes donations in the mere presence of external behaviours which threaten voluntariness irrespective of whether or not the prospective donor would have donated without their presence. Hence, Spain[395] and Hungary[396] require that the agreement to donate is made in the absence of external pressures. Hong Kong's Ordinance states that the Board authorising organ

---

[388]Slovenia (Article 10 of 1996 Law)

[389]E.g. Venezuela (Law of 19 November 1992 at section 12) and the model law of Canada (Uniform Human Tissue Donation Act 1990 at section 7(6)) for non-regenerative tissue.

[390]Belgium (Law of 13 June 1986 at section 8(1)).

[391]Law of 1996 at Article 4(1).

[392]Federal Regulations of 16 August 1976 at section 24 and 26.

[393]Decree No. 139 of 4 February 1988 at section 80.

[394]Law No. 2238 of 29 May 1979 at section 7.

[395]Law No. 30 of 27 October 1979 at section 4(c).

[396]Ordinance No. 18 of 4 November 1972 at section 2(2) see also section 10(4).

LDTs not legislatively defined as between genetic relative or spouses of 3 or more years standing[397] must be satisfied that donor consent was given *without* coercion or offer of inducement[398] The Hong Kong approach is contrasted to the English approach where, under regulation 3 of The Human Organ Transplants (Unrelated Persons) Regulations 1989 [SI No 2480] passed pursuant to HOTA 1989, with organ LDTs not between persons defined as genetically related, one of the things ULTRA must be satisfied of is that removal was not *obtained* by coercion or the offer of an inducement (Regulation 3(2)c).[399] HOTA and pursuant regulations do not specify a burden of proof, but presumably it is on the balance of probabilities[400] that it will be determined whether or not coercion or an offer of inducement led to someone agreeing to removal when otherwise they would not have done so. Interestingly, preventing donations secured by offer of inducement is less about ensuring voluntariness than helping to ensure humanitarian motivation. Inducements could be of commercial value (e.g. if you donate I will help you start your business) or otherwise (e.g. the hint that donation would get the prospective donor back in his family's 'good books').

Given it is normally difficult to tell if external behaviours have overborne the donor's will or not, there is a logic to preventing donations

---

[397]Ordinance No. 16 of 1995 at section 5(4)d.

[398]Ibid at section 5(4)e. There must also be no payment or intention of payment that would contravene the Ordinance and an interviewing procedure is carried out with the prospective donor and recipient to check that these requirements and other ones relating to disclosure have been met (section 5(5) and 5(6)).

[399]ULTRA's satisfaction of these, and indeed any other factors, could be subject to judicial review. No such case has been brought but clearly proving that ULTRA was not satisfied would be very difficult. Regulation 3(2)e adds the requirement that the donor and recipient must have been interviewed by a person who appears to the Authority to have been suitably qualified to conduct such interviews and who has reported to the Authority on the conditions contained in regulations 3(2)a - 3(2)d and included in his report an account of any difficulties of communication with the donor or recipient and an explanation of how those difficulties were overcome. By virtue of regulation 3(1)c the requirements in regulation 3(2) do not apply 'where the primary purpose of removal of an organ from a donor is the medical treatment of that donor'. This would mean that donation as part of domino heart transplants, for instance, would not be subject to the extra requirements of regulation 3(2), although still subject to the other provisions of the law (as to not obtaining removal by coercion etc.).

[400]The test used in showing factual causation under the tort of negligence.

simply on the basis of presence of external behaviours that *threaten* to change that will. Preventing offer of an inducement is more about wanting the donation to be non-profit making, unpaid and motivated by a humanitarian desire to benefit another.[401] The problem with preventing donations made in the presence of an offer of inducement or indeed pressure, manipulation or coercion is that it arbitrarily excludes some prospective donors with 'bona-fide' motivation. A better approach might be to prohibit the behaviours themselves (e.g. Argentinean law prohibits coercion and inducement,[402] most jurisdictions prohibit commercial inducement[403]) but allow donations made in their presence providing that the prospective donor would have donated if they had not been present. WHO Guiding Principle 3, which states consent by the donor should be free of any undue influence and pressure,[404] could be usefully 'fleshed out' in this light.

Under general principles of law a decision brought about by coercion is obviously going to be involuntary but difficulties can arise in determining whether a decision is voluntary or not in cases where there has only been overt persuasion or more subtle influences such as the way one is asked to decide or the context the decision is being made in. The extent of influence and its effect, the balance of power between the parties and the consequences of intervention and non-intervention are all relevant consideration but the ultimate question is whether the influence was of such a character and effect as to undermine the reality of consent. This was one of the issues addressed in the landmark English case of Re T (adult: refusal of medical treatment) [1992] 4 All ER 649. In Re T a mother, who was a Jehovah's Witness, had according to the trial judge influenced her daughter, who was not a Jehovah's Witness, to refuse a blood transfusion. The daughter was a patient who was admitted to hospital 34 weeks pregnant. Her condition worsened such that she was taken into intensive care. The Court of Appeal granted a declaration stating that in the circumstances it would not be unlawful for the hospital to administer a blood transfusion on the basis that the patient did not make

[401]Would offering payment of reasonable expenses be classified as an offer of inducement? This would not normally be the intent of the offer but it could occasionally be an effect, e.g. someone living abroad motivated by free travel.
[402]Law No. 24193 of 24 March 1993.
[403]See chapter 7.
[404]Guiding Principle 3.

a valid refusal to consent to this.[405] Butler Sloss LJ suggested that, 'the degree of pressure to turn persuasion or appeals to affection into undue influence may... be very little'[406] but perhaps Lord Donaldson MR made the most important statement of principle in concluding that the critical question is whether or not the will of the patient has been overborne,

> ...it is wholly acceptable that the patient should have been persuaded by others of the merits of such a decision and have decided accordingly. It matters not how strong the persuasion was so long as it did not overbear the independence of the patient's decision. The real question in each such case is 'Does the patient really mean what he says or is he merely saying it for a quiet life, to satisfy someone else or because the advice and persuasion to which he has been subjected is such that he can no longer think and decide for himself?' In other words is it a decision expressed in form only, not in reality?[407]

In this case, although speculative, it was probably right to infer that on the balance of probabilities the mother's conversations with her daughter influenced the daughter in such a way that she turned from agreeing to a transfusion to rejecting one. However, this should not obscure the ethical dilemma of whether it was acceptable to impose a blood transfusion in these circumstances. Deciding that a consent to a medical intervention is invalid by reason of undue influence raises little dilemma because there are not sound grounds to go ahead. However, imposing a medical intervention (after holding that a refusal to consent to that intervention is invalid) places one foursquare against the right of self-determination.

The danger is that where there has been influence in a certain direction, and the decision-maker has decided in that direction, a judge in the absence of clear evidence of the decision-maker's values will determine whether or not influence overbore the decision-maker's will by reference to his own standards of whether or not the decision is rational. Arguably, though on its facts Re T was a courageous decision reflecting an expression of compassion. It is known that Jehovah's Witnesses are zealous to incorporate people into their way of thinking and use techniques to this end. It is most likely in this context that the daughter came to be

---

[405]All three judges concurred on this although one felt that the decision was voluntary (in the sense that it wasn't brought about by compulsion but invalid by reason of undue influence).
[406][1992] 4 All ER 649.
[407]Ibid.

influenced into thinking that a transfusion was a fate worse than death (eternal damnation) or simply hoped that the transfusion would be forced upon her to avoid both death and perhaps the risk of damnation.

A consequence of Re T might be that a prospective recipient's decision not to receive is overturned due to the determination that the decision has been reached because of external pressure. However, what would be almost inconceivable is a prospective donor's decision not to donate being overturned because it was based on undue influence. This would set to dangerous a precedent, would damage the reputation of transplantation, would subject a person to a physically non-therapeutic procedure against their expressed will and would also be excluded under most jurisdictions simply because most transplant legislation requires express donor consent (e.g. Bolivia,[408] Peru[409] and Cuba[410]) or at least written consent.[411]

In the opposite direction, the danger is that decisions that fit the judicial conception of what is rational will be inadequately scrutinised for voluntariness. A possible example is the case of Poynter v Hillingdon Health Authority (23 April 1997 Unreported) where the parents of a potential recipient of a cadaveric organ were clearly rejecting the reductionistic model of treatment of organ disease. The plaintiffs claimed that the acceptance of the transplantation was the result of pressure, which one can imagine could take place in such a situation. The judge rejected the possibility of this without ever really examining it in detail.

Procedural Prerequisites for Living Donation

It is normal practice for certain procedural formalities to be observed in obtaining consent for medical interventions of a more serious nature. Living donation is a procedure which is non-therapeutic as well as serious and this has doubtless been the reason why procedural formalities in obtaining donor consent are a normal feature of legislation affecting

[408]Requires the donors express consent without any reservations. Regulations of March 1982 at section 3(a).

[409]The donor's consent *and* the recipient's acceptance must be free, conscious and express. Supreme Decree No. 014-88-SA of 19 May 1988 at section 15.

[410]Decree No. 139 of 4 February 1988 at section 80.

[411]Nearly all laws do - see chapter 3.

LDT.[412] Legislation rarely imposes formalities in relation to the recipient.[413]

Most transplant laws prescribe the procedural method by which donor consent is to be given. In many instances it is stated simply that consent is to be given in writing.[414] The manner in which it is to be written is not normally specified. Exceptions include Hungary which requires that the donor make a declaration signifying his consent to the removal in a written document drawn up by a notary and kept in the clinical file of the donor[415] and Romania where the law states that the written consent must be given in the form of Annex Number 1 attached to the Act (this involves the donor signing to say (s)he was informed of the risks, asked for and received no payment and consented without pressure etc.[416]).

Occasionally the donor is given a choice of consent in writing or an alternative method. For instance, the law of Cyprus offers oral consent in the presence of witnesses (with a declaration being recorded in a dedicated register) as an alternative.[417] Article 19(2) of the recent Convention on Human Rights and Biomedicine allows consent to be given in writing or before an official body.

A significant number of laws specify that consent must be evidenced before a specific body or person(s). In some cases it must be given before a legal authority. For instance, in France donor consent must be expressed before the Presiding Judge of the *tribunal de grande instance* (or the judge designated by him).[418] In Spain the written consent of the donor is to be given in the presence of the magistrate responsible for public records in the

---

[412]For exceptions see, for example, Cuba (Decree No. 139 of 4 February 1988 at section 80) and Ecuador (Law No. 64 of 26 May 1987).

[413]For exceptions see, for example, Lebanon where recipient consent must be in written form (Decree No. 109 of 16 September 1983 at section 3).

[414]See e.g. laws of Algeria, Australian state laws of Northern Territory, Queensland, South Australia, Tasmania and Western Australia, Belgium, Bulgaria, Costa Rica, Denmark, Finland, Greece, Lebanon Mexico, Norway, Panama, Poland, Romania, Russian Federation, Slovakia, Slovenia, Spain, South Africa, Sri Lanka, Sweden, Syrian Arab Republic, The Netherlands, The Philippines, Turkey, Venezuela and Zimbabwe.

[415]Ordinance No. 18 of 4 November 1972 at section 2; although this can be an oral declaration in the presence of a notary retained in the clinical file of the donor.

[416]Article 4(1) of the Law of 1996.

[417]Section 7(2) of 1987 law.

[418]Law No. 94-654 of 1994 at Art L-671-3 (*IDHL*, 1994, 45(4), 473-482 at 474).

locality concerned. The consent document must additionally be signed by the other persons present.[419] Countries like Bolivia [420] and Uruguay[421] have reassuringly adopted the requirement of consent before a legal authority in the context of organ market related coercion being a clear and present danger in these countries. However, it could be argued that in countries where the danger of coercion is less significant (e.g. many European countries) a less bureaucratic approach would suffice and avoid the danger of discouraging the overall use of LDT. A more straightforward approach would be to require consent before a medical authority. This could be any doctor or physician,[422] a professional independent of the transplant team,[423] or ideally, in terms of reducing the danger of conflict of interest, someone independent of the recipient's team. Germany's law requires that the information giving process should be undertaken by a physician in the presence of another physician and, where necessary, other expert persons. The content of this information and the declaration of consent by the organ donor is recorded in a document signed by the two physicians and the donor. All donations are scrutinised by a commission which must include an independent physician, a person experienced in psychological matters and a person qualified to exercise the functions of a judge. One of the commission's roles is to ensure that the consent has been freely given.[424]

Some legislative provisions require consent to be before witnesses who do not have to be persons exercising a judicial or medical function. An example of this is the law of Greece where the declaration of willingness to donate must be made in the presence of two witnesses who must both sign the declaration together with the donor.[425] The requirement of witnesses

---

[419]Crown Decree No. 426 of 22 February 1980 at section 4(4)).
[420]Regulation of 15 March 1982 at section 3).
[421]Decree No. 660/991 of 4 December 1991 at section 4.
[422]See e.g. Poland Law of 26 October 1995 at Article 9(1) point 7).
[423]See for example Portugal (Law of 1993 at section 8(2)).
[424]Act of 5th Nov 1997 at section 8(4)2 and 3.
[425]The declaration must be in notarial form or on a form on which the police authority has confirmed the authenticity of the signature of the potential donor or orally, the declaration being recorded in a special register kept by the treatment establishment where the removal is to be performed (Law No. 1383 of 2 Aug 1983 at section 5). See also Algeria Law No. 85-05 of 16 Feb 1985 at section 162, Costa Rica Law No. 5560 of 20 Aug 1974 at section 15, Mexico Federal Regulations of 16 Aug 1976 at section 24, The Philippines Decree No. 856 of 23 Dec 1975 at section 96(e) and Venezuela Law No. 4497 of 19 Nov 1992 at section 12.

could be limited to cases of donation where more vulnerable donors are involved. An example of this is the law of Turkey where only minor and legally incompetent donors are required to give consent in front of witnesses.[426]

Legislation in a few jurisdictions specifies that there must be a certain time lapse between donor agreement and organ removal (e.g. Spain[427] and most Australian state laws[428]). This time lapse is usually 24 hours; enough to help ensure that the potential donor has a chance to reflect and change his/her mind if donating does not reflect his/her true will. Of course in practice there is usually a larger time lapse between agreement and removal partly as a by-product of needing to organise facilities and staff and work-up the potential recipient for the transplant.

Some legislation identifies a person responsible for information giving to the donor. Greece,[429] Turkey,[430] Hungary,[431] Belgium[432] and Panama[433] attempt to assist proficient information giving by requiring the person undertaking the transplant to give the information. The diametrically opposite approach to this is to help ensure that disclosure is not biased in favour of donation by requiring the donor's information giver to be independent of the team conducting the removal. Jurisdictions which take this approach within transplant legislation include: Poland,[434] Spain,[435] Sri

[426]These donors are required to draw up a written document giving consent to the removal and sign it in the presence of at least two witnesses or give an oral undertaking in the presence of at least two witnesses and then sign a declaration which is then countersigned by a physician (Law of 1979 at section 6).
[427]At least 24 hours must elapse between the signing of the consent document before the local magistrate and the removal of the organ. Crown Decree No. 426 of 22 February 1980 at section 4(4).
[428]See Northern Territory Act No. 121 of 1979 at section 9, Queensland The Transplantation and Anatomy Act 1979-1984 at section 11, South Australia The Transplantation and Anatomy Act 1983 at section 10, Tasmania The Human Tissue Act 1985 at section 8(1) and Western Australia Act No. 116 of 1982 at section 9(1).
[429]Law No. 1383 of 2 August 1983 at section 5-6.
[430]Law No. 2238 of 29 May 1979 at section 7.
[431]Ordinance No. 18 of 4 November 1972 at section 2(2).
[432]Law of 13 June 1986 at section 9.
[433]Law No. 10 of 11 July 1983 at section 6.
[434]Law of 26 October 1995 at Article 9(1) point 5.
[435]Crown Decree No. 426 of 22 February 1980 at section 3.

Lanka[436] and Hong Kong.[437] Some jurisdictions, such as Finland[438] and Sweden[439] take what is perhaps an even better legislative approach of requiring that the donor's information giver should be separate from the person who is caring for the recipient.

Withdrawal of Consent in Living Donation

The ability to withdraw consent at any time is integral to the self-determining rights of potential donors and is a general principle of law. Many jurisdictions specifically uphold this principle within transplant law including Algeria,[440] Bolivia,[441] Canada,[442] Columbia,[443] France,[444] Germany,[445] Hong Kong,[446] Hungary,[447] Kuwait,[448] Mexico,[449] Panama,[450]

---

[436]Act No. 48 of 1987 at sections 7 and 8 requires a medical consultant, other than a medical consultant attached to the transplant team, to give information.

[437]This law imposes a requirement of authorisation that the potential donor and recipient have had the procedure, it's risk and the fact that consent may be withdrawn at any time explained to them by a medical practitioner, not being the practitioner who is to remove the organ. This requirement only applies for potential donations *which are not* by a spouse of 3 years standing or a close genetic relative (Ordinance No. 16 of 1995 at section 5(4)c).

[438]Law No. 355 of 26 April 1985 at section 3 states that the information giver must be a physician who is not caring for the recipient.

[439]The responsibility is with the chief physician or the assistant chief physician at the hospital (not being the physician in charge of the care of the recipient patient). Law No. 190 of 15 May 1975 at section 5 read in conjunction with section 3.

[440]Law No. 85-05 of 16 February 1985 at section 162.

[441]Regulations of 15 March 1982 at section 12.

[442]The Uniform Human Tissue Donation Act 1990 at section 9(2).

[443]Ibid at section 9(2).

[444]Section 2 of Decree No. 78-501 of 31 March 1978. See also Article 671-3 of the 1994 law which states that, 'consent may be withdrawn without formality and at any time'. (*IDHL*, 1994, 45(4), 473-482 at p475).

[445]Act of 5th Nov 1997 at section 8(4)2.

[446]Ordinance No. 16 of 1995 at section 5(4)d for donations which are not between spouses of 3 or more years standing or close genetic relatives.

[447]Ordinance No. 18 of 4 November 1972 at section 2(3) stating that, 'at any time prior to removal of the organ, the donor may unconditionally withdraw his consent, in any manner whatsoever'.

[448]Decree-Law No. 55 of 20 December 1987 at section 4.

[449]Federal Regulations of 16 August 1976 at section 26.

Poland,[451] Portugal,[452] Romania,[453] Slovakia,[454] Slovenia,[455] Spain,[456] Tunisia,[457] most Australian states,[458] UK law for donations not between persons defined as genetically related under HOTA (ULTRA must be satisfied that the proposed donor understands his/her entitlement to withdraw consent and has not done so. Medical practitioners submit proposed genetically unrelated donations before ULTRA who must be satisfied that the donor understands his/her right to withdraw consent at any time.[459] Failure on the part of the practitioner to ensure the donor understands this right constitutes a statutory offence[460]) and Hong Kong's Ordinance for organ LDTs not legislatively defined as between genetic relative or spouses of 3 or more years standing[461] (the Board authorising such donations must be satisfied that after giving consent there was no subsequent withdrawal of consent[462]).

---

[450]Law No. 10 of 11 July 1983 at section 19.

[451]The law requires that the potential donor be informed of the consequences of withdrawal of consent during the last phase of preparation of the recipient for the transplant procedure. This is perfectly reasonable if done in a neutral way but it could be done in a manner which pressurises the potential donor to carry on despite no longer really wanting to donate. In this situation the donation could be prevented by the fact that it can be said that consent has no longer been freely given. Law of 26 October 1995 at Article 9(1) at point 8 read in conjunction with point 7.

[452]Law No. 12 of 22 April 1993 at section 8(6).

[453]Law of July 1978 at section 132 now contained in Article 4(3) of 1996 Law.

[454]Law of 24 August 1994 at section 46(1).

[455]Article 10 of 1996 Law.

[456]Crown Decree No. 426 of 22 February 1980 at section 4. Additionally this section states that 24 hours must elapse between the signature of the document and the removal of the organ.

[457]Law No. 91-22 of 25 March 1991 at section 9.

[458]Including Northern Territory No. 121 of 1979 at section 16, Queensland The Transplantation and Anatomy Act 1979-1984 at section 21, South Australia The Transplantation and Anatomy Act 1983 at section 16, Tasmania The Human Tissue Act 1985 at section 22 and Western Australia Act No. 116 of 1982 at section 14.

[459]Human Organ Transplant Regulations 3(2)d.

[460]Of course such a failure would result in liability at common law anyway, but what the existence of this legislative regime adds is the reality of independent scrutiny of this and other issues with all genetically unrelated LDT's.

[461]Ordinance No. 16 of 1995 at section 5(4)d.

[462]Ibid.

Independent Authorisation of LDTs

Some transplant laws include provision for independent authorisation of LDT, partly to ensure the voluntariness of donation. There are variations in who is assigned the authorising role and in their level of independence from the recipient team. Finnish law requires the approval of the National Board of Health;[463] Slovakia's law a special advisory committee opinion;[464] Germany's law a commission as already noted;[465] Hungarian law three physicians not involved in the removal and transplantation procedures;[466] and Syrian Arab Republic law a commission of three medical specialists other than the physicians carrying out the removal procedure.[467] UK, Hong Kong and Indian law also require independent authorisation of LDTs involving certain types of donor-recipient relationship. Some laws require authorisation by an independent body for minor or adult incompetent donation.

Voluntariness With Donors of Restricted Liberty

Paraguay's law prohibits 'detainees' from being donors.[468] Panama's law prohibits donation by persons subject to restrictions on their legal rights such as prisoners and other persons deprived of their liberty.[469] Slovakia's law states that, 'removal may not be performed if the donor is serving a prison sentence.'[470] These restrictions are put in place partly to protect persons from being exploited when they are in a vulnerable position but the approach in Bolivian law is perhaps better in that examines on a de facto

---

[463]Law No. 355 of 26 April 1985 at sections 2 and 3 respectively.
[464]Law No.277 of 24 Aug 1994 at section 46(2). *IDHL*, 1995, 46(2), 151-157 at 155.
[465]Act of 5th Nov 1997 at section 8(4)2 and 3.
[466]Transplant must be justified in the view of these physicians. Ordinance No. 18 of 4 November 1972 at section 1(2).
[467]The requirement is only that they find the operation to be necessary for the recipient. Law No. 31 of 23 August 1972 at section 2(5). The Canadian Model law requires that an independent assessment be carried out in cases where non-regenerative tissue is being donated.
[468]Law No. 836180 of 15 December 1980 at section 279.
[469]Law No. 10 of 11 July 1983 at section 22.
[470]Law of 24 August 1994 at section 46(1), *IDHL*, 1995, 46(2), 151-157 at 155.

basis whether prisoners and other persons of restricted liberty are donating voluntarily.[471] However, it does restrict such donations to immediate blood relatives or relatives by marriage.[472] Similarly under Mexican law prisoners can only donate to a spouse, concubine or relative.[473]

Several common law decisions have examined the voluntariness of medical decision-making in the institutional context. The Michigan Circuit Court in the US case of Kaimowitz v Michigan Department of Mental Health 42 USLW 2063 [1973] (Mich Cir Ct) emphasised that pressure can easily be overbearing in a mental hospital context which starts off as inherently unequal. This was a case where on the facts the patient was held not to have given voluntary consent to psychosurgery. The English Court of Appeal referred to Kaimowitz in the case of Freeman v Home Office (No 2) [1984] QB 524. Freeman was a case involving a prisoner where on the facts the consent was held to be valid but it was accepted that an institutional setting could bear down on a decision in such a way as to make consent invalid.[474]

Clearly in Kaimowitz the court would have been particularly cautious because of the nature of psychosurgery as a serious, invasive and indeed ethically questionable procedure combined with the fact that mental hospitals are not renowned for placing a high value of patient self-determination. Living donation in the institutional context is a serious procedure but where it is done on behalf of a person with whom the donor has a close affinity there is much less reason to be skeptical about its voluntariness that the voluntariness of psychosurgery. Clearly one of the concerns in some jurisdictions would be whether the donor had been offered an inducement - such as early release in the case of a prisoner. Under the UK legislative regime ULTRA would not authorise a donation by a prisoner to a person (s)he was not defined as genetically related to if early release had been offered as an inducement and was acting as the cause for the decision to donate.

---

[471]Regulation of March 1982 at section 5 state that 'persons under special disciplinary condition or otherwise detained in closed institutions may donate organs and tissues only of their own free will'.

[472]Regulations of March 1982 at section 5.

[473]Decree of 25 April 1987 at section 328.

[474]Nethertheless, on the facts, Kennedy and Grubb suggest, 'it could be said that the court dismissed the argument that the 'institutional setting' deprived him of his free will too readily'. Medical Law: Text With Materials, *Butterworths*, 1994, 241.

Voluntariness and Restrictions on Donor-Recipient Relationship

Article 4 of the Council of Europe Resolution 78(29) states that removal of substances which cannot regenerate must be confined to transplantation between genetically related persons barring exceptional cases where there are good chances of success. WHO Guiding Principles take a similar approach, stating that in general donors should be genetically related to the recipients although exceptions may be made in the case of transplantation of bone marrow and other regenerative tissue.[475]

Some jurisdictions limit LDTs from living donors to recipients with whom they have an existing relationship, whether genetic, familial or emotional. Germany's law restricts donation to,

> ...relatives of the first or second degree, spouses, fiancees or other persons with whom the donor obviously entertains an especially intimate personal relationship.[476]

It is not specified whether to be in the 'especially intimate personal relationship' one would have to be having sexual relations or, as is more likely, it would suffice to be close in any way such as good friends or emotionally close distant relatives, godparents etc.

Costa Rican law limits donors to giving to relatives, 'up to the fourth degree of consanguinity or up to the third degree of affinity, or of his spouse'.[477] Portuguese law restricts living donation of non-regenerative substances to relatives of the donor up to the third degree.[478] The law of the Russian Federation is ambiguous but appears to restrict donation from living donors to persons with whom there is a genetic relationship, apart from cases of bone marrow donation.[479] French law generally restricts to members of the nuclear family unit.[480] the exception being donation between spouses in emergency cases.[481] Italian law restricts living kidney donation to the nuclear family unit (including half-brothers and sisters).[482]

---

[475]Guiding Principle 3.
[476]Act of 5 Nov 1997 at section 8(4).
[477]Law No. 5560 of 20 August 1974 at section 15.
[478]Law No. 12 of 22 April 1993 at section 6(2).
[479]Law of 22 December 1992 at section 11.
[480]Article 671-3 ibid.
[481]Law No. 94-654 of 29 July 1994.
[482]Law No. 458 of 26 June 1967.

In Slovenia donation of non-reviving body materials appears to be limited to liver segment and kidney for transplantation into genetic or familial relatives.[483]

Some jurisdictions subject LDTs involving certain donor-recipient relationships to more stringent qualifying criteria. The recent Venezuelan law generally restricts LDT to first degree blood relatives but allows the National Executive to determine that a wider range is acceptable.[484] The new Swedish law restricts LDT to situations where 'the donor is related to the potential recipient or if he is particularly close to him for some other reason' and other persons only in 'special cases'.[485] Russian Federation law[486] and Belarus draft law[487] thoughtfully attempt to exclude pressured donations by excluding donations by a person who is dependent on the recipient.[488]

Some jurisdictions rely primarily on an authorising body to determine and/or apply restrictions on specific classes of donor-recipient relationship. The general approach seems to be to restrict and more closely scrutinise donation by persons who do not have a close blood or at least legal tie with the recipient. The main purpose of such an approach is usually to prevent commercially motivated donations and thereby protect the reputation of transplantation. Trade is more likely to happen outside the genetic relative context. However, a clear subsidiary purpose of such provisions is to ensure voluntariness - the concern being that manipulation and coercion can occur outside the genetic relative context. Coercion and manipulation can, of course, also occur within the genetic relative context - a point that has not gained much recent attention but has been documented in the psychological literature for decades. Close family ties can be more coercive in a subtle and manipulative way than more distant ties which offer more potential to produce more purely altruistic donations.

Hong Kong's Ordinance limits donation to close genetic relatives,[489]

---

[483]Law of 1995 at Article 8.

[484]Law of 19th November 1992 at section 11 (*IDHL*, 1995, 46(3) at 329-330).

[485]Law No. 831 of 8 June 1995 at section 7.

[486]Law of 22 December 1992 at section 3.

[487]Section 8.

[488]Either because of their functions or in any other manner.

[489]Ordinance No. 16 of 1995 at section 5 (1). Section 5(2) defines those who have sufficient genetic relationship as the nuclear family unit plus uncles, aunts and first cousins. These relatives can be full or half blood.

spouses of 3 years standing[490] and those given special authorisation to donate by a board set up under the law[491] (this board can only take referrals from the responsible clinicians, not potential donors and recipients themselves[492]). Among the criteria imposed for donations requiring approval are that a registered medical practitioner, who is not the person removing the organ, must explain to the donor and recipient about the procedure, the risk involved and the entitlement to withdraw consent at any time and this information must be understood.[493] The donor must have given consent without coercion, offer of inducement or subsequent withdrawal of consent.[494] An interviewing procedure is also carried out with the potential donor and recipient principally to check that requirements have been met.[495]

HOTA has a provision similar to Hong Kong - again partly aimed at ensuring voluntariness. Under section 2(1) of HOTA it is an offence for a surgeon to remove an organ from a person who is not genetically related to the intended recipient. Section 2(1)b also prohibits the transplantation of an organ into a recipient who is not genetically related to the donor. The definition of genetic relative excludes people who are distant blood relatives as well as spouses and other persons who are emotionally related.[496] Section 2(3) of the Act allows the Secretary of State to pass regulations providing that the prohibition on LDT between non-genetically related persons, as defined above, shall not apply where:

> (a) such authority as is specified in or constituted by the regulations is satisfied -
> (i) that no payment has been or is to be made in contravention of section 1 above;[497] *and*

---

[490]Section 5 (1) ibid.
[491]Section 5 ibid.
[492]Section 5(4)a ibid.
[493]Section 5(4)c ibid.
[494]Section 5(4)d ibid. There must have been no payment or intention to pay that would be prohibited under the Ordinance (section 5(4)e).
[495]Section 5(5) and section 5(6).
[496]The recipient's genetic relatives are classified as: (a) his natural parents and children, (b) his brothers and sisters of the whole or half blood, (c) the brothers and sisters of the whole or half blood of either of his natural parents, and the natural children of his brothers and sisters of the whole or half blood or of the brothers and sisters of the whole or half blood of either of his natural parents.
[497]i.e. in contravention of section 1 of HOTA which regulates commercial dealings in human organs.

(ii) that such other conditions as are specified in the regulations are satisfied; *and*

(b) such other requirements as may be specified in the regulations are complied with.

The Human Organ Transplants (Unrelated Persons) Regulations[498] passed pursuant to section 2(3) of HOTA set up ULTRA as the body to scrutinise non-genetically related donation. Proposed LDTs between distant blood relatives and emotionally related persons, such as spouses, can be brought before ULTRA and permitted providing certain conditions are fulfilled.[499] General Medical Council Guidance on the application of the Act is that doctors have a duty to establish beyond doubt the presence of consanguinity or a close and enduring relationship between the donor and the recipient.[500]

The key behind the scrutiny of donations that are not close genetic related was Parliament's concern to ensure that all donations are altruistic.[501] However, donation between grandparents and grandchildren is perhaps unwittingly subject to ULTRA authorisation (through not being within the legal ambit of 'genetic relative' donation under the Act[502]); it cannot have been seriously considered that such donations were any more susceptible to commercial motivation or pressure than those involving the direct nuclear family unit.[503]

Indian law allows donations from persons outside the nuclear family unit with the prior consent of the Authorisation Committee where the donation is based on donor affection or attachment to the recipient or any

[498]S.I. 1989 No 2480.

[499]These conditions relate primarily to disclosure, capacity, voluntariness and commerce in donation and are discussed in the corresponding chapters of this book.

[500]The Guidance adds that doctors, 'should consider seeking advice from professional bodies, including national and international transplantation societies, on the tests needed to establish consanguinity and on the circumstances in which unrelated live donor transplants may be considered'. General Medical Council Guidance for Doctors on Transplantation of Organs From Live Donors, *General Medical Council Supplement News Review*, December 1992 at point 7.

[501]HC Deb, 6th July 1989.

[502]See Kennedy and Grubb Medical Law: Text With Materials, *Butterworths,* 1994 (2nd edition), 1092.

[503]The additional point can be made that donations within the family can be the consequence of pressure, guilt and other motivations.

other special reasons.[504] It is not unusual for requirements on the relationship the donor must have with the recipient to operate informally at the centre level in countries without the use of specific legislative provisions. For instance, in Germany it was common practice only to allow intra-nuclear familial genetically related living donations although now a more adventurous approach is being taken in some centres, particularly with the use of spouses.[505]

Prohibiting donations where the donor and recipient have an existing relationship seems overly restrictive. However, subjecting certain forms of donation to the prior approval of an authorising committee is an acceptable step. Practitioners might be encouraged to put forward prospective donors who have affinity but no close genetic relationship if they are able or required to pass on the responsibility of determining the ethics of such donations to an expert body.

Conclusions

In the modern age donors may often feel that their decision was the obvious one and required no deliberation. However, whilst it is true that the benefits of LDT are often readily apparent it is doubtful whether many donors are giving adequate attention to whether LDT is preferable to the alternatives. Added to this are concerns that having decided without deliberation, some donors either feel locked into the process or unconsciously reify their decision. These concerns are serious in their own right and can leave prospective donors more vulnerable to being manipulated by external pressures. A measured response involves recognising these factors but also accepting that there similar issues may be just as likely to arise in other walks of life where serious decisions are being made.

Certainly more research in this area would be valuable both in Europe and elsewhere. In particular benefits would arise from a long range study involve centres from several different countries which would look at the process of decision-making at different points in time for key family members as well as prospective donors and recipients. Both interview and

---

[504]The terms and conditions of operation of which is determined by Central Government. Act No. 42 of 1994 at section 9 ((*IDHL*, 1995, 46(1) at 34-37).

[505]Centres taking a more adventurous approach include Munich and Freiburg.

questionnaire methodologies are of value here.

What may be clearly stated at this point is that enough evidence of concerns about the process has emerged to warrant more thorough attention being placed, in regulation and centre protocols, on ensuring voluntariness of both donor and recipient. Thought needs to be given to the way prospective donors and recipients are approached and to ensuring the context for decision-making is, as far as possible, unbiased. One of the strategies that ought to be employed to encourage well-motivated donation is the donor being offered the opportunity to back out without anyone outside the medical staff knowing the reason.

Most external pressures are not readily perceivable and quantifiable in their impact on the decision-maker but pressure ought in any case to be prohibited. Subjecting certain classes of prospective donor to extra scrutiny (e.g. non-genetically related) is a sensible approach. Ideally, the recipient's position ought to be examined in legislation as well as that of the donor.

5 Minors

Introduction

In the modern era young people have been given more legal control over their own affairs in many jurisdictions. In some cases ages of majority in relation to medical intervention and other areas of life have come down and it has been more widely accepted that when a person is below the age of majority they should nonetheless make decisions where legally competent to do so. It is even widely recognised that letting an incompetent person have some say over their own affairs can be a beneficial thing for them and help ensure that decisions made on their behalf are made in their best interests.

Living organ donation by a minor raises particularly novel and important legal and ethical issues. Such donation cannot be legally defined as medical treatment.[506] It is a medical intervention whose purpose is not to benefit the minor donor but the recipient. It could only be in the best interests of the minor to donate where (s)he gets a psychological benefit from donating that outweighs the physical harm and jeopardy. *In its own right* the plight of the prospective recipient is irrelevant to what is in the minor's best interests. There is always a possibility that those involved in deciding whether or not a particular minor will donate will be influenced by the plight of the prospective recipient and allow donation to go ahead where it is not in the best interests of that minor. Does this matter? When the minor is competent to donate and wants to donate isn't this enough to allow the donation on the same basis as it would be allowed for a competent adult? When the minor is incompetent but gives some meaningful agreement to donation it could be argued that removal against the best interests of the minor could legitimately go ahead where it is the best option, taking into account the interests of the minor and the prospective recipients as a pair. In terms of medical ethics this would respect the right of the minor to be an end in him/herself. A minor is arguably less treated as an end in himself where (s)he is forced to donate

[506]See Re W (A Minor) Medical Treatment [1992] 3 WLR 758 at 767F.

on the grounds of it being in his/her best interests or prevented from donating simply because (s)he is a minor.

In addition to these issues there are questions of what age a person should be treated as becoming an adult for the purposes of consent to organ donation and what is required in terms of maturity and understanding for a minor to be competent to donate. The matter of donation by a minor can require careful weighing of interests and can potentially involve pressures and conflicts of interest. Given these factors and the potential harm and jeopardy involved in donation should it be subject to prior scrutiny or approval by a court or other legal forum?

As we shall see there has been considerable judicial comment on when minors can be used as living organ donor - starting over 40 years ago with the Massachusetts Supreme Judicial Court decision in Masden v Harrison.[507] In addition, transplant legislation in many jurisdictions has taken on the role of regulating use.

Given the intricate ethical and legal considerations it can raise, it is not surprisingly that use of living minors as organ donors has been relatively rare. In the US, twins are looked on favourably because of the potential results combined with the specially close interest the minor donor may have in the recipient's well-being. Other minors are used more cautiously. Spital's 1987 survey of US Transplant Centres found that only 13% of responding centres had performed at least one non-twin minor transplant within the preceding 5 years.[508] Use of *any* living minor as an organ donor is a very rare event in Europe with there being only 7 instances from 1982-1992 - 5 in EUROTRANSPLANT and one each in the UK and Eire.[509] I interviewed the minor donor from Eire in Dublin as part of EUROTOLD's programme of donor and recipient interview/questionnaires. She was nearly 14 years old and had given a kidney to her twin sister. She explained that doctors had made it clear to her that she could change her mind at any time before donation but she had not wanted to,

> ...that thought never occurred to me...I knew I'd have the best match...I couldn't really understand the commotion of it...the doctors explained to me what it

---

[507]Eq. No 68651 (Mass, June 12,1957). Confirmed in the same year by Huskey v Harrison Eq. No. 68666 (Mass., Aug. 30 1957) and Foster v Harrison Eq. No. 68674 (Mass., Nov. 20, 1957).

[508]Unconventional Living Kidney Donors: Attitudes and Use Among Transplant Centers, *Transplantation,* 1989, 48(2), 243-248.

[509]Considerably more minors become cadaver kidney and liver donors.

> would all involve but when I heard...it didn't matter what was involved. With what she was going through of course I was going to do this.

It was clear that she had been informed (the information 'was very good') and had chosen on the basis of an explanation of risks and benefits but, like many adult donors, she hadn't weighed these in any detailed or reflective manner (she felt she didn't really need information because she already knew her decision). Valid consent to the donation was given on her behalf by her parents and authorisation was given by a hospital committee.

Whether she was competent enough at the time of agreeing for her own agreement to constitute a valid consent was a moot point. Hence it is important to ask whether or not the donation was in her best interests. From the interview itself it was clear she had a warm relationship with her sister, that they both valued that relationship highly and they were very close to the point of having some telepathic experiences in relation to each other over long physical distances. Probably she had a large interest in her sister's well-being and hence a large interest in using by far the most efficient reductionistic method of protecting that interest, which was her own donation which had projected graft survival of 37 years, about four times better than the alternatives. Her interest probably significantly exceeded the case not to donate given that the harm and jeopardy (s)he was exposing herself to was no greater than that normally involved in kidney donation.

Professional attitudes in Europe are not universally in favour of minor donation in situations similar to the above. EUROTOLD's Professional Attitudes Questionnaire posed the scenario that,

> ...a 14 year old boy has been on haemodialysis for 3 years but is experiencing severe psychological problems with needling. He is unsuitable for CAPD as a result of previous urological surgery as an infant. His mother is a single parent with three other children, one of them being his identical twin. This patient reacts strongly to mother on cytotoxic crossmatch as a result of a previous transfusion.

Only 36% of respondents would accept the twin, with most preferring to wait for a cadaveric transplantation (39% would await a good cadaver match, 25.4% would await a blood group compatible cadaver graft). Clearly the main concern about using the twin would be her age. EUROTOLD's Transplant Centre Questionnaire surveyed the minimum age at which professionals would accept a donor and found very diverse results. Even after taking out the 4 most extreme responses (involving minimums of 1, 5, 25 and 30 years old) there were still centres that would use a donor as young as 10 and, rather paternalistically, several who would not use donors until age 18 or even age 21. In the US professional attitudes towards the use of minors are similarly mixed. In his 1989 study Spital found that the minimum age 3 out of 74 responding centres would use donors was 11 or below, for 11 centres it was 12-14, for 6 it was 15 and for 50 of the remaining 54 centres it was 18. There were far less qualms about using minor donors when it came to bone marrow donation.[510]

The Age of Majority for Being a Living Organ Donor

The age of majority for medical treatment varies between jurisdictions but will typically be 16 or 18. Those transplant laws specifying an age of majority in the context of living organ donation, may simply confirm the age applying to medical treatment generally in that jurisdiction *or* define a different, usually higher, age. In some jurisdictions, such as Sri Lanka[511] and the Syrian Arab Republic,[512] transplant legislation states that the age of majority is 21.

The legal presumption (rebuttable) is that minors are incompetent. Majority is important partly because it brings with it the legal presumption (rebuttable) that one is competent to decide for oneself. As we shall see, however, it can also be important for other reasons.

Under section 8 of the Family Law Reform Act 1969, English law defines 16 and 17 year olds as adults for the purposes of *medical treatment*.[513] However, interestingly it was stated in Re W (A Minor) Medical Treatment [1992] 3 WLR 758[514] that section 8 does not apply to forms of medical intervention which are not treatment, i.e. non-therapeutic

---

[510]Unconventional Living Kidney Donors: Attitudes and Use Among Transplant Centers, *Transplantation,* 1989, 48(2), 243-248.
[511]Act of 11 Dec 1987 at section 7(2)(b)i.
[512]Law No. 31 of 23 Aug 1972.
[513]Section 8(2) states that in section 8 'surgical dental or medical treatment includes any procedure undertaken for the purposes of diagnosis and this section applies to any procedure (including in particular the administration of an anaesthetic) which is ancillary to any treatment as it applies to that treatment'.
[514]At 767F.

interventions of which living organ donation was specifically mentioned. The age of majority for living organ donation is thus not 16 but 18 in English law.

Minor Competency

It is a well established legal principle that some minors will be competent to give a valid content to certain activities. Under English law the landmark House of Lords decision in Gillick v West Norfolk and Wisbech Area Health Authority (1985) 3 All ER 402 considered a general definition of what constituted competency in a minor.[515] Lord Scarman defined a minor as competent to give consent to the particular intervention at hand when (s)he,

> ...achieves a significant understanding and intelligence to enable him or her to understand fully what is proposed.[516]

This test has been accepted and applied in English law[517] and in several other jurisdictions.[518] As we shall see in the next chapter, competency in adulthood is defined differently[519] although a feature of both contexts is that competency can vary over time.[520]

---

[515]In this case the House of Lords decided that a 14 year old girl had capacity to take the contraceptive pill. The girl did not want to take the contraceptive pill but her mother, being generally opposed to doctors prescribing contraception to minors, brought the case to establish certain points of law on the matter and with regard to a Department of Health circular relating to girls under 16 being prescribed the contraception.

[516]At 423j. Lord Fraser took a similar approach (see 3 All ER 409d & e).

[517]However, a modified approach is taken in cases where a minor has a mental disability (see Re R (A Minor) (Wardship: Consent to Medical Treatment) [1992] Fam 11.

[518]Bainham, The Judge and The Competent Minor, *LQR*, 1992, 108, 194. See Court of Appeal decision in Alberta, Canada in C v Wrent [1987] 35 DLR (4th) 419 (Alta CA).

[519]M.Gunn, The Meaning of Capacity, *Med Law Review,* 1994, 2(1) at 8.

[520]However, in Re R (A Minor) (Wardship: Consent to Medical Treatment) [1992] Fam. 11 a 15 year old girl was forcibly administered anti-psychotic drugs on the basis that she was incompetent even though (s)he had had an earlier period of lucid competency during which she had refused such a treatment.

Despite organ donation not being a treatment, the Gillick principle applies to it according to Re W.[521] The Gillick test doesn't intrinsically exclude the possibility of a minor of any age being competent to donate but it is interesting to ask at what the typical age might be for a minor to be competent to donate an organ. Donation of an organ is a more serious, complicated and hazardous matter that donation of blood or most other tissues. Lord Donaldson in Re W felt that a minor could be competent to be a living blood donor but doubted whether one would ever be competent to be a living organ donor.[522] This view was recently echoed in the case commentary of Re Y (Adult Incompetent: Legality of Non-Therapeutic Procedure) [1996] Med L Rev 204-205 at 206,

> ...given the need to weigh the benefit of the procedure against the risks of doing it, it is not likely that a court would contemplate donation of non-regenerative tissue such as a kidney (by a minor).

On close analysis it can be observed that children do have different decision-making processes to those adopted by adults and this can be particularly significant in determining whether or not a minor is likely to be competent to donate an organ. Piaget suggests that younger children are in a pre-operational cognitive stage of development,[523] a point expanded on by Kohlberg in his cognitive developmental theory.[524] A minor in either of these stages would be legally incompetent to donate an organ. However, the cognitive abilities of children obviously tend to grow as they become older. In reviewing psychological studies of minor decision-making David Price and I concluded elsewhere that,

> ...studies of intellectual development suggest that from 7-8 years the child is capable of certain logical reasoning processes applied to concrete objects or

---

[521]3 WLR 758 at 767 and 772 at para C per Lord Donaldson. This view has gained considerable academic support. See, for example: D.Price and A.Garwood-Gowers, Transplantation From Minors, *Contemporary Issues in Law*, 1996, 1(1), 1-27; Mason and McCall-Smith, Law and Medical Ethics, *Butterworths*, 1991, 373; *and* M.Brazier, Medicine, Patients and The Law, *Penguin*, 1992 (2nd ed), 421.

[522][1992] 3 WLR 758 at 767F.

[523]J.Piaget and B.Inhelder, The Psychology of A Child, *Basic Books*, 1969.

[524]L.Kohlberg, Stage and Sequence: The Cognitive-developmental Approach to Socialization in A.Goslin (ed.), Handbook of Socialization Theory and Research, *Rand McNally*, 1969.

> events in the immediate present. From 11-15 years the ability to reason hypothetically is also formed.[525]

We noted that hypothetical reasoning is an intrinsic aspect of the organ donation decision-making process. This is not to say a minor with hypothetical reasoning abilities will be competent to donate an organ, because an ability does not always come with sufficient maturity and understanding to reasonably apply it to one's own situation. However, in a world where teenagers make many important decisions, including marriage, it does seem unduly pessimistic to suggest that persons under 18 are unlikely to ever have capacity to donate an organ. Several US decisions, including Masden v Harrison[526] (14 year old) and Rappeport v Stott[527] (17 year old), have held that minors can be competent to donate organs. Surely teenagers in England and Wales are not any more immature than those in the US?

Jurisdictions Prohibiting all Minors from Being Living Organ Donors

Jurisdictions like Algeria,[528] Belarus (Draft law),[529] Bolivia,[530] Costa Rica,[531] France,[532] Germany,[533] India,[534] Lebanon,[535] Mexico,[536] Panama,[537] Russian Federation,[538] Spain[539] and Tunisia[540] have adopted the statement

[525] D.Price and A.Garwood-Gowers, Transplantation From Minors: Are Children Other People's Medicine, *Contemporary Issues in Law,* 1995, 1(1), 1-25.
[526] Eq. No 68651 (Mass, June 12,1957).
[527] Civil No.1. 74-57 (Mass, Aug 28, 1974).
[528] Law No. 85-05 of 16 Feb 1985 at section 163.
[529] Section 3.
[530] Regulations of 15 March 1982 at section 4.
[531] Law No. 5560 of 20 Aug 1974 at section 15.
[532] Law No. 94-654 of 29 July 1994 at Article 671-4.
[533] Act of 5 Nov 1997 at section 8(1).
[534] The Transplantation of Human Organs Act 1994 at section 2(f).
[535] Decree No. 109 of 16 September 1983 at section 1(1).
[536] Federal Regulation of 16 Aug 1976 at section 24.
[537] Section 22 of Law No. 10 of 11th July 1983.
[538] Law of 22 Dec 1992 at section 3.
[539] Section 2 of the Crown Decree of 1980.
[540] Law No.91-22 of 25 March 1991 at section 2.

within WHO's Guiding Principle 5 that: 'No organ should be removed from the body of a living minor for the purpose of transplantation'.[541] However, the Guiding Principle also allowed exceptions to be made in the case of other regenerative body materials and many laws have followed the spirit of this by allowing a minor to donate tissues, often on conditions such as it being on behalf of a sibling.[542] The advantage of denying the minor the right to donate organs is that it protects him or her from risk taking. However, it may be thought that at least those minors who are competent ought to be allowed to donate.

Jurisdictions Only Allowing Competent Minors to be Living Organ Donors

Under general principles of law an incompetent minor could become a living organ donor. However, there are some jurisdictions with legislative provision that only allows organs to be donated by competent minors. Examples include Bulgaria,[543] Cyprus,[544] Denmark,[545] Ecuador,[546] Iraq,[547] Kuwait,[548] Norway,[549] Paraguay,[550] Poland,[551] Romania,[552] Slovakia,[553]

---

[541]See Human Organ Transplantation: A Report Under the Auspices of WHO (1987-1991) World Health Organisation, Geneva 1991.

[542]France (Article L 671-4 and 671-5 of Law No. 94-654 of 29 July 1994) and Greece (Section 5 of Law No. 1383 of 2nd August 1983) both state this.

[543]Ordinance No 15 of 30th April 1976 No. 35. Law currently under review.

[544]Law No. 97 of 1987 at section 7(3).

[545]Law No. 402 of 13 June 1990 at section 13(2).

[546]Law No. 64 of 26th May 1987 section 24.

[547]Decree No. 698 of 27 August 1986 at section 2.

[548]Decree-Law No. 55 of 20 December 1987 at section 2.

[549]Law No. 6 of 19 Feb 1973 states that the minor donor must have understood the information concerning the nature of the operation and it's consequences which was provided to him by a physician.

[550]Law No. 826180 of 15 December 1980 at section 276.

[551]Law of 26 October 1995 at Article 9(1)(7). See Transplantation From Living Donors Who are Unable to Give Consent For Organ Harvesting, Marek Safjan, Dorota Safjan, *Trans Proc*, Dec 1996. Copies of this and the Law available from EUROTOLD.

[552]Article 4(1) of the 1996 Law.

[553]Section 46(1) of Law No. 277 of 24 August 1994.

Turkey[554] and Vietnam.[555] The position in England and Wales is that donations not classed as between genetic relatives can only be conducted if the donor 'understands the nature of the medical procedure and the risks, as explained by the registered general medical practitioner, and consents to the removal of the organ in question'.[556] Since incompetent donors could not give a valid consent, in effect 'non-genetic-relative' donation is limited to donors who are competent as defined by general principles of law.

Jurisdictions restricting organ donation to the competent minor usually place special restrictions on this class of donor. For instance, jurisdictions like Norway,[557] Denmark[558] and Bulgaria[559] require parents (or persons exercising parental authority) to consent, thereby allowing them to frustrate a competent child's wish to donate.

Sometimes other approvals may also be required, such as approval by the person responsible for the case of the minor and the Directorate of Health Services in Norway.[560] Denmark[561] requires there to be 'special reasons' to allow the donation which might involve things like the donation having a low level of harm and jeopardy to the prospective minor donor, there being an important relationship between him/her and the recipient and there being particular reason to prefer the donation to other options such as because it offers better graft survival prospects or realistic alternatives are not reasonably available.

Turkey allows the competent minor the same freedom to donate as an adult, which is arguably a fairer approach.

---

554 States that, 'the removal of an organ or tissue from a person under 18 years of age... shall be permissible in cases where the person has drawn up and signed a document in the presence of at least 2 witnesses and in the absence of any pressure of any kind, or where the person has given an oral undertaking in the presence of at least two witnesses and has signed a declaration which is then countersigned by a physician'. Donors under the age of 18 (as well as adults) are prohibited from donating if they are deemed 'unable to take their own decision for mental or psychological reasons'. This appears to be equivalent to a requirement for competency. Section 6 of Law No. 2238 of 29 May 1979.

555 Law of 30 June 1989 at section 30(1).

556 The Human Organ Transplants (Unrelated Persons) Regulations 1989 (SI No 2480) at regulation 3(1) b.

557 Law No. 6 of 19 Feb 1973 at section 1.

558 Law No. 402 of 13 June 1990 at section 13(2).

559 Law of 1996.

560 Law No. 6 of 19 Feb 1973 at section 1.

561 Law No. 402 of 13 June 1990 at section 13(2).

Jurisdictions which prohibit incompetent minors from donating organs do not necessarily prevent them from donating tissues. An example is Romanian law where bone marrow may be donated to a sibling where the appropriate consents have been obtained.[562]

Jurisdictions Allowing Competent and Incompetent Minors to be Living Organ Donors

In the absence of legislation which prevents it, both the incompetent and competent minor may donate organs. However, under general principles of law, and often under legislation, there are conditions on minor donation over and above those applying to adults.

Restrictions on What Organs Can be Donated

The Council of Europe states in Resolution (78)29 that minors should only donate non-regenerative material if they are competent[563] and confirms this approach in Article 20(1) and (2) of its Convention on Human Rights and Biomedicine. A number of jurisdictions also take this stance,[564] including Argentina,[565] most Australian jurisdictions,[566] Belgium,[567] Finland,[568] Portugal,[569] Slovenia,[570] South Africa,[571] Sri Lanka[572] and Zimbabwe.[573] If

[562]Article 5(1) of 1996 law.
[563]Article 6(2).
[564]Some use the word 'replaceable' which is much the same.
[565]Section 14 ibid. Section 18 specifies a list of people who are able to consent in order of priority topped by a spouse.
[566]Queensland The Transplantation and Anatomy Act 1979-1984 at section 12(b) by implication; South Australia Act of 1983 section 12(a); Western Australia Act No.116 of 1982 at section 13(1); Tasmania The Human Tissue Act 1985 at section 7(a). However, the NorthernTerritory Act No. 121 of 1979 at section 9 excludes donation by those under 18 and in New South Wales section 10 of The Human Tissue Act 1983 forbids it by omission from specified permissions.
[567]Law of 1986 (sections 5-7).
[568]Law Number 355 of 26 April 1985.
[569]Law No. 12 of 22 April 1993 at section 6(3) and section 8(3).
[570]Law of 1996, Article 9.
[571]Section 18 (b)(ii).
[572]Act No. 48 of 1987 at sections 8(1).

one interprets the term 'regenerable' strictly it would allow donation of liver segment. It cannot have been intended to allow liver segment when it carries more harm and jeopardy to the donor than donation of a kidney, which would not be allowed under these provisions. It is worth noting in this light that the Council of Europe's Committee of Ministers to Member States in Recommendation No. R (97) 16 On Liver Transplantation From Living Related Donors states in its Appendix at point iv) that minors not having capacity to consent should not be used as liver segment donors.

Restrictions on Who Organs Can be Donated To

Some jurisdictions have transplant legislation which limits the classes of person that a minor may donate to more than it limits who an adult can donate to. For example, Syrian Arab Republic only allows donation to a twin brother.[574] Belgium's law states that the transplant must be on behalf of a sibling.[575] Sweden's law only allows minors to donate to 'relatives'.[576] The Netherlands law of 1996 states that donors of 12-18 years must be donating to a first or second degree relative. Incompetent minor donors are only allowed to donate to a linear relative or sibling under Poland's law of 1995[577] and only to the direct family unit under Slovenian law.[578] Colombian law only allows minors to donate to consanguineous relatives up to the fourth degree.[579]

HOTA basically limits incompetent minors to donating to close genetic relatives because under the Act and associated regulations ULTRA screens all other forms of donation and will only allow them in cases where it is satisfied not only that the donor understands, 'the nature of the medical procedure and the risks, as explained by the registered general medical practitioner' but also 'consents to the removal of the organ in question'.[580]

[573]Act No. 34 of 1976 at section 12(b). In Canada this position is recommended for provinces under section 5(1) and 6(1) of its model law of 1990. See also The Human Tissue Donation Act 1992 for Prince Edward Island.

[574]Law No. 31 of 23 Aug 1972.

[575]Law of 1986 at regulation 8.

[576]Section 8 of 1995 law.

[577]Article 9(1)-9(4)).

[578]Law of 1996 Article 9.

[579]Decree No. 1172 of 6 June 1989 at section 32.

[580]The Human Organ Transplants (Unrelated Persons) Regulations 1989 (SI No 2480) at regulation 3(1) b.

This provision would appear to unfairly discriminate against donation to relatives-in-law who are close to the minor. Hong Kong's law is similar in that it prevents the minor from donating to a person who is not a close genetic relative or spouse of 3 or more years standing. However, an exception is made where the minor is at least 16 and married.[581]

Parental/Guardian Authorisation

Under general principles of law it is a basic principle that if the minor is incompetent to decide on a particular matter someone must do so on his behalf. Normally it will be a parent or guardian who is invested with the legal authority to do so (typically a parent). In the absence of legislative provision to the contrary, the incompetent minor must get the consent of a person normally legally responsible for him/her in order to become a living organ donor.

If the minor is competent (s)he will normally be able to donate without such consent according to English law.[582] In the US the Court of Appeals for the District of Columbia in Bonner v Moran 126 F.2d 121 (1941) suggested obiter dicta that parental consent is required for all minor donations[583] and the Massachusetts Supreme Court was not clear whether or not kidney donation by a 19 year old minor could have gone ahead without parental consent in Masden v Harrison.[584] However, there are US authorities which support the more rational legal approach of not requiring parental consent when the minor is competent. These include Rappeport v Stott[585] where the Massachusetts Supreme Court authorised donation of bone marrow solely on the basis that the 17 year old minor was capable of consenting and an unreported decision in an Alabama court where kidney donation by a 17 year old minor to a 16 year old recipient was authorised solely on the basis of the minor's consent.[586]

Unfortunately, some transplant legislation is framed in such a way that all minors must seek consent of the person normally exercising legal

[581]Regulation 5(4)b of Ordinance No. 16 of 1995.
[582]Re W [1992] 3 WLR 758 at 767 F has reaffirmed the Gillick concept that parents have no right of veto if a doctor chooses to accept a competent minor's choice.
[583]Concerning a possible skin graft from the minor to his severely burned cousin.
[584]Eq. No 68651 (Mass, June 12,1957).
[585]Civil No.1. 74-57 (Mass, Aug 28, 1974).
[586]See G.Smitherson, The Legal Dilemma of Minor Sibling Kidney Donation, *The Alabama Journal of Medical Sciences* 1982, 19(3), 309.

authority in relation to them (see e.g. Cuba,[587] Finland,[588] Malawi,[589] Sweden,[590] Zimbabwe[591] and Belgium's law which requires the consent of the person(s) whose consent to the marriage of the minor is required if the donor is under 18[592]).

Donor Authorisation and the Right Not to Donate

Under general principles of Scottish law a competent minor has the same legal right to refuse medical intervention as an adult. However, in English law Re W,[593] as confirmed in Re R, has established that a competent minor is not sovereign over his/her own medical treatment in the same way as an adult.

Lord Donaldson in Re W stated that a medical practitioner obtaining a consent from someone who can legally consent on the competent minor's behalf (usually a parent/legal guardian) has an insulating 'flak jacket' against legal liability.[594] However, he also went further by stating the same position applies to 16 and 17 year olds. Section 8(1) of the Family Law Reform Act 1969 appears to treat 16 and 17 year olds as adults for the purposes of medical treatment. It states that,

> The consent of a minor who has attained the age of 16 years to any surgical, medical or dental treatment which, in the absence of consent, would constitute a trespass to his person, shall be as effective as it would be if he were of full age and where a minor has by virtue of this section given an effective consent to any treatment it shall not be necessary to obtain any consent for it from parent or guardian.

Section 8 of the Family Law Reform Act was surely intended to make 16 and seventeen year olds sovereign over their own treatment and it was open to Lord Donaldson to respect this intention. However, section 8(3) of the FLRA states that,

---

587 Decree No. 139 of 4 February 1988.
588 Law No. 355 of 26 April 1985.
589 Section 11 The Anatomy Act 1990.
590 Law No. 831of 8 June 1995 at section 8.
591 Act No. 34 of 1976 at section 12(b).
592 Law of 1986 sections 5-7.
593 Re W (A Minor) (Medical Treatment) [1992] 3 WLR 758 (CA).
594 Ibid at 767.

(n)othing in this section shall be construed as making ineffective any consent which would have been effective if this section had not been enacted.

Lord Donaldson interpreted this as meaning that the presumption of sovereignty over medical decision making applied from the age it was before the Act, i.e. 18. Not surprisingly, Re W and Re R have come in for heavy academic criticism.[595] The whole approach of Lord Donaldson undermines the principle of self-determination of competent minors that formed the spirit of the decision in Gillick. His Lordship's approach also conflicts with the policy of the Children Act 1989 under which a child who has sufficient understanding has a right to make an informed refusal to submit to a medical or psychiatric assessment or examination.[596]

Kennedy and Grubb note the disturbing possibility that doctors have a legal basis on which they can now perform a sterilisation or abortion on a young competent woman without her consent.[597] Similarly disturbing is the fact that there might be a legal basis to force a competent minor to donate a tissue or organ. However, the fact that consent exercised on behalf of a minor has to be exercised in his/her best interests would make forced minor living donation exceptional because in forcing the minor you dilute or counteract the psychological benefits that (s)he must get from donation at a level outweighing the physical harm and jeopardy. So far in the US there have not been any cases where a minor has been forced to donate and much of the case law emphasises minor agreement as a necessity. In English law Lord Justice Balcombe in Re W stated obiter dicta that a competent minor could not be forced to donate and the case commentary in Re Y has even hypothesised that the court would, as a rule of thumb, look for agreement in *bone marrow* donation by an *incompetent* donor.[598]

Several jurisdictions use transplant legislation to specifically exclude the spectre of forced minor donation - including Belgium,[599] Colombia,[600]

---

[595]E.g. J.Bridgman, Old Enough to Know Best?, *J of Legal Studies,* 1993, 13(1), 69 *and* Kennedy and Grubb, Medical Law: Text with Materials, *Butterworths,* 1994, 393.

[596]See sections 43(8), 44(7) and Schedule 3, paras 4(4) and 5(5).

[597]Ibid.

[598]Re Y commentary, Med L Rev 205-207 at 207 - discussed further in chapter 6.

[599]Section 5-7 of 1986 law.

[600]The intention of the donor overrides any contrary opinion of his relatives or any other person according to Law No. 73 of 20 December 1988 at section 3.

Finland,[601] Portugal,[602] Slovenia,[603] Sweden[604] and The Netherlands.[605] This doesn't mean that the minor's active agreement has to be obtained in all cases. Finnish law simply imposes a limited duty to consult; the minor's opinion of the intervention is established insofar as is possible having regard to his age and level of development.[606] Portuguese law only requires the minors to agree if they are 'capable of understanding and able to express their wishes'.[607] Meanwhile, Belgian[608] and Slovenian[609] laws do not require consultation with minors under the age of 15 but actually require their consent if they are 15 or over.

Other Prior Authorisations Including Court Authorisation

Under general principles of law it has been stated in a host of US cases that living donation of organs by minors must be subject to prior court approval.[610] Washington is an exception in that the Attorney General's Office there appears to have determined that the written consent of the legal guardian is sufficient authorisation for a minor or other incompetent to donate. It is not entirely clear whether prior court approval would be required were the donor competent.

---

[601] Law No. 355 of 26 April 1985.
[602] Section 8(4) of 1993 law.
[603] Article 11 of law of 1996.
[604] Law No. 831 of 8 June 1995 at section 8.
[605] Section 8(4).
[606] Law No. 355 of 26 April 1985. An expert in child psychology or paediatrics must submit a report to the National Board of Health to accompany the application for approval, which must be submitted to the Board before the living donation in question can proceed.
[607] Section 8(4) of 1993 law. South Australian law (section 13) and Western Australian law (section 13(2)) are similar.
[608] Law of 1986 (sections 5-7).
[609] Article 11 of law of 1996.
[610] Hart v Brown, 29 Conn. Supp. 368, 289 A.2d 386 (Super. Ct 1972); Howard v Fulton-DeKalb Memorial Hosp. Auth., Civil No. B-90430 (Super. Ct., Fulton County, Ga., Nov. 29, 1973); Children's Memorial Hosp. v. Lewis, No. 73CH6936 (Cir. Ct., Cook County, Ill., Nov. 21, 1973); *In re* Richardson, 284 So. 2d 185 (La. App. 1973); *In re* Bostrom, Eq. No. 49385 (Cir. Ct., Montgomery County, Md., June 7, 1974); *In re* Bachman, Fid. No. 20828 (Cir. Ct. Fairfax County, Va., Aug. 9, 1974); Lausier v Pescinski, No. 668 (Wis., Mar. 4, 1975).

There are no English minor organ donation cases but there have been obiter dicta comments on whether prior court approval is required in such cases. Lord Donaldson in Re W seems to imply that court involvement would *not* be mandatory for organ donation at least where the doctor reasonably believes the minor is Gillick competent or obtains the consent of someone legally able to consent on behalf of the minor.[611] The furthest he went was to say that,

> ...a doctor may well be advised to apply to the court for guidance, as recommended by Lord Templeman in a different context in Re B (a minor)(wardship: sterilisation) [1988] A.C. 199, 205-6.[612]

However, David Price and I have suggested that Lord Donaldson's approach in Re W of not requiring court involvement in organ donation may *not* be good law.[613] Indeed, Lord Justice Nolan in Re W contradicts Donaldson's approach. He considered court involvement to be mandatory in the context of a potential abortion procedure and added, 'I would say the same of a case in which a child of any age consented to donate an organ'.[614] In other words he was suggesting prior court approval would be required even if the minor is competent. Clearly organ donation is a serious procedure for even a competent minor to be considering and there are conflicting interests involved.

An analogy can be drawn with incompetent adults. Mr Justice Connell in Re Y merely suggested court involvement was appropriate in adult incompetent bone marrow cases.[615] However, donation of tissues such as bone marrow, whilst it should arguably involve court involvement can be

---

611[1992] 3 WLR 758 at 767. He stated that, 'Organ transplants are quite different and, as a matter of law, doctors would have to secure the consent of someone with the rights to consent on behalf of a donor under the age of 18 or, if they relied on the consent of the minor himself, or herself, be satisfied that the minor was Gillick competent in the context of so serious a procedure which could not benefit the minor'. This means that however desirable court involvement might be with regard to minor donors it is not legally necessary as the doctors will be insulated from liability if they follow Donaldson's instructions.
612[1992] 3 WLR 758 at 767G.
613Price and Garwood-Gowers, Transplantation From Minors: Are Children Other People's Medicine, *Contemporary Issues in Law*, 1996, 1(1), 1-27 at 17.
614Re W [1992] 3 WLR 758 at 782C.
615[1996] Med L Rev 204-205 at 205.

distinguished from donation of organs in that it involves less harm and jeopardy to the donor.

The more analogous situation in terms of seriousness may be compulsory sterilisation of the adult incompetent where the weight of legal authority suggests court involvement is mandatory.[616] In Re F [1990] 2 A.C. 1, Lord Bridge in the House of Lords,[617] along with Lord Justice Neill[618] and Lord Donaldson MR[619] in the Court of Appeal, mentioned that an operation to allow inter vivos organ donation by an incapacitated adult required similar safeguards to contraceptive sterilisation - i.e. including court involvement. The Law Commission, rightly in my view, recommended in Mental Incapacity, its Command Paper on decision making by mentally incapacitated adults, that both organ and bone marrow donation by incompetent adults should be treated as within a 'special category' of procedures under English law requiring the involvement of a Court forum.[620] In the case of incompetent minors, prior involvement of a legal forum ought to be obligatory. If the minor is competent it would still be best to make it obligatory because the forum can play an important role in checking competency and checking that the minor is donating voluntarily.

Transplant legislation in some jurisdictions does away with the requirement for court involvement. In some cases another body is required to authorise donation such as a National Board of Health in the case of Finland[621] and in the case of in Sweden the National Board of Health and Welfare and (rather obviously) the physician empowered to decide on the removal.[622] Slovenian law requires prior ethical committee approval for

---

[616]See Lord Templeman in Re B (a minor) (wardship: sterilization) [1988] AC 199, Lord Griffiths in Re F (mental patient; sterilisation) [1990] 2 AC1 and the majority in the Australian case of Department of Health v JWB & SMB (1992) 66 ALJR 360 (Aust High Ct). Contrast the view that court involvement is just desirable (Lords Brandon and Goff in Re F [1990] 2 AC). The net effect of a series of recent lower court decisions by Sir Stephen Brown P (Re E (a minor) (medical treatment)[1991] 7 BMLR 117 (Fam Div) and F v F [1991] 7 BMLR 135 (Fam Div) and Re SG (a minor) (1991) 6 BMLR 95 (Fam Div)) appears to be that the court will only necessarily involve itself in matters which are non-therapeutic.

[617]Re F [1990] 2 A.C. 1 at 52.

[618]Ibid at 33.

[619]Ibid at 19.

[620]Law Com No. 231 at p85.

[621]Law No. 355 of 26 April 1985.

[622]Law No. 831of 8 June 1995 at section 8.

the donation,[623] something that would happen as a matter of routine in nearly all transplant centres anyway. Belgium's law requires the consent of the spouse of the donor, if (s)he is under 18, married and the spouse is residing with him/her.[624]

The Requirement for Justifications Over and Above those Required For Living Organ Donation by Competent Adults.

Both general principles of law and, in many cases, transplant legislation require justification for using a minor as a living organ donor over and above the justification required to use a competent adult.

Finland's law requires that there is 'special justification' to use a minor. What constitutes special justification is not elaborated. However, it would probably involve factors like the donation being by some margin the best alternative for the recipient and some special relationship between the donor and recipient resulting in the former having a special interest in the well-being of the latter. Donations involving his/her levels of harm and/or jeopardy would probably be looked upon unfavourably. Sweden's law requires the situation to be one where the recipient is unable to get compatible material from another person and again there must be special grounds for removal.[625] Under Queensland's law there must be likely death of a member of the nuclear family without donation by the minor and the risk must be minimal.[626] The Netherlands amongst other conditions specifies that removal from minors under 12 and those over 12 who cannot make a reasonable assessment of their interests in the matter can only be performed if the removal is of non-regenerable material and will not have lasting effects on the donor's health.[627]

As earlier noted, where general principles of law apply decisions made on behalf of a minor must be made in his/her best interests. The best interests test has been used in cases involving incompetent minors as prospective donors as early as the Massachusetts decisions of 1957 such as Foster v Harrison, Eq.No. 68674 (Mas., Aug.30, 1957) and Huskey v Harrison, Eq. No. 68666 (Mass., Aug.30, 1957). Baron states that in the Massachusetts jurisdiction, where most minor donation cases have been

623 Article 11 of 1996 law.
624 Law of 1986 (sections 5-7).
625 Law No. 831of 8 June 1995 at section 8.
626 Sections 12c and d.
627 Law of 24 May 1996 at section 5(2) - see *IDHL*, 1996, 47(4) at 470.

heard, 'the justices have not clearly articulated the legal theory upon which their decrees have been based'[628] He suggests that while some cases consider best interests, some require consent by the minor (thus preventing incompetent donation) *and* some engage in a review of the parents' weighing of the relative costs and benefits of the operation to both children (prospective donor and recipient).[629] In addition, historically the doctrine of substituted judgement was sometimes used to decide affairs on behalf of an incompetent by reference to what (s)he would have done if competent.

Looking at the merits of the different approaches it can be stated that requiring consent is perhaps too strict in that it eliminates donations in a minor's best interests that (s)he might want to undertake. The collective utility is abuse if it is not accompanied by consent, or at least agreement on the part of the minor. The general application of substituted judgement to cases of organ donation by incompetents has been recommended by Robertson for a number of reasons, including the notion that it attempts to continue regarding the incompetent person, 'as an individual with free choice and moral dignity, and not as someone whose preferences no longer mattered'.[630] However, McLean has pointed out that where a person has always lacked competency, 'what he or she would do if competent is simply a matter of speculation'.[631] Hence, as far as incompetent minors are concerned, substituted judgement is only useful if the minor was once competent and is now temporarily incompetent (as in Re W[632]). However, even here its use would be sophistic unless something was genuinely known about the minor's wishes at the time (s)he had been competent.

No matter what the merits and demerits of these approaches are, it is the best interests test that is in fact used in US cases involving proposed donation by an incompetent minor. The substituted judgement doctrine was often thought to have been the basis for allowing donation by a mentally disabled adult in the case of Strunk v Strunk which is discussed

[628]Live Organ and Tissue Transplants from Minor Donors in Massachusetts, *Boston U Law Review* 1975, 55, 159 at p169.

[629]Nathan v Farinelli Eq. No. 74-87 (Mass., July 3, 1974).

[630]Organ Donation by Incompetents and the Substituted Judgement Doctrine, *Columbia LR*, 1976, 76, 48.

[631]McLean, A Patients Right to Know, *Dartmouth Publishing*, 1989 at p68.

[632]See Kennedy and Grubb Medical Law, Text with Materials, *Butterworths,* 1994 at p289. For an example of where substituted judgement was used see Re Lucille Boyd [1979] 403 A 2d 744 (Dc Cir) where the pre-incompetency religious beliefs of the incompetent person suggested that she would have refused treatment.

later in this chapter. However, the judges in Strunk did not clearly state that they were basing their decision on substituted judgement. In this regard Little v Little (Tex Civ 1979), 576 SW 2d 493 at 498, sensibly concluded that,

> ...it is clear in transplant cases that courts, whether they use the term 'substituted judgement' or not, will consider the benefits to the donor as a basis for permitting an incompetent to donate an organ. Although in Strunk the Kentucky Court discussed the substituted judgement doctrine in some detail, the conclusion of the majority there was based on the benefits that the incompetent donor would derive, rather than on the theory that the incompetent would have consented to the transplant if he were competent. We adopt this approach.

The substituted judgement doctrine has subsequently been rejected in a minor organ transplantation case In Re Guardianship of Pescinski (1975) 67 Wis 2d 4 226 NW 2d 180. Justice Calvo neatly sums up the position for incompetent minor donation in Curran v Bosze,[633]

> ...notwithstanding the language used by the courts in reaching their determination that a transplant may or may not occur, the standard by which the determination was made was whether the transplant would be in the best interest of the child or incompetent person.

What the incompetent would have done if competent is just one factor in the overall determination of best interests.

English law has basically rejected the use of the substituted judgement doctrine as a basis for determining medical intervention on minors.[634] Lord Reid did state, obiter dicta, in the House of Lords case of S v S [1970] 3 All ER 107 that a medical intervention on a minor might be justified were it *not against* his/her best interests.[635] However, this view runs against the whole thrust of law relating to children and has gained no currency in

---

[633](1990) 566 NE 2d 1319 (Illinois Sup Ct).

[634]In Re J (a minor) (wardship: medical treatment) (1991) Fam 33 substituted judgement was applied to a neonate but generally the doctrine has lost favour and is only one of several factors that may be taken into account within the overarching context of the minor's best interests. This approach is also the Law Commission's recommended one for adults.

[635]At 110.

subsequent cases including the bone marrow donation case of Re Y. It is the best interests test that applies to donation of an organ by an incompetent minor, just as it does in the US.

Under what circumstances is a living organ donation in the best interests of an incompetent minor? Lord Donaldson in Re W implied that living donation cannot benefit any minor.[636] However, there must surely be cases where the physical harm and jeopardy to the minor are outweighed by a prospective psychological benefit from donating. Certainly, this is generally accepted as the case in the US. However, one of the criteria established by Mr Justice Calvo in Curran v Bosze for living donation by an incompetent minor was that (s)he must be an existing close relationship with the prospective recipient.[637] The rationale underlying this rule is that although it may be psychologically beneficial for an incompetent minor to help another person, doing so is unlikely to be beneficial enough *in its own right* to outweigh the harm and jeopardy to themselves that living donation involves. However, it might be enough if, *in addition*, the minor had a close relationship with the prospective recipient and, hence, a more specific vested psychological interest in the prospective recipient's well-being. Mr Justice Calvo logically added that there must be emotional support available from the person or persons who take care of the child. The case itself involved a petition for testing of three and a half year old twins for possible bone marrow donation to a half sibling which was refused on both the ground of lack of emotional support (the day to day carer of the twins was not in support of the procedure) and lack of close relationship (the twins had only met their half sibling twice and did not know him to any significant degree).

The most useful English case for analysing when living donation might be in the best interests of an incompetent minor Re Y,[638] a case concerning whether an incompetent adult could become a living bone marrow donor. The commentary on Re Y suggested that even in bone marrow cases the courts will look for evidence of a close relationship which will be damaged if the prospective dies. It added that it was unlikely that a court would contemplate even a minimally risky procedure with a child if the child's age prevented him her forming such a relationship with the prospective recipient.[639] However, donation was sanctioned in the case itself in spite of

[636] Re W (A Minor) Medical Treatment [1992] 3 WLR 758 at 767F.
[637] (1990) 566 NE 2d 1319 (Illinois Sup Ct).
[638] Re Y commentary [1996] Med L Rev 205-207.
[639] Ibid at 206.

there not being a fundamental and vital connection between the adult incompetent and the prospective recipient. Seemingly, the court took a liberal interpretation of how close the prospective donor and recipient should be and were influenced in this by the fact that the donation was likely to be so beneficial to the recipient and because, being only bone marrow, it was minimally harmful and jeopardising for the incompetent donor.

When it comes to studies looking at the psychological impact of donation upon minors as a whole, the picture is generally positive. Bernstein and Simmons have concluded that older minor donors tend to gain significant psychological benefits such as increased self esteem.[640] Simmons et al. have emphasised positive attitudes amongst teenage donors and that problems with this group are no more common than with adult donors.[641] Lewis suggests that even younger donors may gain similar benefits.[642] However, the problem comes when one moves from an assertion that donation is generally beneficial to one that it is going to be beneficial in the specific case. Studies suggest that about one third of adults would not donate an organ because of objections to it.[643] Hence, it is hardly reasonable to assume that a minor will come to look favourably upon having donated and it is entirely possible that some might come to consider it to have been an unwanted invasion. Each case really turns on an educated guess which makes it important that one does not 'push the boat out too far'. In addition to the incompetent minor having a serious interest in the well-being of the prospective recipient, there ought to be very powerful reasons for preferring donation by him/her than taking an alternative course of action. The maturity of the incompetent minor must also influence acceptability. The more mature the incompetent minor is the more his/her views about donation can be significantly relied upon and,

---

[640]Bernstein & Simmons, The Adolescent Kidney Donor: The Right To Give, *Am.J.Psychiat,* 1974, 131, 1338, 1340.

[641]At the University of Minnesota 18 donors from age 16-21 were used and evaluated. There was no more evidence of blatant family pressure in this group than in the other age groups and there was only one donor who showed long-term ambivalence about the donation. In general the adolescent kidney donors indicated highly positive attitudes toward the donation and improvement in the self-picture afterward. See Gift of Life at *Wiley and Sons*, 1977 431-3.

[642]Kidney Donation by a 7 Year Old Identical Twin Child: Psychological, Legal and Ethical Considerations, *J Am Acad Child Psychiat,* 1974, 13, 221 at 228-232.

[643]Gift of Life, *Wiley and Sons*, 1977 at 431-3.

where favourable, used as a fairly sound basis for predicting that donation will be in his/her psychological interests and to what degree it is likely to be so. On the other hand, because of likely immaturity, it is easy to see why authors like Hollenberg[644] and Curran[645] are opposed to using very young minors as organ donors. It is obviously a very serious business to open up anyone and take an organ out of them for donation. It must also be considerably more serious, both psychologically and physiologically, when that person is a young child. However, my view is that their must be some cases where the very young minor has such a very strong and direct interest in the well-being of the prospective recipient that even donation of an organ can be justified as almost certainly and clearly in his/her best interests. Clearly, this kind of perspective has been influential in the US where courts have authorised several forms of donation by minors of 7 years of age and even younger. For instance, in Hart v Brown 289 2 Ad 386 (1972) donation of an organ by a minor of 7 years and 10 months to his identical twin was authorised.[646] In Cayouette v Mathieu [1987] R.J.Q. 2230 (Sup. Ct) donation of bone marrow by a 5 year old to his brother who was suffering from leukemia was authorised. Donation of skin by a 3 year old minor to an identical twin was upheld by a Washington Court in McMahon v McMahon (unreported).[647] However, there are cases in the US, such as Camitta v Fager Eq. No. 73-171 (Mass., Sept 5, 1973),[648] where donation has not been allowed because the minors mental state or general immaturity make it doubtful that psychological benefit will occur.

Conclusion

EUROTOLD found that legal restrictions on minor donation were not correlated with transplant professional attitudes towards use of this class of

[644]N.K.Hollenberg, Altruism and Coercion: Should Children Serve as Kidney Donors, *N Engl J Med,* 1977; 296: 390.

[645]W.J.Curran, Kidney Transplantation in Identical Twin Minors: Justice is done in Connecticut, *N Engl J Med,* 1972, 287, 26.

[646]29 Conn. Supp. 368, 289 A.2d 386 (Super Ct 1972).

[647]See P.Herron and I.Marion, Homografting in The Treatment of Severe Burns, *Pacific Med and Surg,* 1967, 75, 4.

[648]In this case the minor had a mental state characterised as a combination of mild retardation and schizophrenia.

donor.[649] Nonetheless, there is no doubt that legislative regulation of minor donation can play a role in facilitating its wider use whilst at the same time helping to ensure that it is not used unethically. Legislation in this area ought to be clear, comprehensive, not overly restrictive and sufficiently straightforward to apply that legitimate use of this class of donor is not discouraged.

The first observation to make about the current legal position is that many jurisdictions are too paternalistic in the determination of the age of majority. 16 or 17 is the age of majority for many jurisdictions in most areas of serious decision-making. It seems a more appropriate age than 18 for majority to donate an organ. Certainly placing the age of majority at 21 is far too paternalistic.

Currently, as we have seen, some transplant legislation prevents organ donation by minors. This provides legal certainty but again it seems overly restrictive. It must be surely concluded that some minors will be legally competent to donate and such donors at least ought to be allowed to donate. To deny them this opportunity would be interfere with their self-determination too much. The Law Reform Commission of Canada in it's Report on the Procurement and Transfer of Human Tissues and Organs looked at the grounds for prohibiting all forms of donation by minors but each of these was countered in the paper, which concluded that,

> ...there are really no compelling arguments against allowing (competent) minors to donate even (paired) non-regenerable organs in certain circumstances.[650]

Competent minors should be allowed to donate the same range of organs as competent adults and to the same range of people. If there is to be any extra restriction on competent minor donation it should be limited to a requirement that it be not just the best option available but *significantly better* than the other options. In the case of organs at least, a court, or quasi-legal forum set up by under legislation, should scrutinise issues of minor competency and proposed donation by incompetent minors.[651]

---

[649]Indeed a negative correlation of -.433 (statistically significant at the 0.1% level) was established between the attitudes of professionals and the restrictiveness/ liberality of the legal framework for minor donation that they operated under.
[650]Working Paper 66, 1992.
[651]D.Price and A.Garwood-Gowers, Transplantation From Minors: Are Children Other People's Medicine, *Contemporary Issues in Law*, 1996, 1(1), 1-27 at 18.

A competent minor ought not to be subject to parental veto as regards the decision to donate. Of course, all other things being equal, professionals are likely to prefer to use adults as donors since they tend to be less vulnerable than competent minors. However, the independent procedure for testing competence should facilitate greater professional confidence in using competent minor donation in instances where it is clearly the optimum remedium.

Some commentators have concluded that minors should only be used as organ donors if they are competent[652] and, as we have seen, some jurisdictions have transplant legislation which takes this approach. This would not be my view although it has to be admitted that the use of incompetent minors as donors is fraught with difficulties. The clear danger is that sympathy towards the recipients plight will influence, and thus distort, decisions about whether donation is in a minor's best interests.

It can be particularly difficult to put aside recipient benefit as a factor *in its own right* where donation by the minor would offer much superior prospects (e.g. of graft survival) to the alternative courses of action. Fortunately, these superior prospects also make donation the most efficient method for a minor to protect any special interest (s)he has in the well-being of the prospective recipient. The ultimate expression of this is often donation to an identical twin.

Another difficult situation to put aside recipient benefit in its own right is where the consequences of the minor not donating are grave, such as even death if there is no dialysis and no likelihood of an alternative transplant. Here again, if the minor has a serious stake in the well-being of the prospective recipient donation will probably be in his/her best interests as the best way of protecting that stake.

As we have seen, one of the potential problems of using the best interests test to decide whether an incompetent minor should donate is that there is a possibility of using the minor without his/her agreement. Perhaps the only circumstances in which the incompetent minor should be used without his/her agreement is where the donation is a necessity, such as because it is the only feasible option for preserving the life or well-being of a prospective recipient who is a key component in the incompetent minor's

---

[652]For instance, D.Daube has suggested that a minor's consent would be a minimum (Transplantation: Acceptability of Procedures and the Required Legal Sanctions, in G.Wolstenholme and M.O'Connor (eds.), Ethics in Medical Progress, *Little Brown*, 1966, 188-201.

own well-being. This prospective recipient would most likely be a parent or sibling of the incompetent minor. However, it is conceivable that it could be someone else with whom (s)he has an especially important relationship.

Where necessity is not present the incompetent ought only to be used as a donor with his/her explicit agreement. The incompetent minors agreement ought to be based on some degree of meaningful understanding, i.e. it should be more than an assent. In practical terms very young minors are unlikely to be able to give such meaningful agreement since to do so requires hypothetical reasoning abilities, at least where it is an organ being donated. These abilities normally appear between the ages of 11-15.

Even tissue donations by an incompetent minor ought to normally be meaningfully agreed to by the incompetent[653] as well as being in his/her best interests. If tissue donations are not meaningfully agreed to they ought to be justified as a necessity for the donor, although the level of necessity might legitimately lessen in line with the degree to which removal of the tissue concerned is less harmful and jeopardising than removal of an organ.

Should legislation be explicit about when a donation could be in the incompetent minors best interests? The best approach would probably be not to prescribe factors that must be present but to provide guidance. The guidance could state that the prospective harm and jeopardy to the prospective incompetent donor must be low and exceeded by the prospective benefit to him/her, the donation must be by a substantial distance the best option for the recipient and the prospective incompetent donor must normally have some direct interest in the well-being of the prospective recipient. It will be surely rare that the use of an incompetent minor as a donor will come to be considered nowadays given that, even if there is no other suitable living donor, waiting for a cadaveric organ will often be a reasonable option.

Since family and medical professionals have a potential conflict in relation to whether an incompetent minor should donate, and because the issue is so important, it should be a court or an equivalently expert and independent quasi-legal forum that evaluates whether or not donation is in the incompetent's best interests and whether or not (s)he has meaningfully agreed to it. The involvement of a quasi-legal forum reduces the chances

---

[653]This was suggested as a rule of thumb for bone marrow donation in the Re Y commentary, *Med L Rev* 205-207 at 207.

of any pressure on the minor,[654] or indeed 'manufacturing' of assent or agreement, going unnoticed. In evaluating best interests and determining whether or not the incompetent has meaningfully agreed, the legal forum could have reference to expert psychological evidence and where appropriate use a social worker to interview a child.[655]

---

[654]Pressures can include family conflicts and feelings of guilt and / or fears of family disapproval that may lead to a minor agreeing to donate when they don't really want to. A minor may be unduly eager to donate out of a desire to appear mature. 6 out of 26 adolescent donors in the Minnesota study donated on this basis (see R.G.Simmons et al., Gift of Life, *Wiley and Sons*, 1977, 177). In some cultural sub groups (e.g. some Asian cultures) vulnerability to compulsive assent may arise through norms of family reciprocation applying to offspring.

[655]L.Delaney has suggested that a social worker could be used (Law and the Altruistic Child in Medicine in D.Lockton (ed), Children and the Law, *Cavendish*, 1993, 39 at 42).

6 Adult Incompetents

Introduction

Buck v Bell (1927) 274 US 200 stated that, '(i)t is better for all the world, if instead of waiting to execute degenerate offspring for crime, or to let them starve for their imbecility, society can prevent those who are manifestly unfit from continuing their kind.'[656] Involuntary sterilization of person's categorised as mentally retarded was an entirely legal feature of the medical programmes of several Western countries right up until a few decades ago. Eugenics as a whole, including racial eugenics practiced under the Nazi regime, has tainted medical history.[657]

These days, medical intervention on the incompetent adult must be in his/her best interests. However, obviously a concern when it comes to living organ donation, as with sterilisation, is that a decision to authorise intervention may be couched in terms of best interests of the incompetent but in fact be unconsciously based on social utility considerations. Judge Samuel Steinfield was doubtless concerned about this when giving his dissenting opinion in Strunk v Strunk 445 S.W. 2d 145 (Ky. 1969) that consent is the sole justification for organ donation,

> ...apparently because of my indelible recollection of a government which to the shame of its citizens embarked upon a programme of genocide and experimentation with human bodies I have been more troubled in reaching a decision in this case than in any other.[658]

Although living organ donation by the incompetent adult is extremely rare, it has been the subject of several interesting US cases and, given that it can benefit the incompetent, it is not surprisingly allowed to occur in many jurisdictions. Generally it will only be allowed under strict conditions of demonstrable benefit and limited detriment, often only with the agreement of a court of other independent body or authority, a parent/legal guardian

---

656(1927) 274 US 200 at 207.
657See R.Lifton, Nazi Doctors: Medical Killing and the Psychology of Genocide, *Basic Books*, 1986.
658445 S.W. 2d 145 (Ky. 1969) at 149.

and, in some cases, the incompetent him/herself. As in the case of minors, showing that the donation is necessary from the point of view of the prospective donor's best interest is often the most difficult task in that one needs to point to the likelihood of tangible psychological benefits from donating that are sufficient to outweigh the physiological harm and jeopardy that the removal of the material will cause.

It was seen in the discussion on minors that there were two categories of psychological factors that can favour donating. Firstly, psychological benefits, such as benefits in self-esteem, and, secondly, protection from psychological harm that could stem from not donating. As with the incompetent minor, it is unlikely that the intrinsic value of engaging in a helping act will be enough to justify the incompetent adult being subject to the harm and jeopardy of donating. It is likely that the incompetent adult will have to show a likelihood of more specific benefit, i.e. from the donation being much the best way of protecting a special vested interest (s)he has in the well-being of the prospective recipient. Again as with minor donation, there is the question of what to do if the prospective donor does not want to donate or cannot give any kind of meaningful agreement. Should donation be excluded under these conditions or allowed, for instance, if there is some special justification?

When is an Adult Competent?

While an adult starts with a presumption of competency to make all medical and other decisions[659] this presumption is rebutted for any given decision that the adult is shown to be incompetent to make due to mental illness or disability or to temporary factors such as shock, severe fatigue, pain or the drugs being used in his/her treatment. Whilst the Gillick test is used in relation to testing aged based competency, a variety of approaches have been used for determining non-age based competency.

In Re C[660] Thorpe J gave weight to the expert witness view of Dr Eastman that adult competency involved comprehending and retaining information, believing it and weighing it in balance to arrive at a choice.

---

[659]See for instance the law of Scotland on this matter discussed in D.M.Walker, Principles of Scottish Private Law, *Clarendon Press*, 1982 (3rd edn), Vol 1.
[660]*NLJ*, 1993, 143, 1642.

This approach fleshes out Bristow J's statement in Chatterton v Gerson [1981] 1 All ER 257 that in order to be able to give valid consent the patient must understand the nature of the procedure and its consequences in broad terms.[661] In Re F [1990] 2 AC 1 the test was ability to understand the nature or purpose of an operation or treatment.[662] This approach is usually referred to as the functional or cognitive approach. The Mental Health Act Code of Practice, applying to detained and informal patients, defines competency in a more detailed fashion as:

- an ability to understand what medical treatment is and that somebody has said that he needs it and why the treatment is being proposed;
- understand in broad terms the nature of the treatment;
- understand its principal benefits and risks;
- understand what will be the consequences of not receiving the proposed treatment; *and*
- possess the capacity to make a choice.

The Law Commission, in its Command Paper entitled *Mental Incapacity*, recommended that a person be defined as incompetent at the material time if (s)he is;

1) unable by reason of mental disability to make a decision on the matter in question, or
2) unable to communicate a decision on that matter because he or she is unconscious or for any other reason.[663]

with the requirement for understanding and retaining information being viewed as met where a person is, 'able to understand an explanation of that information in broad terms and simple language'.[664] Concerned that a person should not only be able to retain and understand information but utilise it in the decision-making process, the Commission recommended that,

> ...a person should be regarded as unable to make a decision by reason of mental disability if the disability is such that, at the time when the decision needs to be

---

[661][1981] 1 All ER 257 at 265 see also Re T (Adult: Refusal of Treatment) [1992] 4 All E.R. 649.

[662][1990] 2 AC 1 at 55 per Lord Brandon.

[663]Law Com No 231, *HMSO*, 1995, Draft Bill, clause 2(1)) at 37.

[664]Ibid at 39.

> made, he or she is unable to make a decision based on the information relevant to the decision, including information about the reasonably foreseeable consequences of deciding one way or another or failing to make the decision.[665]

Gunn states that it is,

> ...essential that a test for capacity sets a standard which allows as many people as possible to make their own treatment decisions.[666]

It seemed that the Commission had this type of view in mind when they took on board evidence that incompetency should not simply be deduced by the nature of the choice a person makes,

> ...a person should not be regarded as unable to make a decision by reason of mental disability *merely* because he or she make a decision which would not be made by a person of ordinary prudence.[667] (ital. added.)

It is well known that medical professionals tend to obtain consent in a perfunctory manner so will they pick up all the cases where an adult's competency is in doubt - particularly cases where there is no history of mental illness or disability? The answer must surely be that they will miss some. In this light it must be of prima facie concern that the EUROTOLD Transplant Centre Questionnaire found that only 31.4% of responding European centres with a LDT programme undertake a donor psychiatric/psychological evaluation (41% when weighted by catchment population). Of course, this concern may be mitigated by the fact that in some centres a less formal evaluative process may be in operation with the possibility of a psychiatric expert being brought in where the competency of the prospective donor is in doubt.

Jurisdictions Prohibiting Living Organ Donation by Adult Incompetents

Several jurisdictions have legislation which is framed in such a way that they might even result in *some competent persons* being unable to be organ

---

[665]Law Com No 231, *HMSO*, 1995, Draft Bill, clause 2(2)(b) at 39.
[666]Gunn, The Meaning of Capacity, *Med Law Review,* 1994 (Spring), 2, 8-29 at 8.
[667]Law Com No 231, *HMSO*, 1995, Draft Bill, clause 2(4), p39.

donors because of their 'mental state'. In France, a 1994 law prohibits donation by adults who are the subject of legal protection measures.[668] This is supplemented by a general requirement for consent which would indirectly restrict donation to persons with sufficient competence.[669] In Mexico there is prohibition on persons in a state of diminished awareness in *addition* to persons who are incompetent according to the 1976 Mental Health Act. Some laws *might* result in some competent persons not being allowed to be organ donors: Zimbabwe prohibits donation by persons mentally disordered or defective;[670] Sri Lanka,[671] Northern Territory,[672] Western Australia,[673] Tasmania[674] and Queensland[675] persons not of sound mind; *and* Paraguay persons with a disability prescribed by law.[676] These laws can be viewed as an unacceptable restriction on the autonomy of adults who may be de facto competent to donate even with their mental 'difficulty' or 'condition'. On the other hand one would want special protection of potentially vulnerable adults if they were to become organ donors.

Bolivia,[677] Cuba,[678] Cyprus,[679] Ecuador,[680] Panama,[681] Poland,[682] Romania,[683] Russian Federation,[684] Slovakia,[685] Spain,[686] Syrian Arab Republic,[687] Tunisia[688] and Turkey[689] specifically exclude use of adult

---

[668]Law No. 94-654 of 29 July 1994 at Article L.671-4.
[669]Article L. 665-11 ibid.
[670]Act No. 34 1976 at section 13(3).
[671]Act No. 48 of 1987 at section 7(2)(b)(ii).
[672]Law No. 121 of 1979 at section 8(1)(b).
[673]Act No. 116 of 1982 at section 8(1)(b).
[674]Act of 1985 at section 9(c)(ii).
[675]The Transplantation and Anatomy Act 1979-1984 at section 10(b).
[676]Law No. 836180 of 15 December 1980 at section 279.
[677]Section 4 of Regulations of 15 March 1982.
[678]Law No. 41 of 13 July 1983 at section 80.
[679]Section 7 of Law No. 97 of 1987.
[680]Law No. 64 of 26 May 1987 at section 1.
[681]Law No. 10 of 11 July 1983 at section 10(1).
[682]Law of October 26, 1995.
[683]1996 Law at Article 4(1).
[684]Law of 22 December 1992 at section 3.
[685]Section 46(1) of Law of 24 August 1994 - see *IDHL*, 1995, 46(2), 151-154.
[686]Law No. 30 of 27 October 1979 section 4(b).
[687]Law No. 31 of 23 August 1972 at section 2(3).
[688]Law No. 91-22 of 25 March 1991.

incompetents as donors. Some legislation arrives at the same result by requiring the donor to have proper judgement (e.g. Slovenia[690] and Algeria[691]), to be capable of giving consent[692] or simply to give consent.[693] Greece requires that the donor must not have been declared incompetent by a court or be in the care of a guardian appointed by a court.[694]

Under HOTA donor consent is one of the conditions ULTRA must be satisfied is met in order to authorise donation between persons classed as non-genetically related. It is also one of the conditions under Hong Kong law for authorisation of donation between genetic relatives or spouses of 3 or more years standing.[695] The Hong Kong approach isn't much of a restriction anyway because it is only ever likely that an incompetent adult would be requested to donate to a spouse or close relative and in such cases consent would be given on his/her behalf under the relevant principles of general law.

Jurisdictions Allowing Living Organ Donation by Incompetent Adults

Some jurisdictions allow organ donation by an incompetent adult albeit not as many as allow organ donation by minors. Where adult incompetents are allowed to donate there are typically requirements and restrictions on doing so, similar to those placed on incompetent minors.

Jurisdictions Requiring Court Involvement

In Portugal liver segment appears to be the only organ that an incompetent adult can donate. Regenerative materials as a whole can be donated but this is subject to court authorisation.[696]

Under general principles of English law, we have already seen in the last chapter that Mr Justice Connell in Re Y merely suggested court

---

[689]Law of 1979 at section 7.
[690]Article 10 of Law of 1996.
[691]Section 183 of law of 1985.
[692]Germany's Act of 5th Nov 1997 at section 8(1).
[693]E.g. Belgium, Denmark, Norway, Belarus Draft law, Lebanon, Venezuela, Peru, Vietnam, South Africa and South Australia.
[694]Law No. 1383 of 2 August 1983 at section 5(a).
[695]Hong Kong Ordinance No. 16 of 1995 at section 5(4).
[696]Law No. 12 of 22 April 1993 at section 6(3) and 8(5).

involvement was appropriate in adult incompetent bone marrow cases.[697] However, as argued in that chapter, donation of tissues such as bone marrow, whilst it should arguably involve court involvement, can be distinguished from donation of organs in that it involves less harm and jeopardy to the donor. An analogy was drawn in the last chapter between donation of an organ by an incompetent and compulsory sterilisation of the adult incompetent and we saw that in Re F (mental patient; sterilisation) [1990] 2 A.C. 1, Lord Bridge in the House of Lords[698] along with Lord Justice Neill[699] and Lord Donaldson MR[700] in the Court of Appeal, mentioned that an operation to allow inter vivos organ donation by an incompetent required similar safeguards to contraceptive sterilisation where the weight of legal authority suggests court involvement is mandatory.[701]

In its Command Paper, *Mental Incapacity*, The Law Commission can be applauded for recommending that both living organ and bone marrow donation by incompetent adults be treated as within a 'special category' of procedures under English law requiring the involvement of a court forum.[702] The Commission noted that this would involve amending existing regulations under HOTA which require donors not classed as genetically related to be competent.[703] It is possible to justify donation by an incompetent adult to a non-genetically related person under certain circumstances. For instance, an incompetent could have a special interest in protecting the well-being of a spouse, partner or even friend such that

---

[697][1996] Med L Rev 204-205 at 205.
[698]Re F [1990] 2 A.C. 1 at 52.
[699]Ibid at 33.
[700]Ibid at 19.
[701]Lords Brandon and Goff in Re F [1990] 2 AC 1 regarded court involvement as merely desirable. Lord Griffiths thought in should be mandatory and this was Lord Templeman's view in Re B (a minor) (wardship: sterilization) [1988] AC 199 and was subsequently the view of the majority in the Australian case of Department of Health v JWB & SMB (1992) 66 ALJR 360 (Aust High Ct). The net effect of a series of recent lower court decisions by Sir Stephen-Brown P (Re E (a minor) (medical treatment)[1991] 7 BMLR 117 (Fam Div) and F v F [1991] 7 BMLR 135 (Fam Div) and Re SG (a minor) (1991) 6 BMLR 95 (Fam Div)) appears to be that the court will only necessarily involve itself in matters which are non-therapeutic.
[702]Law Com No. 231 at p85.
[703]The Human Organ Transplants (Unrelated Persons) Regulations 1989 (SI 1989 No. 2480) - reg 3(2)(b).

donation to that person would under circumstances be warranted as the best means of protecting that interest.

In the US, whether or not court involvement is obligatory depends on which state one is in. Many cases have been brought in Massachusetts where court involvement is obligatory. In the state of Washington the state attorney can authorise organ donation by an adult incompetent.

Limits on What Can be Donated

Both the Council of Europe's Resolution (78)29 and Article 20(1) and 20(2) of its Convention on Human Rights and Biomedicine limit incompetent adults to donating regenerative material and subject this to strict conditions. We saw in the last chapter that if one interprets the term regenerable strictly it would allow donation of liver segment but the Council of Europe's Committee of Ministers to Member States in Recommendation No. R (97) 16 On Liver Transplantation From Living Related Donors states in its Appendix at point iv) that adults not having capacity to consent should not be used as liver segment donors. In jurisdictions discussed below the types of organ that can be donated are not specifically restricted on grounds of incompetence but donation has to be in the best interests of the incompetent, which makes it more difficult for more maleficent forms of organ removal to be justified.

The Need for Consents/Authorisations and Justifications

Under general principles of law donation must be consented to by the person legally entitled to act on the incompetent's behalf. Legislation in many jurisdictions leaves this as the sole consent required either by default or by re-affirmation (e.g. Hungary,[704] Colombia[705] and Malawi[706]). However, a few jurisdictions have used transplant legislation to impose additional consents, agreements and/or authorisations usually within an overall context of further confining when donation can occur.

Swedish law[707] requires that the incompetent is related to the potential recipient, that medically compatible biological material is not obtainable

---

[704]Law No. 18 of 4 Nov 1972 at section 13.
[705]Decree No. 1172 of 6 June 1989 at section 30.
[706]Anatomy Act No. 14 of 1990 at section 11(b).
[707]Law No. 831 of 8 June 1995 at section 8 (*IDHL*, 1996, 47(1), 28-30 at 29).

from an alternative person, that donation is not against the incompetent's wishes and has been consented to by the guardian or legal representative and authorised by the National Board of Health and Welfare under conditions of special justification and support of the physician empowered to decide on the removal. Swedish law may not be as stringent as it appears since it is difficult to imagine a donation by an adult incompetent being justified as in his/her best interest if it does not meet the above requirements. The Canadian Uniform Human Tissue Donation Act 1990 requires an independent assessment to be made where such donation by an incompetent adult is proposed. In Finland a psychiatrist gives an account of the mental condition of the donor and his suitability as a donor. It would appear that 'unsuitable' donors are excluded.[708] It is probably the case that there would need to be special justifications for a psychiatrist to view donation by an incompetent adult as suitable.

As with minors, an important issue is whether donation should occur without the incompetent's meaningful agreement. We have seen that the Council of Europe Resolution and Swedish transplant legislation go some way towards this approach by barring donation where the incompetent has objected. Colombian law seems to protect the incompetent from forced donation through providing that the intention of the donor overrides any contrary opinion of his relatives or any other person.[709] In the absence of legislation requiring it, the general law will not treat the incompetent's wishes as sacrosanct but they are taken into account in assessing the incompetent's best interests. This can include consideration of the views that the incompetent expressed previously.[710]

There have been some cases where the incompetent's objection to a medical treatment has been overridden. In Re W [1992] 3 W.L.R. 758 there were extremely strong grounds to respect the refusal of treatment of a mentally ill incompetent minor because she had also rejected treatment in an earlier phase in which she had been competent. However, the Court of Appeal took the approach that treatment should be forced upon her. One central factor in the decision was the view of the Court that she would be seriously jeopardised if not treated (she had a serious eating disorder). However, given the generally restrictive approach that Re W takes to self-

---

[708]Ordinance No. 724 of 23 August 1985 at section 2.

[709]Law No. 73 of 20 December 1988 at section 3.

[710]On the significance of the patient's previous known views see the US case of Re Conroy [1985] 486 A.2d 1209 which held that the significance of such views will vary according to their remoteness, consistency, thoughtfulness and specificity.

determination, it is clear that in establishing best interests an incompetent's objection to a form of treatment is likely to hold sway only in cases where the alternative to that treatment is considered almost as effective, or that the issue is of such a minor character that upholding the incompetent's view will do little jeopardy.

It seems that the English courts are likely to underestimate the value of respecting the autonomy of incompetent's in medical decision-making and the damage that can stem from forcing treatment upon them. However, the Law Commission took a more enlightened approach. It recommended that action contrary to an adult incompetent's objection should be limited to the 'taking of steps which are necessary to avert a substantial risk of serious harm to the (incompetent) person concerned'.[711] In LDT this would probably mean that an adult incompetent's objection to donating an organ would only be overridden if there was a significant risk of serious psychological harm to the incompetent from not donating. The justification for forced donation would have to be more than saying the incompetent will not accrue psychological benefit if (s)he misses the opportunity to help another. There must be some specific connection whereby the incompetent has a strong personal interest in the well-being of the prospective recipient and not donating must involve significant risk of serious damage to this interest - such as because the therapeutic alternative(s) were considerably inferior.

It has to be said that in LDT the judges are likely to be especially cautious about overriding the objection of an incompetent because it is not a procedure designed for the incompetent's benefit. To force donation involves concluding not only that the psychological value of donation outweighs the *combined* disadvantages of using force and the physical harm and risk of donating. There have been no cases where donation has been forced but it would be appropriate for legislation to clarify whether it can be and, if it can be, in what circumstances. There is always too much of a danger of objection not been taken seriously under general principles of law.

Another thing legislation should do is consider what should happen where an incompetent is so severely ill or disabled as to make his/her view meaningless. Here one would say it may be legitimate for donation to go ahead if it is in the incompetent's best interest but that a finding of best interests would have to rely primarily on the likelihood of donation

---

[711]Draft Bill clause 5, Law Comm No. 231 at 62.

avoiding psychological harm because it would be more speculative and unlikely that the incompetent could accrue actual psychological benefits (e.g. in self-esteem) from donating.

We have seen that under general principles of law consent on behalf of minors must be exercised in their best interests rather than in some other fashion such as substituted judgement. The substituted judgement doctrine has also been rejected in non-age related incompetency cases. Lord Goff took the view in Airedale NHS Trust v Bland [1993] 1 All ER 821 that substituted judgement forms no part of English law in relation to incompetent adults. However, this approach has been criticised and the weight of legal authority is against it.[712] The common sense view is that substituted judgement can be a factor within the overall determination of best interests.[713]

The best interests test has been specifically reaffirmed as applicable to deciding cases involving the prospective use of adult incompetents as living donors. In Re Y (Adult Incompetent: Legality of Non-Therapeutic Procedure) [1996] Med L Rev, 204-205 Mr Justice Connell in the High Court of Justice, Family Division used the best interests test in determining the legality of an adult incompetent donating bone marrow to her sister.[714] In the context of organ donation specifically the Kentucky Court of Appeals considered using substituted judgement in Strunk v Strunk 445 SW 2d 145 (Ky 1969)[715] but they did not base their decision on it according to Little v Little (Tex Civ 1979), 576 SW 2d 493,

> It is clear in transplant cases that courts, whether they use the term 'substituted judgement' or not, will consider the benefits to the donor as a basis for permitting an incompetent to donate an organ. Although in Strunk the

---

[712]The approach in Airedale is criticised by Kennedy and Grubb Medical Law, Text with Materials, *Butterworths,* 1994, 289. The authors doubt whether Lord Goff in Bland was sound in his reliance on Re F (mental patient: sterilisation)[1990] 2 AC 1 (HL) as authority for substituted judgment not applying in English law. Lord Mustill also criticised substituted judgment in Bland but his comments were more relevant to the specific case of a non-sentient patient.

[713]See for example Lord Donaldson MR in Re T (adult: refusal of treatment) [1992] 4 All ER 649 (CA).

[714]Page 204. The US bone marrow case of Curran v Bosze (1990) 566 N.E. 2d 1319 (Ill.Sup.Ct) was used as authority.

[715]The New York case of In The Matter of Willoughby, A Lunatic 11 Paige 257 (N.Y. 1844) provided authority that the substituted judgement doctrine applied in the US. For further discussion of the doctrine see Annot, 24 A.L.R. 3d 863 (1969).

> Kentucky Court discussed the substituted judgment doctrine in some detail, the conclusion of the majority there was based on the benefits that the incompetent donor would derive, rather than on the theory that the incompetent would have consented to the transplant if he were competent. We adopt this approach.[716]

What does best interests mean in the case of an adult incompetent? Lord Donaldson in the Court of Appeal in the sterilisation case of Re F [1990] 2 A.C. 1. suggested that doctors exercising a choice on behalf of a patient should apply the same principles as those which would be applied by a 'reasonable' adult considering his own medical treatment.[717] This does not tell us very much. When the case went to the House of Lords Lord Brandon took the view that a treatment would be in the patient's best interests where it was carried out to save his life or ensure improvement/prevent deterioration in his physical or mental health.[718]

Several academics have seized on this to argue that Re F was confining best interests to medical factors.[719] This would result in donation of tissues or organs by an incompetent adult being unlawful unless incidental to a medically necessary removal. This result is contradicted by the sanctioning of incompetent adult bone marrow donation in Re Y, and in any case the intrinsic nature of a best interests test must be not to confine itself but take into account everything in determining the best course of action for the incompetent. There would be some benefit in legislation stating what factors must be taken into account within the overall consideration of the best interests and here it is difficult to improve upon the Law Commission's recommendation that in deciding what is in a person's best interest regard should be had to:

1) the ascertainable past and present wishes and feelings of the person concerned, and the factors that person would consider if able to do so;
2) the need to permit and encourage the person to participate or to improve his or her ability to participate, as fully as possible in anything done for and any decision affecting him or her;

---

[716]Little 576 SW 2d at 498.
[717][1990] 2 A.C. 1, 18.
[718]Ibid at 55.
[719]A.Grubb and D.Pearl, Sterilisation - Courts and Doctors as Decision Makers, *CLJ, 1989,* 380, 382; D.Morgan, *J.S.W.L.*, 1990, 204, p206; Kennedy and Grubb, Medical Law: Text With Materials, *Butterworths,* 1994, 1087.

3) the views of other people whom it is appropriate and practicable to consult about the person's wishes and feelings and what would be in his or her best interests;
4) whether the purpose for which any action or decision is required can be as effectively achieved in a manner less restrictive of the person's freedom of action (Draft Bill, clause 3(2)).[720]

The main features of this approach are a notion of substituted judgment in point 1, an emphasis on the beneficial impact of maximising the incompetent's participation in decision-making in point 2, an emphasis on drawing widely on relevant sources of evidence in point 3 and, in point 4, an emphasis on taking the option least restrictive for the incompetent.

In terms of living organ donation the above principles might translate into taking the prospective donor's known views and wishes during any period where (s)he was competent into account, an emphasis on the incompetent's current views and wishes, drawing evidence from the incompetents family and other sources and, finally, using the least restrictive option might translate into not using the incompetent as a donor where there is an acceptable alternative. These are useful principles but living donation is rather an unusual situation and it might be best if legislation laid down specific guidelines or requirements in relation to establishing when donation can be in an adult incompetent's best interests. So far there have been several cases involving prospective donations by adult incompetents but these have not settled on any one set of rules or guidelines as to when donation is in the incompetent's best interests.

In English law Mr Justice Connell in Re Y states 3 obvious principles: that donation must benefit the adult incompetent to a degree outweighing detriment; benefit from the procedure to the prospective recipient is only relevant in so far as it serves the best interests of the incompetent; *and* benefit goes beyond the purely medical to include 'emotional, psychological and social benefit'.[721] In the case itself the benefit was contended to be derived from the fact that if the incompetent did not donate his sister would die, placing extra burden on her family and in particular her mother who was already ill and would have to face the death and look after the plaintiff's daughter. The relevance of this in terms of the incompetent was mainly that she was close to her family and would be

---

[720]Law Comm No 231 at 44-45.
[721]Re Y [1996] Med L Rev 204-207 at 205.

harmed by the fact that with the burden of a death they would cease or dramatically reduce visits to her (she was institutionalised). The harm done would outweigh the small disadvantages of bone marrow donation. Additionally, she would benefit from the donation through the gratitude of her family.[722]

The evidence of benefit in Re Y has rightly been described in the case commentary as 'not...particularly strong'.[723] Even if the evidence was strong enough to justify bone marrow donation it would not be strong enough to justify organ donation. Indeed Mr Justice Connell himself stated that Re Y should not be considered, 'a useful precedent in cases where the surgery involved is more intrusive'.[724] The most useful precedents are US adult incompetent organ donation cases.

The first such case was Strunk v Strunk 445 SW 2d 145 (Ky) 1969) where the Kentucky Court of Appeals held by a 4-3 decision, that it had the power to permit a kidney to be removed from a person deemed an incompetent ward of State upon the petition of his committee[725] for the purpose of being transplanted into his brother, who was 'dying' of a kidney disease, on the basis that the donation was in the incompetent's best interests. Some of the dissenting minority felt that evidence in the case was insufficient to 'conclusively demonstrate' a 'significant benefit' to the incompetent, but that if the evidence ever did rise to that 'pinnacle' the transplant should be allowed. The dissenters were also concerned by the testimony that a cadaver kidney could be used.

The majority in Strunk did not articulate the precise reasons why they allowed donation to go ahead. The Commonwealth of Kentucky Department of Health, acting as custodian for Jerry, the incompetent, felt that donation would be of psychological value for him[726] and this clearly influenced the Court, which could see that Jerry was close to the prospective recipient, his brother, who represented Jerry's main link outside of institutionalisation. The view was taken that the continued close relationship between Jerry and his brother was important to Jerry's

---

[722]Commentary note - ibid at 205-206.
[723]Ibid.
[724]Ibid.
[725]Which in this case was his mother.
[726]Transcript of the case entitled 'In the matter of Jerry Strunk, an incompetent,' Aug 19, 1969 at p113. The transcript is on file with Franklin County Court. See also Joe C Savage, *Kentucky Law Journal*, 1970, 58, 132.

rehabilitation and treatment.[727] Also, Jerry was the only viable living donor[728] and his donation was clinically a vastly superior option to an average cadaveric donation.[729] Clearly, donating was the best way for Jerry to protect a significant interest in the well-being of his brother but what the case illustrates is that it did not have to be the *only* way.

In In Re Richardson (La App 1973) 284 So 2d 185 the Louisiana Court of Appeal distinguished Strunk from the case before it which involved a 17 year old incompetent with a mental age of 3 or 4 whose parents were consenting to his being the donor to his sister:

> We find the facts in (Strunk), particularly the conclusion relative to the best interest of the incompetent, are not similar to the facts in the instant case and we also find that both the procedural and the substantive aspects of the majority opinion are not in accord with Louisiana law ...(which) is designed to protect and promote the ultimate best interest of a minor....since our law affords the unqualified protection against intrusion (sic) into a comparatively mere property right, it is inconceivable to us that it affords less protection to a minor's right to be free in his person from bodily intrusion to the extent of the loss of an organ unless such loss be in the best interest of the minor. Of course that statement and our conclusion are restricted to the facts of the present case.[730]

The main factual distinction between Richardson and Strunk was that in Richardson the prospective recipient was not such a key person in the life of the incompetent. Strunk is also distinguishable from Re Guardianship of Pescinski [1975], 67 Wis 2d 4, 226 NW 2d 180 where donation by a 37 year old incompetent to his brother was prevented simply because it was held the incompetent would derive no benefit from it,

> ...an incompetent particularly should have his own interests protected. Certainly no advantage should be taken of him. In the absence of real consent on his part, and in a situation where no benefit to him has been established, we fail to find any authority for the county court, or this court, to approve this operation.[731]

---

[727]Transcript Note 41, p13-14 ibid.

[728]Medical testimony stated that other relatives had been tested and none of them were well enough matched to be living donors (Transcript Ibid).

[729]90% chance of graft survival after 2 years due to 'top quality match' between the brothers as distinct to 40% with a cadaver.

[730]Richardson, 284 So 2d at 187.

[731]Pescinski, 67 Wis 2d at 8-9, 226 NW 2d at 182).

This decision simply reflected an 'exercise of judicial restraint under particular circumstances'.[732] However, with improvements in cadaveric donation it is probably true that there are less situations in which donation by the incompetent can be justified. On the conditions for donation to be in the incompetent's best interests, Richardson was fairly strict in stating that in addition to psychological benefit being shown, the procedure must be urgent, have no reasonable alternatives *and* have minimal contingencies.[733] However, subsequently in Little v Little 576 SW 2d at 499 donation by an incompetent was authorised without these conditions being met. In Little the contingencies of donation were minimal but authorisation occurred without the procedure being urgent and the court was satisfied by the incompetent's donation being the best option even though it wasn't the only reasonable option. Little placed importance on the consent of the incompetent's parents, a close relationship between donor and recipient and the involvement of the court.[734]

The conclusion we can derive is really that there are differing judicial interpretations of what justifies a donation as being in the best interests of the incompetent. The requirement in Richardson for the donation to be the only reasonable option seems too strict. What matters is that the incompetent has an important psychological stake in the well-being of the prospective recipient, and that donating is sufficiently better at protecting this interest than the other options to outweigh the level of harm and jeopardy it causes the incompetent.

Conclusion.

Many transplant laws have missed the opportunity to comprehensively address the issue of adult incompetent donation. Any opportunities to remedy this position should be taken since legislation would provide greater transparency and, potentially, greater certainty. What kind of stance should be taken?

Organ LDT is an invasive procedure, particularly for someone who doesn't fully understand it and is thus incapable of giving fully consensual

[732]Supreme Court of Wisconsin in In Re Guardianship of Eberhardy (1981) 102 Wis 2d 539 at 565.
[733]Gullotta J at 188.
[734]Ibid at 498-499.

agreement. However, it seems reasonable to allow donation by an adult incompetent under strictly defined conditions. The consent of someone empowered to act on behalf of the incompetent is an obvious one and ought to be supplemented by the scrutiny of a body independent of the family; perhaps the preferable approach being one that is also independent of the medical team and qualified to consider the difficult issues, e.g. a judicial or quasi-judicial body. This body could be the same as that used for minors and could also judge competency in adult in more marginal or uncertain cases referred on by practitioners.

Aside from these criteria, the incompetent's view should be considered wherever unless (s)he has insufficient capability to give a meaningful view. An objection should only be overridden where donation is a necessity to protect the incompetent from significant risk of serious psychological harm such as would arise if the incompetent had an important stake in the well-being of the prospective recipient and not donating would seriously undermine that well-being because there were no other reasonable options. If the incompetent wants to donate, the psychological stake in the well-being of the prospective recipient is still important but what matters is not that donation is the only reasonable option but that it is sufficiently better at protecting the stake than the other options to outweigh the level of harm and jeopardy it causes the incompetent. For an incompetent to be viewed as having an important stake in the well-being of the prospective recipient it should not be necessary to prove close genetic relationship nor should it be assumed that an important stake will simply follow from close genetic relationship. The key to finding an important stake is a close affinity between the two persons with the prospective recipient being a valuable part of the incompetent's life such that not only may there be special benefit to be derived from donating but the incompetent's psychological well-being is at least to some degree interwoven with the well-being of the prospective recipient.

A wider point that can be raised is about the way the views of the incompetent adult are elicited. In Strunk the emphasis was on psychiatric evaluation of the capabilities of Jerry, the incompetent, such as through I.Q. and other tests. The psychiatric testimony stated that Jerry understood that, 'the operation would hurt and that he might have to be in hospital for two weeks' and continued, 'I believe he does understand that the giving of a kidney is a helpful act because of his brother's ill health'.[735] Strunk was

[735] Pages 74-75 of the Transcript.

decided at a time when inquiries by some academics were suggesting that psychiatric testimony tended to be relied on too heavily in medical cases and was in any case often questionable.[736] Whilst evaluating capabilities is important, there is perhaps today a greater recognition that it is also important to facilitate the awareness and understanding of the incompetent so that (s)he can arrive at a more meaningful perspective. In chapter 3 we saw how Barnard had recommended a person-centred model of negotiation in communication between the patient and practitioner,

> ...patients possess a positive potential for growth and health...A major role of the physician is to assist the patient to reclaim or renew his or her own strengths and tendencies toward growth. In certain circumstances this may entail the application of technical modes of healing. In all cases, however, it will require the effort of helping the patient to clarify personal needs and goals, and to select, with the help of the physician, plans and actions consistent with and supportive of personal values.[737]

In modified form this type of approach would apply as much, if not more so, where the patient is incompetent. With an incompetent person this facilitative might best be played by a psychotherapist or psychological counsellor rather than a physician or psychiatrist. In this context it is interesting to note the success of person centred therapists in working with, 'unmotivated, deeply disturbed and often highly uncommunicative persons' such as schizophrenics,[738] and disturbed children.[739] Some transplant centres, such as Dublin, have a counsellor or psychotherapist available for all prospective donors and recipients.

---

[736]See e.g. T.S.Szasz, Law, Liberty and Psychiatry: An Inquiry Into The Social Uses of Mental Health Practices, *MacMillan,* 1963.

[737]The Personal Meaning of Illness in Client-Centred Dimensions of Medicine and Health Care, *Client-Centred Therapy*, J.Shlien (ed.), 337-351, 350-351.

[738]See, for instance, E.T.Gendlin, Client-Centred Developments in Psychotherapy With Schizophrenics, *Journal of Counselling Psychology,* 1962, 9, 205-211 and Sub-verbal Communication and Therapist Expressivity: Trends in Client-Centred Psychotherapy with Schizophrenics, *The Wisconsin Psychiatric Institute Bulletin,* 1961(1); C.R.Rogers, Some Learnings From a Study of Psychotherapy With Schizophrenics, *Pennsylvania Psychiatric Quarterly,* 1962, 3-15.

[739]V.Axline, Play Therapy, *Houghton Mifflin,* 1947.

7 Commerce and Compensation

Introduction

Within the context of modern reductionistic medicine, body materials have become an item of 'value' for medical research and treatment. The transfer of materials between persons or other legal bodies stems from this simple fact. Combined with this fact is the reality that people making transfers want to obtain some value out of doing so.

In some cases a person may simply hope to gain in a non-economic sense from donation such as from the experience of transferring something that may benefit medical research or a specific recipient of the body material. In some other cases a person may hope to gain economically from transfer. They may first of all wish to be paid for the time and effort they have put in, in relation to the body material concerned, whether this is in relation to donation, extraction, distribution or implantation. The donor may also want to receive money for what the material was worth to him/her. Finally, any or all the parties involved may wish to make additional money or what in capitalistic terms would be called profit.

Under free market conditions profit can be made wherever somebody is prepared to pay an amount over and above what might be described as the intrinsic or fair value of the material and labour. This is particularly likely to be the case where there is not enough material to meet the demand for it, i.e. a shortage. Indeed, where there is a shortage there will often be people who are prepared to ask for profit, or pay it, even if this is illegal.

Under conditions of shortage we have seen profiteering from various organs and other body materials occurring on a significant scale for decades. Key international bodies as The Council of Europe, The Transplantation Society, the World Health Assembly and WHO regard the commodification of most body materials as unacceptable.[740] Italy was the jurisdiction to first to regulate against it in 1969. Most of the jurisdictions

[740]For details see WHO, Legislative Responses to Organ Transplantation, *Martinus Nijhoff*, 1994, Appendix.

in Europe,[741] North America,[742] Central America,[743] South America[744] and Australia,[745] along with a few in Africa[746] and Asia,[747] have followed suit.

Prohibitions are often focused on 'trade,' 'commerce' or 'payment' but in isolation these terms are somewhat vague. One of the objectives of this chapter is to closely examine what kinds of financial exchange are prohibited and also what types of exchange, if any, it is ethically legitimate to prohibit. This is both a matter of the rights of those involved in providing materials and the rights of those wanting to utilise them.

Legal Regulation

Prohibitions on Payment

In most cases legislative prohibitions relating to payment are imposed on all the parties involved. However, in a few cases they appear only to affect the donor, such as Panama's law which states that the *donation* of organs should in principle involve no renumeration'[748] (ital. added) and Lebanon's law which states that, 'no form of compensation shall be provided in relation to the *donation* of tissues and organs'[749] (ital. added). Algeria's law only prohibits financial transactions in relation to removal and transplantation.[750] It does not specifically prohibit financial transactions in transfer but a court might hold these to be generally illegal on the basis of

[741]Including, Belarus (Draft Law), Belgium, Cyprus, Denmark, Finland, France, Germany, Hungary, Italy, Luxembourg, Poland, Romania, Russian Federation, Slovakia, Slovenia, Spain, Ticino (Swiss canton), The Netherlands, Turkey, Yugoslavia and the UK.

[742]Many states in the USA have adopted the prohibition on commercial dealings in organs within the National Organ Transplant Act 1984 at section 10. Some Canadian states have adopted prohibition from the Canadian model law.

[743]Including Costa Rica, Cuba, Guatemala, Honduras, Mexico and Panama.

[744]Including Argentina, Bolivia, Brazil, Chile, Colombia, Uruguay and Venezuela.

[745]Including Queensland, South Australia, Northern Territory, Capital Territory, New South Wales, Tasmania, Western Australia and Victoria.

[746]Including South Africa, Tunisia, Malawi, Syrian Arab Republic, Iraq, Kuwait and Lebanon.

[747]Including Hong Kong, India, Singapore and Sri Lanka.

[748]No. 10 of 11 July 1983 at section 4 prohibits remuneration for organs.

[749]Decree (No.109) of 16 September 1983 at section 4.

[750]Law No. 85-05 of 16 Feb 1985 at section 161.

being contrary to public policy.

One of the main issues that arises is what types of payment laws are aiming to prohibit. The Council of Europe's Resolution (78)29 prohibits parties from making profit in relation to organs and tissues.[751] Belgium's law also takes this approach.[752] Article 22 of the Council's Convention on Human Rights and Biomedicine is directed against commodification of body materials which is probably the same thing as profit. It states that 'the human body and its parts shall not, as such, give rise to financial gain'. Most transplant legislation takes a similar approach to this. For instance, Russian Federation law prohibits the buying and selling of organs;[753] Germany's law prohibits trade;[754] the law of Kuwait states that organs may not be sold or bought in any fashion nor any material benefit be obtained in relation to them;[755] the law of Honduras prohibits all payments in respect of human organs and tissues;[756] Sri Lanka's law states that no person can buy, sell or otherwise dispose of for valuable consideration any body or any tissue or part thereof;[757] Iraq's law prohibits sale or purchase of materials;[758] Costa Rican law prohibits 'any remuneration or compensation for organs and anatomical materials removed for therapeutic or research purposes'[759] along with the procuring of organs with a view to financial gain;[760] Brazil's law prohibits organs and other materials removed for transplantation, therapy or research from being the subject of commercial transactions;[761] Colombian law prohibits remuneration or compensation for those organs or anatomical parts which are intended to be transplanted;[762]

---

[751]Article 14.

[752]Law No.32 of 13 June 1986 at section 4(1).

[753]Law of 22 December 1992 at section 1.

[754]Act of 5th Nov 1997 at section 17. A Commission examines all LDTs and includes within it a person qualified to exercise judicial functions and a person experienced in psychological matters. Donation is not allowed if there are 'real, substantiated grounds' to suppose that the organ is the subject of trade (Section 8(4)3).

[755]Decree-Law No. 55 of 20 December 1987 at section 7.

[756]Section 5 of Decree No. 131 of 23 Nov 1982.

[757]Act No. 48 of 11 Dec 1987 at section 17.

[758]Resolution No. 766 of 9 June 1981 at section 3.

[759]Law No. 5560 of 20 August 1974 on Human Transplants section 13.

[760]Section 14 ibid.

[761]Constitution of Federative Republic 5 Oct 1988 section 199.

[762]Decree No. 1172 of 6 June 1989 at section 17.

Denmark's law makes it an offence to offer or receive payment or any other valuable consideration in respect of removal or transfer, or to knowingly collaborate in any such transaction;[763] Hungary's law states that donation of an organ may be made only in the absence of payment and no person may request or get any form of renumeration;[764] Poland has a similar provision[765] and Malawi's law prohibits supply for gain or profit for any purpose.[766]

Compensation for what the loss of the material is reasonably worth to the donor appears to be excluded in the above provisions. In principle, they would allow payments that didn't relate to the material itself, such as for the time and effort of the parties involved along with any legitimate expenses or financial losses (e.g. donor's loss of earnings). As far as those organising or carrying out the removal and transplantation are concerned such payment would be expected. However, under free economic conditions it would not necessarily be easy to discern whether payments to those involved in organising and carrying out the removal and transplantation were just for their time and effort or also included a profit element. In practice, transplantation is normally provided within the context of nationalised or private insurance and in this context there should be no money passed over from the recipient, i.e. it would be free at the point of delivery. The amount of money given to transplant centres, their staff and others involved in the process is open to view. Nonetheless, the WHO felt that it was still important to assert that payments should be in proportion with actual labour. Guiding Principle 8 states that it,

> ..should be prohibited for any person or facility involved in organ transplantation procedures to receive any payment that exceeds a justifiable fee for the services rendered.

Whilst those involved in organising and carrying out activities are never expected to give their time and effort on an unpaid basis, the earlier mentioned legislative provisions that appear to allow the donor to be paid for his/her labour should be read cautiously in the light of the fact that there is a widely held expectation that the donor will give up his or her time free of charge as a charitable act. This expectation was behind

[763]Law No. 402 of 13 June 1990 at section 20(3).
[764]Ordinance No.18 of 4 November 1972 at section 2.
[765]Articles 18 and 20 of Law of 26 October 1995.
[766]Law No.14 of 1990 at section 16.

the statement of The Council of The Transplantation Society, in its 1985 Guidelines, that the transplant team should establish the altruistic, non-profit, motivations of the donor and limit 'payment' to reimbursement of lost work earnings and expenses.[767] Similarly, WHO Guiding Principle 5 appears to limit the donor to obtain payment for reasonable expenses incurred in donation. Article 22 of the Convention on Human Rights and Bioethics is only specifically directed at requiring parties to prohibit financial gain from the body material itself. The Explanatory Report to the Convention implies that those undertaking technical acts relating to the material (i.e. removal, transplantation etc.) can be reasonably remunerated but those donating are prohibited from doing so and instead limited to receiving, where applicable, compensation for loss of income and expenses incurred. Some legislation is also unequivocal in preventing the donor from getting anything but compensation for expenses or lost income, for example, Spain's law.[768] Cuban law requires donation to be 'performed for humanitarian reasons' which would probably be interpreted as excluding the donor from being paid for labour.[769] The same issue arises in Turkish law, which goes on to state that donation must be consistent with humane aspirations[770] after stating that removal or purchase or sale of any organ or tissue for profit or any other kind of remuneration is prohibited.[771] Cypriot law is more unequivocal in that it states that,

> ...all donations or offers of biological materials for diagnostic, therapeutic or research purposes *must be gratuitous*; commercial agreements or transactions are prohibited[772] (ital. added).

So is Chile's law which states that the donor must actually testify that (s)he has received no benefit.[773] Greece's law prohibits all financial exchanges between all of the parties involved[774] which would appear to even prohibit those involved in organising and carrying out activities from being paid, but presumably they wouldn't need paying for these activities specifically

[767]See *Lancet*, 1985, 2, 715-6.
[768]Crown Decree No. 426 of 22 February 1980 at section 5.
[769]Law No. 41 of 13 July 1983 and Decree No. 139 of 4 February 1988.
[770]Law No. 2238 of 29 May 1979 at section 7(e).
[771]Ibid section 3.
[772]Section 4 of Law No. 97 of 1987.
[773]Section 3(f) of Regulations issued on 3 June 1983.
[774]Law No. 1383 of 2 Aug 1983 at section 2.

because they would be getting an overall salary for their medical and/or administration work from the Greek state.

Another point that is worthy of specific note is the recipient's position in relation to obtaining organs. Obviously recipients are generally covered by prohibitions on payment, i.e. in most cases they cannot purchase an organ. WHO Guiding Principle 9 goes a little further than this by also recommending that they should not be allowed to influence distribution in any fashion by money,

> In the light of the principles of distributive justice and equity, donated organs should be made available to patients on the basis of medical need and not on the basis on financial or other considerations.

This approach would lead to slipping some cash to someone to get a little higher on a transplant list being prohibited. It would also, in effect, mean that transplantation services as a whole would have to be free at the point of delivery. If access isn't free at the point of delivery some people would get less access or no access because they wouldn't have the money to pay for transplantation services. This has historically occurred on some occasions in the US. For example, Dworkin reports that as recently as 1993 over 50 artificial body parts were distributed this way in the US as well as a number of natural bodily substances.[775]

Some countries have specifically provided for access free at the point of delivery to the recipient (e.g. Spanish law) and in general the principle that people should be able to access healthcare as a whole irrespective of wealth has been gaining increasing standing internationally. For example, Article 3 of the Council of Europe's Convention on Human Rights and Biomedicine provides that parties to it to take appropriate measures, taking into account health needs and available resources, to ensure equitable access to health care of appropriate quality, with the Convention's explanatory report stating that equitable, whilst not being synonymous with equality, implies being able to obtain a satisfactory standard of care. In some countries most core health services are provided free after being paid for out of taxpayers' money. Countries like the US have a nationalised provision (Medicare in the US) as a back-up for those who do not have the means of paying or insurance to cover payment. However, some countries leave people entirely to make their own arrangements through insurance,

---

[775]Gerald Dworkin, Markets and Morals: The Case for Organ Sales, *Mt Sin J Med*, 1993, 60(1), 66-69 at 67.

paying as and when they need services or going without.

We can surmise that in the absence of legislation prohibiting certain forms of payment, profit making would at least generally be prohibited under general principles of law on grounds of public policy. Whether or not legislative prohibition exists we can surmise from the anti-commerce attitude of The Transplantation Society and widespread condemnation of trade that practitioners involved in the commercial exchange of organs would be subject to disciplinary action by the relevant medical authority for being involved in payments that the authority has laid out as, or would define as, ethically unacceptable. A good example of a framework for professionals is the General Medical Council's 'Guidance for Doctors on Transplantation of Organs from Live Donors' which advises practitioners what they must do in the light of restrictions on payment and related activities laid out under HOTA. The Council makes the basic statement of principle that it,

> ...regards it as unethical and improper for a doctor to take part in any way in the trading of organs or the transplantation of organs obtained from donors whose consent has been given as a result of any form of undue influence. A doctor who behaves in this way is liable to disciplinary proceedings by the Council.[776]

The Council's guidance was based on their belief that:

> (i) human organs should not be the subject of commercial transactions: any donation of organs must be made altruistically, as a gift; *and*
> (ii) where human organs are bought or sold, transplantation will be governed by money rather than by the medical interests of the donors and recipients, with the vulnerable and the poor inevitably exposed to exploitation.[777]

The duties placed on doctors include:

- satisfying themselves that the donation has occurred without financial or other material benefit or undue influence of any kind (point 7).
- In no circumstances may doctors participate in or encourage in any way the trade in human organs from live donors. They must not advertise for donors nor make financial or medical arrangements for people who wish to sell or buy organs (point 6).

---

[776] *General Medical Council Supplement News Review,* December 1992 point 2.
[777] Point 3 ibid.

- A doctor independent of the transplantation team must assess the motivation of the donor (point 7).
- Each member of the team must retain and exercise individual ethical responsibility towards the patient (point 8).

Prohibition on Activities Ancillary or Preparational to Certain Forms of Payment

In some legislation prohibitions are focused not just on preventing certain forms of payment but on preventing activities ancillary or preparational to these payments. Several jurisdictions (including many Australian states,[778] France,[779] Hong Kong,[780] India,[781] Poland,[782] Romania,[783] Russian Federation,[784] Turkey[785] and the UK[786]) explicitly prohibit the solicitation of business for organs, such as via commercial advertisement intended to promote donation of elements and products of the human body for the benefit of a specific person, establishment or agency. Section 1 of HOTA, detailed in Figure 4 on the next page, classically exemplifies this type of restriction. It prohibits supply, offering to supply, soliciting supply, negotiating/initiating of arrangement for payment/supply/offer of supply and prohibition on various aspects of advertising with a commercial purpose and managing/controlling a body of persons (e.g. a company) involved in such activities. An interesting feature is that the prohibitions on such activities in Great Britain apply even if it is intended that the organs will be transplanted elsewhere. In other words this is designed to discourage such things as newspaper adverts telling people they can get an organ at a price in, say, a South American or Asian country.

[778]See e.g. Western Australia Act No. 116 of 1982 at section 30; Northern Territory Act No.121 of 1979 at section 24(1) unless authorised by the minister of health (section 24(3)); Capital Territory Ordinance No.44 of 1978 part VII; and New South Wales Act No.164 of 1983 part VI.
[779]Article 665-12 of Law No. 94-654 of 29 July 1994.
[780]Ordinance No. 16 of 1995 at section 2 (*IDHL*, 1995, 46(3), 325-327 at 325.
[781]Act No. 42 of 1994 at section 2k (*IDHL*, 1995, 46(1), 34-38).
[782]Article 20 of Law of 26 October 1995.
[783]Law of 1996 at Article 4(2).
[784]Law of 22 December 1992 of the Russian Federation at section 1. See also section 4 of Belarus Draft Law of 1995.
[785]Law No. 2238 of 1979 at sections 3 and 4 respectively.
[786]Section 1 of HOTA 1989.

Figure 4: Section 1 of HOTA 1989

Section 1(1) states that 'A Person is guilty of an offence if in Great Britain he-

(a) makes or receives any payment for the supply of, or for the offer to supply, an organ which has been or is intended to be removed from a dead or living person and is intended to be transplanted into another person whether in Great Britain or elsewhere;

(b) seeks to find a person willing to supply for payment such an organ as is mentioned in paragraph (a) above or offers to supply such an organ for payment;

(c) initiates or negotiates any arrangement involving the making of any payment for the supply of, or for an offer to supply, such an organ; or

(d) takes part in the management or control of a body of persons corporate or unincorporate whose activities consist of or include the initiation or negotiation of such arrangements'.

(2) without prejudice to paragraph (b) of subsection (1) above, a person is guilty of an offence if he causes to be published or distributed, or knowingly publishes or distributes, in Great Britain an advertisement-

(a) inviting persons to supply for payment any such organs as are mentioned in paragraph (a) of that subsection or offering to supply any such organs for payment; or

(b) indicating that the advertiser is willing to initiate or negotiate any such arrangement as is mentioned in paragraph (c) of that subsection.

(3) In this section 'payment' means payment in money or money's worth but does not include any payment for defraying or reimbursing:

(a) the cost of removing, transporting or preserving the organ to be supplied; or

(b) any expenses or loss of earnings incurred by a person so far as reasonably and directly attributable to his supplying an organ from his body.

(4) In this section 'advertisement' includes any form of advertising whether to the public generally, to any section of the public or individually to selected persons.

(5) A person guilty of an offence under subsection (1) above is liable on summary conviction to imprisonment for a term not exceeding three months or a fine not exceeding level 5 on the standard scale or both; and a person guilty of an offence under subsection (2) above is liable on summary conviction to a fine not exceeding level 5 on that scale.

Hong Kong has a similar multi-faceted prohibition to section 1 of HOTA. It prohibits buying, selling, negotiating, managing and advertising organs on a commercial basis.[787]

---

[787]Ordinance No. 16 of 1995 at section 2 (*IDHL*, 1995, 46(3), 325-327 at 325).

A few legislative provisions restrict the influx or outflow of organs partly as a function of controlling trade. For example, South Africa restricts import[788] and Malawi prohibits the unauthorised export of organs.[789]

Regulation in Respect of Relationships Between Donors and Recipients

Certain jurisdictions only allow a person to donate to someone if they have a certain type of relationship with them. We saw in chapters 5 and 6 that there were specific restrictions in some jurisdictions on who a minor and adult incompetent could donate to. We also saw in chapter 4 that there were some laws which even restrict who competent adults can donate to. For example, several jurisdictions, including India,[790] the UK and Hong Kong[791] prohibit organ donation to strangers. One of the reasons why some jurisdictions prevent a person from donating to a stranger is that they might be doing so involuntarily but it is also designed to prevent economically motivated donations which are more likely between people who do not know each other.

Some jurisdictions prohibit donation to additional classes of person. For example, in Portugal[792] organ donation to anyone outside a relative of third degree is prohibited and in France[793] organ donation to anyone outside the nuclear family unit is prohibited. These prohibitions are not warranted out of concern for voluntariness and it is doubtful that they are necessary to protect against economically motivated donation. A better approach is perhaps the one taken in India,[794] UK and Hong Kong[795] which supplement the exclusion of organ donation to strangers with the requirement that organ donations not on behalf of close genetic relatives (and spouses of 3 or more years standing in the case of Hong Kong[796]) must be specially authorised by a quasi-legal Authority which, amongst other things, tests for commercial motivation with the goal of screening out

---

[788]Section 28 of the Human Tissue Act No. 65 of 1983.
[789]Law No.14 of 1990 at section 20.
[790]Section 8 of Act No. 42 of 1994, *IDHL*, 1995, 46(1), 36.
[791]Ordinance No. 16 of 1995, *IDHL*, 1995, 46(3), 326.
[792]Law No. 12 of 22 April 1991 at section 6(2).
[793]Law No. 94-654 of 29 July 1994, Article 671-3.
[794]Section 8 of Act No. 42 of 1994, *IDHL*, 1995, 46(1), 36.
[795]Ordinance No. 16 of 1995, *IDHL*, 1995, 46(3), 326.
[796]Ibid at section 5(1).

donors who have an economic motivation. In the UK, for example, section 2(3) of HOTA states that the Authority (i.e. ULTRA) must, amongst other things, be satisfied that no payment has been made in contravention of section 1 of the Act to grant authority for non-genetically related donation.[797] Continuing this theme, regulation 3(2)c of The Human Organ Transplants (Unrelated Persons) Regulations 1989 requires ULTRA to be satisfied that the donor's consent was not caused by an offer of an inducement.[798] This type of scrutiny will help to sift out donations where people are trying to conceal an economically motivated intent behind a 'manufactured' emotional or legal relationship. The development of the HOTA 1989 took place within the context of The Presidents of The International Transplantation Society and British Transplantation Society alleging in 1985 that,

> British surgeons are transplanting kidneys into Indian and Pakistani patients who have paid living donors to give up a kidney.[799]

and later reports of Turkish peasants being flown in to London and paid to be kidney donors.[800] During the passing of HOTA these events formed a background for the then Under Secretary for Health stating that Parliament could not,

> ...rule out the possibility of non-genetic relationships being formed solely for the purpose of the operation or of pressure - economic or otherwise - being brought to bear upon a donor to submit to a transplant operation.[801]

---

[797]This requirement is repeated in regulation 3(1)a of The Human Organ Transplants (Unrelated Persons) Regulations 1989.

[798]Regulation 3(1)c limits the scope of 3(2)c to those cases in which the organ is *not* being removed primarily for medical treatment of that donor. This would mean regulation 3(2)c would not apply to what are called domino transplants, i.e. where donations are incidental to a therapeutic removal.

[799]The Times (London), May 13, 1985 at 32 column 1.

[800]Transplanting Organs from Living Donors: An International Regime or More Free Enterprise, *Finnish Yearbook of International Law*, 1990. In one case, at the exclusive private London hospital Wellington Humana, two Turkish people had been paid £2,000 each to donate their kidneys. Dr Raymond Crockett was struck off by the General Medical Council for his involvement in this affair (*The Independent* (London), Jan 18, 1989, p2 columns 1-3).

[801]The then Parliamentary Under Secretary of State For Health in the House of Commons (HC Deb, 6 July 1989).

Philosophically speaking it is doubtful that someone can be economically pressured into donating. Offering a person money to do something does not put pressure on them to do it. If they feel pressure by being offered money it is their own desire for the money that is pressuring them not the money itself or the person offering it. Nonetheless, it is true that non-genetic relationships can be 'manufactured' for the purpose of donation and that the prospective donor in this position may on some occasions have been pressurised and/or manipulated into 'agreeing' to donate either by medical personnel or intermediaries who stand to make money out of the donation.

Kishore takes the unusual position that there should be no restrictions or at least exclusions in relation to consanguineous proximities between donor and recipient. Part of his reasoning is that,

> Families are not unconnected or antagonistic fragments of society. After thousands of years of continuous efforts the individuals on this search have attained a state of organic and functional integration. Atomisation of society on the basis of consanguineous proximities is a reversal of this holistic trend.[802]

Kishore's point is to some degree valid and indeed most countries do allow certain body material to be even donated to a stranger. However, most often this is material which by its nature can be donated anonymously into a pool, such as semen, bone marrow and blood. Because it is donated into a pool there is no communication between the donor of the material and its recipient(s) and this limits the possibilities for economic exchange.

Organs cannot be donated in a pool system and in addition there is the fact that strangers are very much more likely to want to do such a serious thing as donate an organ for economic reasons than for non-economic ones. Denying strangers the opportunity to donate an organ is thus a pragmatic and balanced action if one wants to avoid economically motivated donation. At the same time allowing distant relatives and emotionally related persons to donate, subject to scrutiny, is ethically reasonable and practically necessary, particularly in the context of organ shortages. Hence, for example, ULTRA allowed a prospective lung LDT recipient to receive a lung lobe from a friend in 1996 when only one of the two needed for the LDT to be conducted was available within the family.

---

[802]Organ Donation: Consanguinity Vs Universality - An Analysis of Indian Law, *Trans Proc*, Dec 1996.

Donor Compensation for Losses

Aside from the question of economic value for his activities the donor will be faced with the need to be defrayed or reimbursed for financial expenses and losses reasonably associated with the fact of having donated and compensated for physical harms. The anti-trade stance of international bodies and transplant legislation does not come into conflict with such defrayment or reimbursement. Jurisdictions like Hong Kong,[803] India,[804] Luxembourg,[805] The Netherlands,[806] Ticino (a Swiss Canton),[807] Tunisia[808] UK,[809] USA[810] and many Australian state laws[811] simply point out that this compensation or reimbursement is acceptable. However, some international bodies have suggested that the donor should be able to get such defrayment or reimbursement as a matter of right. On this point, the Council of Europe in Resolution (78)29 states that,

> ...loss of earnings and any expenses caused by the removal or preceding examination may be refunded. The donor, or potential donor, must be compensated independently of any medical responsibility, for any damage sustained as a result of a removal procedure or preceding examination, under a social security or other insurance scheme.[812]

---

[803]Ordinance No. 16 of 1995 at section 2 (*IDHL*, 1995, 46(3) at 325).
[804]Act No. 42 of 1994 at section 2 *(IDHL*, 1995, 46(1), 34-38 at 34).
[805]Law of 25 November 1982 at section 16 allowing for reimbursement of loss of revenue and other expenses that may be occasioned by organ removals.
[806]Law of 24 May 1996 - section 7 states that the donor may be compensated for the expenses referred to in section 2 which are compensation for expenses including lost earnings deriving directly from the removal of the organ.
[807]Law of 18 April 1989 at section 15.
[808]Law No. 91-22 of 25 March 1991.
[809]Section 1(3) b of HOTA allows reimbursement or defrayal of, 'any expenses or loss of earnings incurred by a person so far as is reasonably and directly attributable to his supplying an organ from his body'.
[810]Section 10 of The National Organ Transplants Act explicitly allows the donor's expenses to be paid. This approach has been legislatively adopted in many states.
[811]Northern Territory Act No. 121 of 1979 at section 24(5), South Australia The Transplantation and Anatomy Act 1983 section 35(4), Tasmania The Human Tissue Act 1985 at section 27(3) and Western Australia Act No. 116 of 1982 at section 29(3).
[812]Article 9.

Most jurisdictions will provide the donor, and often also the recipient, with free medical care in relation to the transplantation. Some are also explicit about compensating the donor for physical harms that were not the inevitable result of the removal itself. In Slovenia[813] and the Belarus draft law[814] this is done by indemnity according to the rules of invalids insurance. In Slovakia law requires health establishments engaging in organ removal to take out a special insurance policy against liability for damages that may be caused to a living donor during organ removal.[815] Portugal's law similarly requires insurance to be taken out by transplant centres[816] with the donor being compensated for any injury suffered except those that are a direct cause of the intervention itself.[817] These provisions may be an improvement on legal recourse under general principles of law in that the donor would appear to be able to get compensation without proof of negligence - certainly Portugal's law even makes it explicit that no proof of negligence is required.[818]

What none of the transplant laws do is compensate the donor for the inevitable physical consequences of the removal, such as pain and suffering and scarring of the wound site. In addition, there are only a handful who provide for the donor to be defrayed or reimbursed for direct financial expenses and losses. These include: French law, under which arrangements are made to reimburse living donors of their necessary costs;[819] Belgium's law, where provision is made for 'the costs and loss of income directly resulting from the provision of an organ';[820] Spanish law, where provision is similarly made for 'coverage of any costs incurred as a result of the donation and operation';[821] *and* Panama's law, which pays various expenses of the donor and 'loss of earnings during his absence from work by reason of examinations and other necessary procedures'.[822]

---

[813]Law of 1996 at Article 4.

[814]Article 11 of draft law of 1995 (copy held at EUROTOLD).

[815]Law of 24 August 1994 at section 46(3). *IDHL*, 1995, 46(2), 151-157 at 155.

[816]Section 9(2) ibid.

[817]Section 5(2) ibid.

[818]Section 9(1) ibid states that donor will be compensated irrespective of misconduct.

[819]Article 665-13 of Law No. 94-654 of 29 July 1994 (*IDHL*, 1994, 45(4), 473-482 at 474).

[820]Law No. 32 of 13 June 1986 at section 4(2).

[821]Crown Decree No. 426 of 22 February 1980 at section 5.

[822]Law No. 10 of 11 July 1983 at section 4.

These provisions would clearly provide for expenses like costs of home help/childcare, travel and subsistence where reasonably associated with donation, as well as lost earnings. An example of a provision providing only the latter is Finnish law which simply gives the donor a right to a daily allowance where (s)he has to take a day or more off work.[823]

A few governments make special non-legislative arrangements for donor expenses and lost earnings to be paid for[824] but in general the absence of legislative provision in this area can cause problems. Whilst hospitals can voluntarily offer the donor compensation it is unlikely that many of them are doing so as a matter of course. EUROTOLD's Transplant Centre Questionnaire found that only 42.86% of responding European transplant centres with an LDT programme actually discussed the financial implications of donation with the donor and only 35.29% made financial help available - presumably some of these doing so under legislation but in any case the significant fact is that it appears that the majority of donors are left to find their own methods of compensation for financial and physical loss. The main issue for many donors in this position will be to get compensation for time off work if they are employees. This compensation will be in the context of sick pay/benefit provision that employers are required to give by legislation or under their own sick pay/benefit scheme. I have examined global sick pay provisions in the context of the living donor in detail elsewhere[825] but the main issues are important enough to be briefly outlined here.

Like any employee, the donor will have to meet the qualifying conditions applying to the sick pay/benefit scheme (s)he is working under in order to obtain benefit. A typical condition is that the employee must not be culpable for his/her illness. The donor may run into the problem that his/her sickness was brought on by the choice to donate. However, the law is likely to treat the donor sympathetically because (s)he has acted in a

---

[823]Law No. 780 of 25 August 1994 at section 11 (*IDHL*, 1995, 46(1), 33). The daily allowance is in accordance with the provisions of Health Insurance Law (364/63).

[824]In the UK there is Circular No. 308 of 7 September 1989, 'On the Arrangements for The Payment of Costs and Reimbursement of Expenses Incurred by the Removal from Living Donors of Human Organs or Bone Marrow Intended for Transplantation.'

[825]Austen Garwood-Gowers, An Investigation into the Ethical and Legal Issues in Living Donor Organ Transplantation, *De Montfort University*, December 1997, 252-257.

reasonable manner by choosing to donate and is not culpable in this sense. Occasionally a condition is that a person has to reach a certain status before being able to claim. For example, being employed for a certain period, finishing a trial period or being temporary. However, more often one's status in these terms does not affect the ability to get provision but limits the amount of support given. Another factor is that sick pay/benefit is rarely 100% of the employee's normal wage - more typically it is 75-90% of this wage. In many cases it may also only start on the second day off work or after a number of days off. It will also end after a certain period. Elsewhere I have noted that many schemes operate long enough to cover the whole time off that most donors will need. However, there are a small minority of donors who will require a longer time off than even the more generous schemes provide for and a larger minority who will be in this position with the less generous schemes.

In all it can be concluded that most donors in most jurisdictions will be able to get defrayment or reimbursement for most of their losses and expenses. However, when defrayment or reimbursement is not provided as a matter of right there is no guarantee that donors will be made aware of what they can get and no guarantee that they will not suffer significant loss even if they are made aware. These factors will result in a significant minority of donors suffering financial hardship through donating. In EUROTOLD's donor-recipient interview/questionnaires a quarter of donors (19 out of 76) reported moderate to severe financial consequences of donation. In 2 cases the recipient was left to help out the donor with expenses, which in one case was reported to have contributed greatly to stress within the family. 17.7% of the 474 Norwegian donors questioned in Westlie et al.'s study said they had personal expenses associated with donation; many met these with insurance but a significant minority lost vacation time or had to draw on their own or family financial support (23.6%), a few having to be helped out by the recipient. 16.2% of donors replied 'yes' or 'to a certain extent' when asked if the donation caused financial hardship. 3.2% said that donation had influenced their personal income/career although it was not specified as to whether or not this influence was a negative or constructive one.[826]

A final issue is the effect donation may have on employment security and the ability to obtain life and, where applicable, health insurance. Fortunately, in terms of job security donors are rarely at risk of dismissal

[826]Quality of Life in Norwegian Kidney Donors, *Neph Dial Trans*, 8, 1146-1150.

for donating, employment regulations will tend to protect them though legal protection is often weaker in cases where workers are only recently employed, temporary or on trial. EUROTOLD's donor-recipient questionnaires found that donation had little impact on employment status, and only occasional adverse impact on work performance and income. In terms of life insurance 6.4% of the Norwegian donors surveyed by Westlie et al. who had tried to obtain life insurance had difficulties doing so.[827] Problems with life and health insurance can be avoided by taking the US approach of agreeing insurance for donors on a national level with insurance companies.

Ethical Issues

If a jurisdiction undertakes activities relating to removal, transfer and use of body materials without a framework of regulation or without regulation being properly enforced the outcome is normally very bad practice. There are probably 100,000 or more removals and transplantations of body material in this context each year and many of them are done in a context where the well-being of donors and recipients is placed beneath the desire to make money.

In terms of recipients, G.M.Abouna studied 110 people from Kuwait who had bought kidneys and their transplantation in countries without a properly enforced framework of regulation, such as India and the Philippines. He observed 59 of them at the Kuwait Transplant Centre. 6 were known to have died shortly after the operation, 13 to have lost grafts through complications, 14 others to have had serious surgical complications and almost all the remaining patients had come with acute rejection, sepsis or other medical problems. Some had communicable diseases including incidences of AIDS.[828] K.V.Johnny studied 53 other Kuwaiti patients who had mainly gone to India between 1985-1990 to buy a kidney and its transplantation. 4 patients had lost their grafts, 3 had died from reasons relating to their transplant and a shocking further 6 had hepatitis B and 7 tuberculosis.[829] Al Khader reported results of 20 people

---

[827]Ibid.

[828]Commercialization in Human Organs: A Middle Eastern Perspective, *Trans Proc,* 1990, 22(3), 918-921.

[829]Values Gained and Values Lost in Live Unrelated Renal Transplantation, *Trans Proc*, 1990, 22(3) (June), 915-917.

returning to Saudi Arabia after buying a kidney and its transplantation in Bombay where donors were also paid. 95% of the returnees required admission to hospital in Saudi Arabia to treat rejections and infections or to adjust immunosuppression. A total of 25% had significant renal artery sterosis and fully 40% lost their grafts. One patient acquired Malaria.[830] Similar results come from patients transplanted in Bombay who came from Oman and Dubai. In the survey period of September 1984-December 1986 9 out of 36 patients from Oman died, 6 of these within the first 100 days and the other 3 within a year. At least 2 more had lost grafts and were back on dialysis in Oman. Of 27 patients from Dubai 6 died within 3 months and 4 others had rejections and were back on dialysis within this period.[831] Dr B.N.Colabawalla's view on the position of receiving a kidney from a paid donor in India is that it is full of potential hazards,

> ...most of such donors come from a strata of society where their health and nutrition are already compromised due to economic stringency. Many of these donors may not have been adequately investigated for transmissible diseases and hence pose a danger to the recipient. In this context it is worth noting that of late some reports have documented the occurrence of AIDS in recipients who have received kidneys from this category of donor.

He also suggests that there can be serious problems from the donor's perspective - many of the Indian donors having difficulties in reaching an informed understanding of what was involved.[832] This was partly because of low levels of social and literacy skills. However, clearly if someone is low on such skills it can be easier to manipulate them. There are many situations where the basic ethical principle of beneficence is missing in the sense that the material being donated does more harm to the donor than it could give benefit to the recipient; activities like living donation and donation of cornea fall into this category and only take place because there are medical professionals and others who are prepared to exploit the financial desperation of the donor or manipulate/force him or her.

Studies such as Abouna's have confirmed the common sense likelihood that without properly enforced regulation people are significantly at risk of

[830]Al Khader et al., XI Int.Cong.Trans.Soc.Helsinki, Aug 1986, Abstract No.S11.4.
[831]P.J.Morris, Kidney Transplantation, 1988, 3rd edition, p72.
[832]B.N.Colabawalla, Commerce and trade in Human Organs. Presented at the 2nd International Conference on Organ Transplantation, Kuwait, 1990 (Copy at WHO).

being coerced into donating.[833] News reports of such coercion are numerous and they often involve organised criminal gangs or Mafia taking organs from people going about their regular business or going to hospital for a routine operation.[834] Evidence also exists of the practices of buying and selling of children (especially orphans) so that they can be cut up (dead or alive) for their organs.[835] There are also rumours of psychiatric patients disappearing. In one case the population of a mental institution was found to have diminished to an abnormal degree over a period of years and when bodies were excised from the grounds they were suspiciously incomplete in certain vital respects. One of the things that led to the state authorities taking action was that a mother had contacted them after being told by the institution that her son was missing because he had run away. Since her son had no legs the mother was naturally very skeptical as to the veracity of this story.

Clearly there must be proper regulation which is properly enforced but should this simply focus around safety issues and the assurance of informed and voluntary donor consent or should it also place restriction on the financial exchanges that can be made in relation to body materials? There are no examples of a properly enforced system of regulation which has allowed organs to be freely bought and sold. However, there are examples of donors being allowed to sell blood within a properly regulated and enforced system of blood donation.

The foremost comparison of 'voluntary' and 'regulatorily controlled commercial' blood donation systems was conducted 25 years ago by Titmuss. Titmuss preferred the former to the latter which he highly criticised as:

- highly wasteful of blood with the demand and supply position being characterised by chronic and acute shortages;
- administratively inefficient and lowering of scientific standards;

---

[833]Commercialisation in Human Organs: A Middle Eastern Perspective, *Trans Proc,* 1990, 22(3), 918-92.

[834]For example, Mukesh Kosla has reported that, 'there are cases of poor patients who have gone for a simple operation having had a kidney removed' (*This Week*, 1989, September 24, 51). The Times of India of 3rd February 1990 reported that 3 young men died at the hands of a 'kidney gang'.

[835]*Sydney Morning Herald*, Wednesday 26 September 1990. See also the United Nations Economic and Social Council Commission on Human Rights 47th session Agenda item 12 report submitted by Mr.Vitit Muntarbhorn on the sale of children.

- more costly (in the US commercial system 'five to fifteen times more costly than voluntary systems in Britain');
- tending to be lower quality with more likelihood of contaminated blood;[836]
- having other negative consequences like eroding community and limiting personal and professional freedoms.[837]

This work was followed by an ongoing blood donation debate between Arrow and Singer. Arrow maintained that except for the danger of post-transfusion hepatitis Titmuss had not shown the inefficiencies in the US system of blood donation were due to commercialisation.[838] However, Singer shows how Arrow had not even noticed some of the important empirical evidence presented by Titmuss, including the proper contrasting of the British voluntary system with the US commercial system and on the link between wastage and commerce.[839]

More recently, Fagot-Largeault, in examining the recent crisis in the voluntary blood donation system in France, has suggested that a voluntary system, 'removes some adverse effects but creates others'.[840] Fagot-Largeault's overall finding was that higher health and safety standards resulting from paying blood donors in France.[841] On the other hand, John Keown, in a paper defending the principle of voluntary, unpaid donation in EC directive 89/381 uses the ground of safety as one of five arguments.[842] Keown accepts that 'non-payment no more ensures safety than payment precludes safety' but argues that it is prudent to have a voluntary unpaid system for several reasons. These include the fact that it is not possible to screen out problems with 100% success, that viruses are likely to be found

---

[836]The Gift Relationship: From Human Blood to Social Policy, *Pantheon Books* 1971. In a recent survey of 10,000 plasma donors N.B.Paull found that over 30% donated more than 18 times in a period of only three months (Safeguarding Donors: First, Do No Harm, *J Am Blood Res Ass*, 1993, 11 (Spring), table 4).

[837]Ibid. See also P.Rodriguez, Paying Donors and the Ethics of Blood Supply, *J of Med Eth,* 1989, 20, 31-35.

[838]Gifts and Exchanges, *Phil and Publ Affairs,* 1972, 343-362 at 361.

[839]Altruism and Commerce: A Defence of Titmuss Against Arrow, *Phil and Publ Affairs,* 1973, 2, 312-320 at 314.

[840]Fagot-Largeault, Does Non-commercialisation of the Human Body Increase Graft Security, Chapter 2 in Organ and Tissue Transplantation in The European Union, Y.Englert (ed), *Martinus Nijhoff,* 1995 at 13.

[841]Ibid.

[842]The Gift of Blood in Europe: An Ethical Defence of EC Directive 89/381, *J Med Eth* 1997, 23, 96-100 at 98.

in heaviest contamination in commercial blood and plasma products and that this makes theoretical sense because paid donors tend to be less well off and have a financial interest in concealing any ill health.[843]

Whether it would be possible to have a properly regulated system of legal trade in organs without adverse health and safety consequences is difficult to say. On the one had within a regulatorily controlled commercial system of donation organ donation would be different to the position for blood donation in as much as it is routine for organ donors to undergo detailed health and safety checks. One concern is that standards of checks might naturally slide in a system of regulated commercial donation.

Some prospective donors motivated by money would probably want to conceal contra-indications to their donating. However, professionals would have all the usual professional incentive to rigorously check health standards and no financial incentive not to. The number of donors who would successfully be able to conceal contra-indications might be small.

The concern about a slide in values as a whole, including such problems as donors being manipulated or coerced, really comes into play when parties other than the donor are allowed to get special incentives for their involvement in removal, transfer or transplantation activities. Here an effect would be felt if the incentives were of a character such that there was significant benefit to be derived from cutting corners. The most obvious example would be where those involved were able to make profit out of the material itself but the problem could also arise where the pay of the parties involved is heavily reliant on the amount of transplantation conducted (as opposed to them just getting a salary unconnected to the amount of transplantations conducted).

Proponents of a more commercialised approach to organ transplantation have tended to argue that it can increase supply.[844] The effect of this would obviously be positive in that it would reduce shortages where these exist and allow clinicians to be more selective about who becomes a donor

---

843 Ibid.

844 See for example R.L.Horton and P.J.Horton, Supplying Organs For Transplantation, *Journal of Health Politics, Policy and Law,* 18(1), 175-188; J.Peters, Life or Death: The Issue of Payment in Cadaveric Organ Donation, *JAMA,* 1991, 265, 1302-1305; H.Hansmann, The Economics and Ethics of Markets for Human Organs, *Yale University*, 56-85; G.Dworkin, Markets and Morals: The Case For Organ Sales, *The Mount Sinai Journal of Medicine*, 1993 (Jan), 60(1), 66-69.

where shortages don't exist. Clearly some people who would not donate an organ if they were not paid would do so if they were paid. In addition there is sense to the view of Barnett et al., that if you also give special incentives to those organising transplantation it will encourage them to more automatically ask people to donate and hence get additional organs.[845] Barnett et al. recommend a free functioning market with procurement firms having an incentive to collect as many organs as profitable and donors profiting from their action.[846] However, I have already suggested that this type of incentive could lead to corner cutting.

In more general terms it must also be noted that for a more commercialised approach to increase supply it must in addition to bringing new donors on-line keep hold of people who already donate, or at least the vast majority of them. I have previously observed that it cannot be taken for granted that everyone who chooses to donate currently would continue to do so under a more commercialised approach.[847] The main reason it cannot be taken for granted is that procurement relies on favourable public opinion towards transplantation and most of the public are against a more commercial approach. It seems to engender mistrust.[848] Prottas paints a cataclysmic picture of the potential effects of a more commercialised approach:

> Hostility to payment is strongest among those in the population presently most willing to donate, about 80% reject any payment system. Among families that have actually donated, an even greater percentage reject the idea of payment. If the percentage of people who refuse to participate in a paid system approaches these numbers, then a market system is a catastrophe. It would result in far fewer organs at far higher cost...even much smaller refusal rates would have a marked impact.[849]

---

[845]Barnett et al., Improving Organ Donation: Compensation Versus Markets, *Inquiry,* 1992, 29, 372-378 at 372.

[846]Ibid at p374.

[847]A.Garwood-Gowers, To Pay or Not to Pay: That is the Question? An Analysis of the Economic Rights of Donors, in D.Price and H.Akveld (eds.), Living Organ Donation in the Nineties: European Medico-Legal Perspectives, *EUROTOLD,* 1996, 163-173.

[848]See F.Cantarovich, Values Sacrificed and Values Gained by the Commerce of Organs: The Argentine Experience, *Trans Proc* 1990, 22(3), 925-927.

[849]J.Prottas, Buying Human Organs - Evidence that Money Doesn't Change Everything, *Transplantation,* 53(6), 1371-1373.

This view of the consequences of a more commercial system might be a little extreme. It also doesn't take into account that public opinion is not so weighted against a more commercial approach when it involves mild incentives. An NFK/UNOS study found marginally over half of the respondents in favour of 'mild incentives'.[850] It is also the case that the public may come to accept certain incentives even more readily if researchers educate them more about the distinctions between different levels of commercialisation. In one US survey, the majority of respondents stated that their major reason for being opposed to incentives was that they were against buying 'buying organs'.[851] This suggests that they had not come to distinguish between incentives that commodify the organ and incentives that do not. However, it is also true that we should not assume that most or even the majority of those who currently choose not to become living donors or to bequeath their organs would suddenly do so if money was involved. A large proportion of people who don't currently donate have consciously chosen not to. We saw in chapter 1 that in many cases this was because they object to transplantation. In some other cases people don't want a deceased relative's organs to be used because it will involve mutilation.[852] Some people's objections, at least to bequeathing their organs, might be put aside for money, but what proportion is uncertain.

Removal, transfer and use of body materials can also be examined more directly from the perspective of the rights of those involved and affected by such activities. One of the arguments advanced is that people have a right to get payment for donating. Radcliffe-Richards suggests that preventing donor payment,

> ...obviously runs against the fundamental liberal principle that although people's freedom of action may legitimately be curtailed to prevent their harming others, it may not be curtailed to prevent their harming themselves. Anyone who takes this principle to be absolute, as many do, must obviously rule out paternalistic intervention completely.[853]

---

[850]Jim Warren, Financial Incentive Controversy Continues, *Dialysis and Transplantation*, March 1993, 156-158.
[851]B.Teo, Organs For Transplantation: The Singapore Experience, *Hastings Centre Report,* 1991, Nov-Dec:10-3.
[852]J.Prottas, H.Batten, The Willingness to Give: The Public and The Supply of Transplantable Organs, *J Health Polit Policy Law.*
[853]For Him That Hath Not, in W.Land and J.Dossetor (eds.), Ethics, Justice and Commerce in Organ Replacement Therapy, *Kluwer*, 1990.

She adds that arguments that potential vendors are being subtly coerced, or are too ill informed to make rational decisions can only justify intervention in particular cases.[854] Andrews takes this approach a step further by arguing that, 'humans have the right to treat certain physical parts of their bodies as objects for possession, gift and trade'.[855] She is one of a significant minority of writers in favour of profit making for donors and organisers.[856]

All participants have a clear ethical right to obtain payment for their labour. In addition the donor has a strong right to obtain money for the material; the minimum right being to be paid or compensated for what (s)he has given up. Not providing any of the above payments is a severe breach of rights; if an activity goes on people ought to be able to obtain a legitimate payment for what they put into that activity and preventing them from doing so is effectively an infringement of their right to determine the ways in which they make their livelihood. This would result in more costs to whoever has to pay (e.g. the recipient, state or insurance companies) but such cost is irrelevant in as much as nobody has the right to expect people to give things up - whether labour and/or material - without being fairly paid for doing so. However, the approach Andrews takes is that those involved ought to be able to obtain profit, which implies that they have the right to derive as much money as they can from those that pay. This is essentially part of a laissez faire view of capitalistic economics where the law might be concerned to ensure that exchanges are not made by force but does not concern itself with what type of deal is struck. On the one hand, contract law has traditionally been based on this approach. On the other, most jurisdictions have introduced regulation into markets for goods and services to ensure that competition is maintained and to ensure that the interests of the purchaser/ultimate consumer are protected (as well as the environment in many cases). In organ transplantation those who would be purchasing materials would typically be in a weakened bargaining position by the fact that there is more demand than supply. An interventionist approach would at minimum seek to protect them from unconscionable bargains and more likely cap prices.

Another side of the debate about payment is whether prospective recipients should be able to access organs and other body materials and the

---

[854]Ibid.

[855]Andrews, My Body, My Property, *Hastings Center Report,* 1986, 16, 28 at 36.

[856]The Body as Property: Some Philosophical Reflections - A Response to J.F.Chidress, *Trans Proc*, 1992, 24(5) October, 2149-2151.

services of their transplantation irrespective of their wealth. Obviously an approach where there is equal access irrespective of wealth has advantages of social cohesion and this is one reason Titmuss has recommended distribution of blood should be nationalised with free access.[857] In organ transplantation this approach also avoids the problems of lower standards that can arise in a system where recipients have to pay. However, money does not grow on trees - in other words someone has to pay for free access and those who pay through tax or compulsory national insurance lose the freedom to do what they please with that proportion of their money. Some of them may not even agree with dialysis and transplantation or as a whole the reductionistic medicine that tends to dominate national health services.

Conclusion

It has been stated that trade in organs has been exaggerated by the media.[858] However, trade is clearly a significant global problem even in some of the countries prohibiting it.[859] For some countries enforcement is an issue and at the end of the day some trade is almost inevitable in conditions of scarcity. One argument is that since anti-trade laws are circumvented they should be abolished.[860] However, there is no sense in legalising something that is detrimental when by doing so we increase its incidence. The more appropriate approach is to remove the cause of trading by using acceptable forms of procurement, such as living donation, to eliminate organ shortages. What also needs to occur is a clearer demarcation of what forms of payment are and are not ethically acceptable.

---

[857]R.Titmuss, The Gift Relationship, *Pantheon Books,* 1971. Compassion demands that at least some vulnerable members of society are protected, e.g. children.

[858]See e.g. H.Kreis, Chapter 10 in Organ and Tissue Transplantation in the European Union: Management of Difficulties and Health Risks Linked to Donors, Y.Englert (ed), *Martinus Nijhoff,* 1995. A review of this book is produced by A.Garwood-Gowers, *IDHL*, 1996, 47(1), 126-7.

[859]For instance Argentina, Brazil, Russian Federation and India. Some national legislation such as the Human Organ Transplants Act 1989 (section 1) prohibits its nationals from buying an organ abroad but most laws do not. However, this and other limitations in prohibitions on 'trade' in organs can only partially explain why the trade continues.

[860]Kishore, Organ Donation: Consanguinity Vs Universality - An Analysis of Indian Law, Manuscript with EUROTOLD.

There is a strong right for everyone legitimately involved in the process, including the donor, to be able to get reasonable payment for what they do. However, the argument that they have the right to greater payment than this is not convincing because there is a need to fairness as between all parties particularly when a scarce resource such as this is involved. The view that additional incentives will improve supply is contentious and there are potent dangers that such incentives would lead to a slide in standards.

The failure of most jurisdictions to provide for compensation of donor losses as a matter of right is odd. It leaves some donors suffering a 'double whammy' of physical damage and financial hardship from their activities and this is totally unacceptable. Also odd is the widely held perception that donors should give their time, effort and material without fair payment for them. Titmuss[861] and Keown[862] emphasise the value of altruism and social solidarity both of which are commonly a factor for donating in an unpaid system.[863] However, if we carry through this approach to its logical outcome we would expect people to do all 'socially useful activities' on an unpaid basis. It would be a sorry and topsy-turvy world that only let us get financial reward for doing harmful or useless things! Harris[864] and Radcliffe-Richards[865] must be correct in their view that paying a donor doesn't necessarily lead to the donor being exploited. Indeed, expecting the donor to give on an unpaid basis is exploitative. The donor should have the following rights to payment in donation from whoever is responsible for the costs of transplantation:

- the right to fair compensation for the loss of what the material was reasonably worth to the donor and for the pain, intrinsic and non-intrinsic physical detriments that stem from the donation;
- the right to free medical care and regular check-ups in relation to the consequences of donating;

---

[861]The Gift Relationship, *Pantheon Books*, 1971.

[862]The Gift of Blood in Europe: An Ethical Defence of EC Directive 89/381, *J Med Eth* 1997, 23, 96-100 at 96-7.

[863]Keown's review of studies of why people donate blood in an unpaid system has illustrated this (ibid.) as to a lesser extent have surveys of motivation in living donation (see chapter 4).

[864]September 1991 talk at the Bioethics and Profit Making Conference at Manchester University.

[865]'For Him that Hath Not, in W.Land and J.Dossetor (eds.), Ethics, Justice and Commerce in Organ Replacement Therapy, *Kluwer*, 1990.

- the right to fair compensation for his/her time and effort involved in donation related activities from testing right through to the completion of recuperation. This 'labour' could be paid at a nationally determined rate - perhaps similar to rates normally given to medical research volunteers. However, for any relevant portion of this 'labour' which takes place during the time where the donor would otherwise have been undertaking remunerative work the donor will have the right to compensation at a rate matching his normal wage subject to a ceiling (e.g. the national average wage rate); this compensation again provided by those responsible for the costs of transplantation in the event that no other party (such as an employer) wishes to take responsibility;
- the right to defrayment/reimbursement of reasonable costs arising in activities pursuant or incidental to the donation. These may include such costs as travel to and from the centre, childcare/baby-sitting expenses and accommodation expenses;
- the right to compensation for discrimination stemming from having donated (for example, in relation to job security and obtaining security) and where reasonable legal protection from such discrimination; and
- prospective donors who do not become actual donors should have the rights that are applicable from the above also. For example, compensation for labour involved in testing or for time taken off work for this.

It has been pointed out that prospective donors are sometimes desperate for money.[866] However, the significance of this is not so much as an argument in favour of paying them as a warning that medical professionals need to be cautious in whom they accept as donors. Obviously, if donors are going to be paid they should not be rejected simply because part or even all of their motivation is commercial. Hence, jurisdictions with requirements as to altruistic or humanitarian motivation would need to shed them. However, there is still a case for saying that donors should have at least a genuine emotional relationship with the recipient, i.e. not be a stranger or a person who is pretending to be emotionally related. It is not that strangers would per se be unacceptable but if they were allowed to donate it would be too easy for their unacceptable use to go unnoticed. Even if all the transplant centres could be forced to apply high ethical standards to stranger donation it would be difficult to regulate against unethical activity on the part of others who might covertly or overtly involve themselves in the process. For example, to transplant centre professionals, a stranger might appear to want to donate but behind the scenes there may be people

[866]Radcliffe-Richards, Organs for Sale, 1995.

manipulating, coercing, blackmailing or simply 'fleecing' him or her. There is already significant illegitimate involvement of gangsters and Mafia in transplantation globally and giving an additional means for such activity to take hold could result in serious further damage to donors and recipients and undermine confidence in transplantation services.

When it comes to cadaveric donation, L.R.Cohen has explored the possibility of a futures market for cadaveric donation where donors choose during their life-time what to do with a sum of money given at their death. He says he can,

> ...think of no reason why anyone who now signs an organ donor card would decline to do so if informed that in the process they could also specify their designee (which could be a charity) who would receive a sum of money as a result.[867]

Another suggestion is that the funeral expenses of the dead donor could be paid.[868] These types of approach might increase the number of organs currently obtained and avoid the slide in values that would arise if there were a free market for cadaveric organs. However, the objection is that by bequeathing an organ a person is doing very little - they are just signing a card - hence giving them or their relatives an incentive of any significant size amounts to profit making.

---

[867]L.R.Cohen, A Futures Market in Cadaveric Organs: Would it Work? *Trans Proc*, 1993, 25(1), 60-61.

[868]T.G.Peters, Life or Death: The Issue of Payment in Cadaveric Organ Donation, *JAMA,* 1991, 266, 1302-1305.

8 A Change of Approach

Introduction

Wherever transplantation is considered the gold standard for treatment of organ disease, utility drives the impulse to procure sufficient organs to meet demand. Yet rights should be considered inviolable, including the living person's rights to determine treatment of their body upon death as well as in life. The right not be used for the purposes of others is a basic tenet of civilised society and any contravention of it represents a step away from pluralism toward totalitarianism. The acceptance of this approach excludes any procurement methods that assume consent to donate in the absence of refusal.

Kidney transplantation is at a global cross-roads in relation to LDT. One direction is to accept the maleficent consequences of growing waiting lists by continuing the path of limited LDT use. The other is to increase LDT dramatically, gaining the quality of life and economic rewards that can come from much higher rates of transplantation without contravening donor rights or strict limits to donor maleficence. Whichever direction is taken by those involved it should be taken consciously with a clear perspective of the ethics of procurement as a whole and the legitimate use and limits to use of LDT.

Attitudes and Their Relationship With LDT Use

In the case of the United States, Spital's studies indicate an increasingly positive attitude amongst transplant centres to the use of LDT. Spital found a positive change in attitude towards living donation between his 1987 study (reported 1988)[869] and his 1993 study (reported 1994).[870] In the 1993 study 64% (127) of US transplant centres responded and one of the remarkable features was how positive they were even towards using living

[869]Unconventional Living Kidney Donors - Attitudes and Use Amongst Transplant Centres, *Transplantation,* 1989, 48 (August), 243-248.
[870]Unrelated Living Kidney Donors, An Update of Attitudes and Use Among U.S. Transplant Centers, *Transplantation*, 1994, 57(June), 1722-1726.

unrelated donation (LURD). 88% of these responding would accept spouses as donors, 63% would accept friends and 15% would even consider altruistic strangers. Commenting on the relationship of this study with his study 6 years ago Spital stated,

> ...it became clear that support for unrelated living kidney donation had increased, as the great majority of centers now believe that emotionally related donors are acceptable. On the other hand, while more of these donors are being used, they still account for only a small fraction of all kidney transplants. It appears that the medical successes and favourable ethical arguments have generated broad support for some types of unrelated living donors, but more in principle than in practice, as there still seems to be some hesitation to actually proceed.[871]

However, despite the hesitancy toward using LURD, Spital noted that there still have been changes in patterns of use including 22 of the responding centres having actually used friends as living donors compared with only 3 in the survey 6 years before, although this still only amounted to 40 such transplants in the previous year. The number of centres now using spouses was more than twice that in the previous survey. Of the small number of centres accepting the idea of strangers as donors in principle none had actually used them in practice. Opposition appeared to revolve around the difficulties of being certain of altruistic as opposed to financial motives in such a situation and also factors like the lack of available guidelines, possibility of psychopathology and the view that it was unethical.

Another important feature of Spital's 1993 study was that over half of the responding centres preferred living related donation to cadaveric, while only 8% took the reverse view. This represented a sea change from 1987,

> ...while a 1985 survey revealed that 54% of responding U.S. transplant centers preferred living related donors just two years later that number had fallen to only 36%. Now the present data show that over the past six years this previous downward trend in the popularity of living donors has reversed.[872]

Spital suggests that the basis of these changes is as follows:

> Besides its obvious potential to mitigate the organ shortage, other considerations supporting unrelated living kidney donation may be summarised

[871]Ibid at 1723.
[872]Ibid at 1725.

> as follows: (1) the risk to a healthy living donor is very low and is independent of the relationship to the recipient; (2) the more distant the relationship of the donor to the recipient, the less likely there is to be psychological coercion, and the more likely the altruistic donor is to be a true volunteer; (3) the fear that unrelated donors harbour psychopathology has been disproven by studies demonstrating that altruism is generally what motivates these remarkable people to give; (4) in other areas of life, taking risks to help people is generally considered heroic, not crazy; (5) motivation should not even be an issue when the donor is closely related to the recipient emotionally; (6) like having related donors, many unrelated donors benefit psychologically from donating through meaningful and persistent increases in self-esteem; *and* (7) surveys of the public have shown that the great majority are willing to donate to their spouses and most believe that donations by friends and even strangers should be permitted.[873]

While these are clear arguments for looking on living donation favourably, probably the single most important reason for the changes in attitude has been the fact that waiting lists have been increasing in size. Much of the US transplant profession has felt it has had to be more pro-active about using LDT in order to limit the spiralling of waiting lists. The interesting question in Europe is why only a few of the countries with spiralling waiting lists have sought to significantly increase LDT use. This is particularly baffling given European transplant centre attitudes toward LDT, whilst not as positive as those in the United States, are still very positive.

EUROTOLD surveyed 190 European Transplant Centres by Questionnaire and of the 56% responding the vast majority had a living donor programme (86% or 85% when weighted by catchment population). Asked whether they foresaw an expansion of their living donor programme, 55% of those centres responding answered 'yes' with only 10% answering 'no' (29% said 'maybe'). There was a 66% 'yes' response and only a 6% 'no' response when results were weighted by catchment population (28% 'maybe'). Respondents from centres with an LDT programme answered the question of who they would consider as a living donor as follows: parents 98.8%; siblings 98.8%; spouse 54.5%; relative by marriage 23%; grandparent 54%; son/daughter 52.9%; friend 10.3%; *and* other 3.5%.

Perhaps the most interesting factor was that 54.5% of respondents with an LDT programme would consider using spouses; a percentage exceeding

[873]Ibid at 1725.

that for grandparents and son/daughter matches. Presumably this is based on the clinical significance of age matching, with spouses tending to be a closer match and more preferable as living donors in this regard. However, age matching is clearly a secondary factor at times; parents are almost universally considered yet are not any more age matched than son/daughter donations, which are not so accepted. Presumably, son /daughter donations are partly considered to be less appropriate on a psychological basis. However, this perception would not normally be shared in some cultures (particularly Asian) where the family is more typically seen as a unit with mutual rather than more one-way caring responsibilities. Lesser use of 'offspring' donations may also be due to practical considerations, such as the possibility that they may have their own dependents to look after. A closer examination of attitudes in this area would be valuable as there could be underutilisation occurring.

The EUROTOLD Transplant Attitudes Questionnaire found the most positive attitudes toward LURDs amongst transplant professionals in Europe were found in Armenia, Slovakia and Norway, with fairly positive attitudes found in Denmark, Poland, Switzerland and Italy. Meanwhile, EUROTOLD's interview/questionnaires with donors and recipients found that they had an even more positive attitude towards LURD. The most poignant example of this was that as many were in favour of strangers donating (as against a mere 15% of practitioners in Spital 1993 US survey[874] and 3.5% of European centres in the EUROTOLD questionnaire).

Although there is significant scope to increase spousal donation the European professional attitudes data suggests other forms of LURD are unlikely to be significantly relied upon in the near future. However, this is not statistically that relevant since LURD as a whole only ever plays a bit part of 10% or less of even the most ambitious living donor programmes. There must be other reasons why only a few of the European countries with spiralling waiting lists have significantly increased LDT in the 1990s. One of the factors bearing on this may have been a carry over from the 1980s when, with the advent of cyclosporine, there must have been a mood of hope that cadaveric transplantation would be able to meet demand for organs and hence a logically more restrictive attitude towards LDT amongst the transplant community. Indeed, a study of 148 European Transplant Centres in the early 1980s found that 22% of surveyed doctors

[874] A.Spital, Unrelated Living Kidney Donors, An Update of Attitudes and Use Among U.S. Transplant Centers, *Transplantation*, June 1994, 57(12), 1722-1726.

thought LDT was ethically unacceptable.[875]

In some cases, practice and the framework for practice (clinical guideline, protocols and legislation) may not immediately reflect the changes in attitude that have occurred toward LDT in the context of the realisation of CDT procurement being in most cases insufficient to meet 90s demand. Certainly some legislative provisions concerning LDT use are not clear enough and some are not very positive about use, expressing a bias towards LDT or unrealistic restrictions on maleficence. The precise relationship of legislation to professional attitudes and practice is not entirely clear nut obviously there will be one. EUROTOLD Transplant Centre Questionnaire responses even showed a positive correlation between the restrictiveness/liberality of LDT regulation and transplant centre perception of whether LDT was legal or not (.3468 at 0.1% level). Remarkably, 5 in 10 Spanish centres responding to the Centre Questionnaire thought LDT was unlawful, along with 3 in 8 from Italy, 2 in 12 from France, 3 in 5 from Belgium, 1 in 4 from Austria and 1 in 14 from Germany. It may be more than coincidence that none of these countries have high levels of LDT p.m.p.

During the 1990s in Europe it is really only Denmark, Estonia and to a limited extent Austria that have increased LDT use significantly. In Belgium, Eire and Spain the use of living donors has declined, which is understandable given the extent to which CDT has been able to meet demand in these countries. However, most European countries including, notably, the UK, Germany and France, have not increased LDT use significantly despite markedly rising waiting lists.

Attitudes and the Point in Treatment at Which CDT and LDT are Considered

EUROTOLD found that only 40% of the centres which responded to its Centre Questionnaire would consider using CDT before dialysis. 51% would consider CDT when dialysis was needed and 9% only when the patient has been on dialysis for some time.

One of the factors influencing some centres not to use pre-dialysis CDT may be distributive justice; if there are insufficient kidneys to meet demand then it might be fairer for people only to get them at or near to the point of necessity. If you delay giving a person an organ until necessary then on the

[875] Editorial, *Lancet*, 1982, ii, 696.

face of it you also delay the time at which the organ will stop functioning and this means you preserve their life/well-being longer and/or delay the time at which they will need another organ. This obviously benefits the individual patient as well as the whole patient community. However, there is a point at which delaying becomes counterproductive because the person waiting for a transplant deteriorates sufficiently on dialysis to start reducing the level of likely survival of a graft.

When it comes to living donation there is no distributive justice rationale to delay consideration of use. Not surprisingly, more of the centres responding to the EUROTOLD Centre Questionnaire would use LDT before dialysis than would use CDT before dialysis (60% v 40%). Under conditions of organ shortage the patient community actually benefits from a sensible use of LDT at whatever point it is conducted (one less person waiting for CDT).

Obviously professionals are concerned to use LDT only where necessary in terms of the specific interests of the prospective donor and recipient at hand. In this sense there can be a rationale for waiting to see if a reasonable CDT turns up; 10.67% of centres with an LDT programme responding to the Centre Questionnaire said they would only use LDT after a period of dialysis. However, if the waiting list is long and the chances of a suitable cadaveric organ arriving quickly slim then there will generally be clear sense in going ahead with LDT. The sooner one does so the greater one can exploit the benefits of early transplantation to the recipient; pre-dialysis LDT being the 'gold standard' in this sense.[876]

Not surprisingly, EUROTOLD found a small correlation (.233) between the living donor rate per million population of centres and attitudes toward pre-dialysis. Generally the countries with the most favourable attitude towards pre-dialysis transplantation were those who conducted a high amount of LDT p.m.p. (Cyprus, Norway, Sweden and Holland but cf. Albania which doesn't use transplantation and Italy which has low CDT and LDT rates). Those with the most restrictive attitudes tended to do less LDT p.m.p. (Belgium, Spain, Slovakia and Hungary).

---

[876]Confirming the view expressed by P.K.Donnelly in Pre Dialysis Living Donor Renal Transplantation - Is it Still The Gold Standard for Cost, Convenience and Graft Survival? *Trans Proc*, 1995, 27(1)).

A Framework for Regulation of LDT

LDT is unlike an average medical procedure and many of its unique features point toward the view that its regulation should not be left to the general law. As Price concludes,

> (t)he absence of legislation concerning LDT creates uncertainty, variability of practice and an absence of transparency.[877]

There is a trend toward comprehensive legislation[878] which is to be welcomed but many provisions remain confused particularly on questions of maleficence, beneficence and disclosure. There is work to be done if legislation is to play its full role in maximising legitimate use.

Transplant centres and individual professionals obviously have a choice about whether or not to use LDT and this choice should be respected along with prospective LDT participants being able to choose a centre that does do LDT. However, centres that consider LDT to be acceptable ought to adopt an approach that facilitates legitimate use as far as is possible within the boundaries of the need for it.

EUROTOLD's Centre Questionnaire found that currently 67% of centres with LDT programmes had a protocol for evaluation of donors (73% when weighted by catchment population) but only 37% had written guidelines as to use of living donors (49% when weighted by catchment population). Both guidelines and a protocol should be standard for centres using LDT in order to help provide professionals with a clear reference point for evaluating when LDT should be used and issues within its use such as approaching prospective donors and ensuring they are making voluntary and sufficiently informed decisions. Guidelines and a protocol could also provide a clear framework for the consideration of forms of LDT perceived as more marginal in terms of the benefits to the recipient or in terms of the donor being incompetent or being only emotionally or distantly genetically related to the recipient.

---

[877]The Texture and Content of Living Donor Transplant Laws and Policies, *Trans Proc*, 1996, 28(1), 378-379 at 379.

[878]See Questioning Attitudes to Living Donor Transplantation, *EUROTOLD Project Management Group Final Report,* ch2 at p36 (this part written by D.Price).

Recommendations for Regulation of Beneficence and Maleficence in the Choice of When to Use LDT

1. A patient may receive LDT where, after taking into account the harm and jeopardy to the donor, it represents an equal or superior therapeutic option to its alternatives.
2. Where there is a waiting list for cadaveric organs the likely waiting time for the patient and its consequences for him/her should be factored into the consideration of whether LDT is an equal of superior option to CDT.
3. For LDT to be used the likelihood of death for the donor must not significantly exceed the likelihood of death from a standard operation. The level of inevitable harm stemming from the donation must be within reasonable limits. In terms of harms that may stem from donation, the risk of serious harm must be low and taken as a whole the risks must be within reasonable limits.
4. Safety checks for the donor must be of a high standard.
5. Regulations or Codes of Practice may periodically give concrete guidance on the above matters.
6. Where the donor is not competent to consent, additional stipulations as to benefit and limits to maleficence may be made.

The extreme rarity of mortality from kidney donation and the apparently low levels of short and long-term risks mean it would meet the above limits to maleficence under normal circumstances as would some other forms of living donation like liver segment or lung lobe. Living donor pancreas vessel donation might be ruled out altogether or limited to circumstances where it is the only clinical option that may save the life of the prospective recipient and has a reasonable likelihood of success.

Recommendations for Procedural Requirements

1. Donors must, by signing a form or by a method of equal veracity, state that the donation is a voluntary not-for-profit act done in accordance with their true will.
2. Recipients must evidence their voluntary consent by signing a form (or an equally veracious method) stating that the organ LDT reflects their true will.
3. A duration of at least 48 hours (or exceptionally 24 hours) must have elapsed between agreement and removal.
4. Professionals giving information to, or asking for consent of, the prospective donor shall not be the same people who are involved in caring for the prospective recipient.
5. Further procedural requirements may be used in jurisdictions with organ trade problems and for cases where the donor is not a close genetic relative of the recipient.

Recommendations for Regulating Professional-Participant Communication

1. Professionals shall make all reasonable attempts to inform the prospective donor and recipient of the clinical risks and benefits of the procedure for both parties. The information should discuss physical and psychological consequences in broad terms and highlight specific areas of significance such as the risk of serious injury or death, less serious risks of common occurrence and harms of a significant nature. A reasonable attempt must be made to ascertain and meet any particular information needs a donor or recipient may have.
2. Professionals shall make all reasonable attempts to inform the prospective donor and recipient of any major social and economic implications that LDT is known to have. A reasonable attempt must be made to inform at least the donor of the major methods by which costs incurred in the process of being a living donor (such as from lost earnings and travel expenses) can be defrayed or reimbursed. Where the donor has a legal right or opportunity to claim payment for the his/her time and effort (s)he shall be informed of this.
3. Information offered, and the methods for its communication (e.g. audio visual, tape recorded, multi-media, signed, paper-written and spoken), must reflect a reasonable attempt to ascertain and address the needs, abilities and disabilities of the prospective donor and recipient. The information may draw on different sources - such as different professionals within the centre, former LDT donors and recipients and literature.
4. All prospective donors and recipients must be properly informed irrespective of their wishes. Information can only be withheld where it is of a nature which is likely to harm the donor or recipient (e.g. because of a phobia). When withholding information on this basis, the medical professional must ensure that (s)he still gives a balanced picture in terms of benefits and detriments of the prospective LDT and the alternative courses of treatment.
5. The medical professional must make efforts to ensure that the nature and significance of information communicated is understood. At the very least (s)he must reasonably believe that the donor and recipient have sufficient understanding of the benefits and detriments of the prospective LDT and the alternative courses of treatment to be able to clearly determine which choice is preferable. The medical professional should make these checks before asking the donor and recipient to decide. If they have decided without being asked, the medical professional should make the check at the earliest opportunity.

The emphasis in this framework is on medical professionals helping both donors and recipients to make choices in the light of adequate awareness of what they involve. The interdependence of donor and recipient is recognised.

Recommendations for Regulation of Use of Minors and Adult Incompetents as Donors

1. A court, or an authority set up under legislation, should examine all cases. Practitioners could also use this court or authority in cases where they are uncertain of a prospective donor's competence.
2. The age of majority should be 16, 17 or 18.
3. Competent minors shall not be donors without their consent. Their consent shall override any parental/guardian objection. A clinician should have a significant reason to prefer their donation over therapeutic alternatives.
4. Living organ donation may be conducted on an incompetent person when it is in his/her best interests and is significantly superior to other options. The relevant legal consent(s) must have been given in accordance with general principles of law. The donation may only proceed without the meaningful agreement of the incompetent in the event of donating being a necessity to protect the incompetent's best interests.

This regime allows donation by minors and incompetent adults within rational circumstances and places their right to refuse at the centre of consideration.

Use of Different Classes of Donor in Terms of their Relationship with the Recipient

1. Prior to undertaking a donation the practitioner must ascertain the nature of the relationship between the donor and recipient. Scientific screening tests shall be used in relation to claims of genetic relationship.
2. Proposals for LDTs that are not between close genetic relatives or spouses of 3 or more years standing should gain authorisation from an authority set up under law. This authority should ensure that donation is a voluntary, non-profit motivated gift and not normally authorise donations between strangers.

A framework of this kind is often viewed as important both to providing confidence in LDT use as a whole and specifically encouraging legitimate use of LDT between distant genetic relatives and significantly emotionally related persons.[879] While there is no *clinical* reason to discriminate against strangers per se, doing so will help avoid profit motivated donations.

---

[879]This view has been stressed by Bob Pilling, Chair of ULTRA, in David Price's 1996 communication with them. In personal communication with EUROTOLD, Ferenc Perner of the Budapest transplant centre has also expressed this view.

Recommendations for Regulation of Voluntariness of Donor Consent

1. Practitioners must make reasonable attempts to ascertain that the act of donation reflects the true will of the donor. To this end a psychological evaluation should be made, including evaluation of a short written or otherwise evidenced statement by the donor of his/her reasons for wanting to donate.
2. Practitioners must make reasonable attempts to ensure that the process leading up to donation presents as neutral and unbiased a climate as possible for prospective donors to consider their decision.
3. The donor must be able to revoke the decision to donate (verbally, in writing or by any other method) at any point before the procedure commences (the same provision should exist for the recipient).

One of the criticisms of living donation is that the fact of being informed itself creates a pressure to donate.[880] However, approaching the donor is reasonable if done with care. Centre protocols should address matters like who makes the initial approach to the prospective donor (e.g. family, recipient, a medical professional), whether prospective donors are offered 'a way out without losing face' (e.g. professional stating that donation was not possible for medical reasons), at what point in the process are prospective donors asked to make a decision and by whom and who will explore donor motivation (e.g. counsellor, psychiatrist, psychologist).

Recommendations for Regulation of Commerce and Compensation.

1. Making profit from organs shall be prohibited but law may provide for the donor to be compensated for the loss of the value of the material donated.
2. Reasonable payment may be made for labour to donors and those legitimately involved in the organisation and practice of transplantation at government sanctioned hospitals. Donors must as of right at least receive compensation for losses as follows: Those associated with time off work (both for self-employed and employed); cost of convalescence care; childcare requirements; reasonable hotel/travel expenses under limits set out by the government; *and* reasonable compensation (under limits set out by government) of normal and unusual harms arising from the donation process.
3. Legislation shall require employers and financial organisations to pay compensation for, respectively, prejudicial treatment of the donor in the workplace and obtaining life insurance.

---

[880]See C.Byk, Living Organ Donation European Perspectives, in D.Price and H.Akveld (eds.), Living Organ Donation in The Nineties: European Medico-Legal Perspectives, *EUROTOLD*, 1996, 53-62.

The above approach ensures that donors suffer no economic detriment from the act of donation. It also allows for the possibility of donors being paid for labour and compensated for loss of material and harm. These latter suggestions would doubtless need further examination.

Final Comments and Suggestions for Future Research

International bodies must continue to move away from an approach where LDT was considered as almost a last resort to one where it is recognised as a major source of procurement. It has become a matter of urgency for centres to more toward a more Norwegian type of approach to living donation in order to avert the maleficent consequences of ever-growing waiting lists.

Much of the research now being connected in relation to transplantation is in cloning, artificial organs and xenotransplantation. In LDT specifically one of the developing area is non-renal forms of donation where in many cases ongoing empirical analysis is required to more closely evaluate beneficence and maleficence and begin to evaluate participant and practitioner attitudes and experience. In all forms of LDT the processes used to provide participants with information, levels of participant understanding and reasoned decision-making and the context of decision making - including motivations, pressures and voluntariness - are all areas that could beneficially be revisited with an emphasis on European as well as US data. Continued periodic survey and analysis of centre and practitioner practices and attitudes would also be useful.

Bibliography

G.M.Abouna, Negative Impact of Trading in Human Organs on the Development of Transplantation in the Middle East, *Trans Proc*, 1990, 22(3), 918-921.

Ad Hoc Committee on Nephrology Manpower Needs, Estimating Workforce and Training Requirements for Nephrologists Through the Year 2010, *J Am Soc Nephrol*, 1997, 8(9), 1-32.

Advisory Group on the Ethics of Xenotransplantation, A Report by the Advisory Group on the Ethics of Xenotransplantation, *Department of Health*, 1997.

H.Akveld, Living Organ Donation. Who Pays the Bill?, in Price and Akveld (eds.), Living Organ Donation in The Nineties: European Medico-Legal Perspectives, EUROTOLD, 1997, 143-153.

D.Albrechtsen et al., Kidney Donation From a Spouse: An Alternative to Years of Dialysis Waiting For a Graft That May Never Turn Up, *Trans Proc*, 1990, 22(4), 1435.

P.Alderson, In the Genes or In the Stars? Children's Competence to Consent, *J Med Eth*, 1992, 18, 119-124.

J.Alexander et al., The Use of Marginal Donors for Organ Transplantation: The Older and Younger Donors, *Trans Proc,* 1991, 23(1) at 905.

Alfani et al., Living Unrelated Kidney Transplantation: A 12-Year Single Centre Experience, *Trans Proc*, 1997, 29, 191-194 at 193.

Al Khader et al., XI Int.Cong.Trans.Soc.Helsinki, August 1986, Abstract No. S11.4).

C.F.Anderson et al., The Risks of Unilateral Nephrectomy: Status of Kidney Donors 10-20 Years Postoperatively, *Mayo Clin Proc,* 1985, 60, 367-374.

Andrews, My Body, My Property, *Hastings Center Report,* 1986, 16, 28 at 36.

Andrews, The Body as Property: Some Philosophical Reflections - A Response to J.F.Chidress, *Trans Proc*, 1992, 24(5) October, 2149-2151.

Anon., *New Scientist,* 1989, 25.

Arrow, Gifts and Exchanges, *Philosophy and Public Affairs* 1972, 343-362 at 361.

S.E.Asch, Effects of Group Pressure Upon The Modification and Distortion of Judgements in H.Guetzkow (ed.), Groups, Leadership and Men, *Carnegie Press*, 1951).

V.Axline, Play Therapy, *Houghton Mifflin,* 1947.

Bainham, The Judge and the Competent Minor, *LQR,* 1992, 108, 194.

D.Bakker, Living Related and Living Unrelated Organ Donation - A Clinician's View on the Ethical Aspects, in Price and Akveld (eds.), Living Organ Donation in The Nineties: European Medico-Legal Perspectives, EUROTOLD, 1997, 24-30.

Bandura, Principles of Behaviour Modification, *Holt, Reinhart and Winston,* 1969.

Bar Council, Bar Council Report of Organ Transplants, *BMJ,* 1971 (September), 716.

Barnard, The Personal Meaning of Illness, in J.Shlien (ed.), Client-Centred Dimensions of Medicine and Health Care, *Client-Centred Therapy*, 337-351 at 350-351.

Barnett et al., Improving Organ Donation: Compensation Versus Markets, *Inquiry,* 1992, 29, 372-378 at 372.

C.C.Baron, Live Organ and Tissue Transplants From Minor Donors in Massachusetts, *Boston U Law Review*, 1975, 55, 159.

Bart et al., Study of Shortage, *Transplantation*, 1981, 31, 379.

W.J.Bay et al., Prognosis After Donor Nephrectomy: An Update, *Int J Art Org,* 1987, 10, 9-13.

W.Bay & L.Herbert, The Living Donor in Kidney Transplantation, *Annals Intern Med,* 1987, 106, 719-727.

G.M.Beekman et al., Analysis of Donor Selection Procedure in 139 Living Related Kidney Donors and Follow-up Results For Donors and Recipients, *Nephrol Dial Transplant,* 1994, 9, 163-8.

T.Beauchamp in A History and Theory of Informed Consent, *Oxford University Press*, 1986.

D.J.Bem, Self Perception: An Alternative Interpretation of Cognitive Dissonance Phenomena, *Psychological Review*, 1974, 81, 506-520.

M.Benjamin, Supply and Demand for Transplantable Organs: The Ethical Perspective, *Trans Proc*, 1992, 22(5), 2139.

P.Berloco, *Trans Proc,* 1985, 17(2), 13-17.

S.I.Benn, Freedom, Autonomy, and the Concept of a Person, Proceedings of the Aristotelian Society LXXVI, 1976, 123f.

Bernstein and Simmons, The Adolescent Kidney Donor: The Right to Give, *Am J Psychiat*, 1974, 131, 1338.

J.F.Blumstein, The Case For Commerce in Organ Transplantation, *Trans Proc*, 1992, 24(5), 2190-2197.

V.Bonomini, Ethical Aspects of Living Donation, *Trans Proc,* 1991, 23, 2497.

V.Bonomini et al., Is Living Donation Still Justifiable, *Neph Dial Trans,* 1990, 5, 407-409.

D.Brahams, The Outcry Over the Humana Affair, *Lancet,* 1985, 1, 285.

M.Brazier (ed.), Street On Torts, 8th Edtn, *Butterworths,* 1988.

M.Brazier, Patient Autonomy and Consent to Treatment: The Role of the Law? *L.S.*, 1987, 7, 169.

M.Brazier, Medicine, Patients and The Law, *Penguin,* 1992 (2nd ed.).

Jo Bridgman, Old Enough to Know Best?, *Journal of Legal Studies,* 1993, 13(1), 69.

C.E.Broelsch et al., Liver Transplantation Including the Concept of Reduced Size Liver Transplants in Children, *Ann Surg,* 1988, 208(4), 410-420.

British Transplant Society, Report of the BTS Working Party on Organ Transplantation, *BTS*, 1995.

Lord Brown-Wilkinson, All ER Annual Review, 1997, 314.

F.P.Brunner et al., Combined Report on Regular Dialysis and Transplantation in Europe, 1988. *Nephrol Dial Transplant,* 1989, 4 (supp 4), 5-29).

Bunzendahl et al., Retrospective Evaluation of Psychosocial Factors in Former Living Related Kidney Donors, in W.Land and J.Dossetor (eds.), Organ Replacement Therapy: Ethics, Justice and Commerce, *Springer Verlag,* 1991, 57.

C.Bustza et al., Pregnancy After Donor Nephrectomy, *Transplantation* 1985, 40, 651-654.

R.W.Busutill, Living Related Liver Donation: CON, *Trans Proc,* 1991, 23, 43-45.

C.Byk, Living Organ Donation: European Perspectives 49-57 in Price and Akveld (eds.), Living Organ Donation in The Nineties: European Medico-Legal Perspectives, EUROTOLD, 1997.

F.Cantarovich, Values Sacrificed and Values Gained by the Commerce of Organs: The Argentine Experience, *Trans Proc* 1990, 22(3), 925-927.

A.L.Caplan, Is Xenografting Morally Wrong?, *Trans Proc,* 1992, 24(2), 722-727.

Canadian Transplant Study Group, *Am J Kidney Dis,* 1985, 5, 328-332.

Casabona, The Living Donor in Spanish Law, Copy Held at EUROTOLD.

Channel 4, The Decision: Whose Kidney Is It Anyway?' *Channel 4*, Tuesday 20 February 1996 at 9pm.

J.F.Chidress, The Body as Property: Some Philosophical Reflections, *Trans Proc*, 1992, 24(5), 2143-2148.

Cho et al., Transplantation of Kidneys From Donors Whose Hearts Have Stopped Beating, *New Engl J Med*, 1998, 338(4), 221-225.

R.Cialdini et. al., Low Ball Procedure For Producing Compliance: Commitment then Cost, *Journal of Personality and Social Psychology*, 1978, 36(5), 463-476.

M.P.H.D.Cleiren, Life After Giving. A Research Into the Experience of the Next of Kin of the Organ and/or Tissue Donor, *D.S.W.O. Press,* 1992.

Commercialisation in Human Organs: A Middle Eastern Perspective, *Trans Proc,* 1990, 22(3), 918-92.

A.Cohen, A Market Proposal for Increasing the Supply of Cadaveric Organs, *Clin Trans*, 1991, 5, 467-474.

L.R.Cohen, A Futures Market in Cadaveric Organs: Would it Work? *Trans Proc*, 1993, 25(1), 60-61.

R.B.Colvin et al., *Lab Invest,* 1982, 46, 275-281;

D.K.C.Cooper et al. (eds.), Xenotransplantation: The Transplantation of Organs Between Species, *Springer Verlag,* 1991.

A.Chanutin et al., Experimental Renal Insufficiency Produced By Partial Nephrectomy, *Arch Intern Med,* 1982, 49, 767-787.

F.Th.De Charro et al., Donor Recruitment in Europe in De Charro et al. (eds.), Systems of Donor Recruitment, *Kluwer,* 1992, 5.

W.Cramond et al., Psychological Screening of Potential Donors in a Renal Homotransplantation Programme, *Brit J of Psychiatry*, 1967, 113, 1213-1221.

W.J.Curran, Kidney Transplantation in Identical Twin Minors: Justice is done in Connecticut, *N Engl J Med*, 1972, 287, 26.

J.H.C.Daeman, Non Heart-Beating Donor Program Contributes 40% of Kidneys For Transplantation, *Trans Proc*, 1996, 28(1), 105-106.

M.Daly, Gyn/Ecology: The Metaethics of Radical Feminism, *Beacon Press*, 1978.

D.Daube, Transplantation: Acceptability of Procedures and the Required Legal Sanctions, in G.Wolstenholme and M.O'Connor (eds.), Ethics In Medical Progress, *Little Brown*, 1966, 188-201.

Edmund Davies LJ, The Patients Right to Know the Truth, *Proc Roy Soc Med*, 1973, 533 at 535.

L.Delaney, Law and the Altruistic Child in Medicine, in D.Lockton (ed.), Children and the Law, *Cavendish*, 1993, 39 at 42.

E.Deltz, Medical Risk and Benefit in Small-Bowel Segment Donors in Land and Dossetor (eds.), Organ Replacement Therapy: Ethics, Justice and Commerce, *Springer Verlag*, 110-116.

P.K.Donnelly et al., Transplants From Living Donors in the United Kingdom and Ireland: A Centre Survey. *BMJ*, 1989, 298, 490-493.

P.K.Donnelly et al., Matching For Age in Renal Transplantation, *New Engl J Med*, 1990, 322(12), 851-852.

P.K.Donnelly, Pre-Dialysis Living Donor Renal Transplantation - Is it Still the Gold Standard for Cost, Convenience and Graft Survival? *Trans Proc*, 1995, 27(1)).

L.Dossey, Space, Time and Medicine, *Shambala*, 1982.

J.F.Dunn, Living Related Kidney Donors: A 14 Year Experience, *Ann Surg*, 1986, 203, 637-643.

Gerald Dworkin, Markets and Morals: The Case for Organ Sales, *Mt Sin J Med*, 1993, 60(1), 66-69.

Ronald Dworkin, Taking Rights Seriously, *Duckworth*, 1977.

Edelstein, The Hippocratic Oath: Text, Translation and Interpretation, *Supplements to the Bulletins of the History of Medicine*, 30(1).

E.Edwards, No Defence for a Sado-Masochistic Libido, *NLJ*, 1993, 143, 552.

D.Ehenrich and B.English, Witches, Midwives and Nurses: A History of Women Healers, *The Feminist Press*, 1973.

David Eisenberg et al., Unconventional Medicine in the United States: Prevalence, Costs and Patterns of Use, 328:4, *N Engl J Med*, 1993, 246.

R.M.Eisendrath, Psychologic Considerations in the Selection of Kidney Transplant Donors, *Surg Gynec Obstet*, 1969, 129, 243-248.

R.M.Eisendrath, The Role of Grief and Fear in The Death of Kidney Transplant Patients, *Am J Psychiatry*, 1969, 126, 381.

N.C.Elder et al., Use of Alternative Health Care by Family, 1997 (Mar-Apr), *Arch Fam Med*, 6, 181.

B.A.Elick *Trans Proc,* 1990, 22, 343-344.
Elliot, Doing Harm: Living Organ Donors, Clinical Research and The Tenth Man, *J Med Eth,* 1995, 21, 91-96.
EUROTOLD Project Management Group, Questioning Attitudes to Living Donor Transplantation, *EUROTOLD*, 1996.
R.W.Evans and D.L.Manninen, US Public Opinion Concerning the Procurement and Distribution of Donor Organs, *Trans Proc*, 1988, 20(5), 781-5.
Faden and Beauchamp, A History and Theory of Informed Consent, *Oxford University Press*, 1986.
J.Fabre, Organ Donation and Presumed Consent, *The Lancet*, 1998, 352 (July 11) at 150.
Fagot-Largeault, Does Non-commercialisation of the Human Body Increase Graft Security, in Y.Englert (ed.), Organ and Tissue Transplantation in The European Union, *Martinus Nijhoff,* 1995 at 13.
Feest and H.Riad et al., Protocol for Increasing Organ Donation After Cerebrovascular deaths in a District General Hospital, *Lancet,* 1990, 335, 1133-1135.
C.H.Fellner, J.R.Marshall, Twelve Kidney Donors, *J.Am.Med.Assoc,* 1968, 206, 2703-2707
C.H.Fellner and J.R.Marshall, Kidney Donors - The Myth of Informed Consent, *Am J Psych*, 1970.
C.H.Fellner and J.R.Marshall, Kidney Donors Revisited, *Am J Psychiatry,* 1977, 134, 575-576.
C.H.Fellner and S.H.Schwartz, Altruism in Disrepute: Medical Versus Public Attitudes Toward The Living Organ Donor, *The New Eng J Med*, 1971 (March 18), 582-585.
L.Festinger, A Theory of Social Comparison Progress, *Human Relations,* 1954, 2, 117-140.
R.D.Foss, Blood Donation and the Foot-In-The-Door Technique: A Limiting Case, *Journal of Personality and Social Psychology*, 1979, 37(4), 580-590.
J.L.Freedman and S.C.Fraser, Compliance Without Pressure: The Foot in The Door Technique, *J of Personality and Soc Psych,* 1966, 4, 195-202.
J.R.P.French and B.Raven, The Bases of Social Power, in D.Cartwright and A.Zander (eds.), Group Dynamics, *Harper and Row,* 1968.
B.Freedman and K.Glass, *Law, Medicine and Health Care*, 1990, 18 at 395.
H.Gabel and K.Lindskoug, A Survey of Public Attitudes Toward Cadaveric Organ Donation in a Swedish Community, *Trans Proc*, 1988, 20(3), 431.
Gaber et al., *Trans Proc*, 1990, 22, 340-341.
R.Gabriel, A Patient's Guide to Dialysis and Transplantation, 1990 (4th edn.).
A.Garwood-Gowers, Review of Organ and Tissue Transplantation in the European Union: Management of Difficulties and Health Risks Linked to Donors, Y.Englert (ed.), *Martinus Nijhoff,* 1995, in *IDHL*, 1996, 47(1), 126-127.

A.Garwood-Gowers, To Pay or Not to Pay: That is the Question? An Analysis of the Economic Rights of Donors, in D.Price and H.Akveld (eds.), Living Organ Donation in the Nineties: European Medico-Legal Perspectives, *EUROTOLD*, 1996, 163-173.

A.Garwood-Gowers, An Investigation into the Ethical and Legal Aspects of Living Donor Organ Transplantation (PhD), *De Montfort University*, 1997.

W.Gaylin, On the Borders of Persuasion: A Psychoanalytic Look at Coercion, *Psychiatry*, 1974, 37(Feb), 1-9.

General Medical Council Guidance for Doctors on Transplantation of Organs From Live Donors, *General Medical Council Supplement News Review*, Dec 1992.

E.T.Gendlin, Client-Centred Developments in Psychotherapy With Schizophrenics, *Journal of Counselling Psychology*, 1962, 9, 205-211

E.T.Gendlin, Sub-verbal Communication and Therapist Expressivity: Trends in Client-Centred Psychotherapy with Schizophrenics, *The Wisconsin Psychiatric Institute Bulletin*, 1961(1).

D.Gieson, International Medical Malpractice Law, *Martinus Nijhoff*, 1988, 609.

D.Gieson, Civil Liability of Physicians for New Methods of Treatment and Experimentation: A Comparative Examination, *Med Law Review*, 1995 (Spring), 3, 22-52 at 29-30.

D.Gieson and J.Hayes, The Patient's Right to Know - A Comparative Analysis, *Anglo Am Law Rev*, 1992, 21, 101.

D.Gieson, Vindicating the Patient's Rights: A Comparative Perspective, *Journal of Contemporary Health Law and Policy*, 1993, 9, 273-309.

D.Gieson, From Paternalism to Self Determination to Shared Decision-Making, *Acta Juridica*, 1988, 107.

R.Gillon, Philosophical Medical Ethics, Oxford University, 1986.

R.J.Ginsberg et al., Modern Thirty Day Operative Mortality for Surgical Resections in Lung Cancer, *J Thorac Cardiovascul Surg*, 1983, 86, 654-58.

S.M.Gore, Intensive Care Unit Funding: Survey of Staffing and Bed Occupancy in November 1989, *Care of The Critically Ill*, 1991, 8, 79-80.

S.M.Gore et al., Organ Donation From Intensive Care Units in England and Wales: Two Year Confidential Audit of Deaths in Intensive Care, *BMJ*, 1992, 304, 349-355.

A.Grubb and D.Pearl, Sterilisation - Courts and Doctors as Decision Makers, *CLJ, 1989*, 380, 382.

Gunn, The Meaning of Capacity, *Med Law Review*, 1994 (Spring), 2, 8-29.

M.Haberal et al., Living Related Liver Transplantation in an Adult and A Child in W.Land and J.Dossetor (eds.), Organ Replacement Therapy: Ethics, Justice, Commerce, *Springer Verlag*, 1991, 83-91.

M.Haberal et al., Living Donor Transplantation: Single Centre Experience, *Trans Proc*, 1996, 28(1), 65-7.

H.Hansmann, The Economics and Ethics of Markets for Human Organs, *Yale University*, 56-85.

J.Harris, The Value of Life, *Routledge and Kegan Paul*, 1985.
R.M.Hakim et al., *Kidney Int,* 1984, 25, 930.
P.Herron and I.Marion, Homografting in The Treatment of Severe Burns, *Pacific Med and Surg*, 1967, 75, 4.
Hessing et al., Psychological Aspects of Organ Procurement System, in W.Land and J.Dossetor (eds.), Organ Replacement Therapy: Ethics, Justice and Commerce, *Springer Verlag,* 1991, 287-290.
J.Hirvas and M.Enckell et al., Psychological and Social Problems Encountered in Active Treatment of Chronic Uremia, *Acta Med Scand,* 1976, 200, 17-20.
M.Hoette et al., *Kidney Int,* 1986, 29, 430.
B.Hoggett. Parents, Children and Medical Treatment: The Legal Issues, in P.Byrne (ed.), Rights and Wrongs in Medicine, *Kings Fund (OUP),* 1986, 158.
N.K.Hollenberg, Altruism and Coercion: Should Children Serve as Kidney Donors, *N Engl J Med,* 1977; 296: 390.
J.Hors et al., France Transplant in R.Matesanz et al. (eds.) *Transplant,* 4 (Produced with the Council of Europe), Paris.
R.L.Horton and P.J.Horton, Supplying Organs For Transplantation, *Journal of Health Politics, Policy and Law,* 18(1), 175-188;
T.H.Hostetter et al., Hyperfiltration in Remnant Nephrons: A Potentially Adverse Response to Renal Ablation, *Am J Physiol,* 1981, 241, F85-F93.
A.Hutchinson and P.Singer, Xenotransplantation: is it ethically defensible? *Xeno*, 1995, 3, 58.
I.Illich, Limits to Medicine: Medical Nemesis and the Expropriation of Health, *Penguin*, 1976.
The Independent (London), Jan 18, 1989, at 2 columns 1-3.
International Digest of Health Legislation (various editions).
International Forum for Transplant Ethics, The Case For Presumed Consent in Organ Donation, *The Lancet*, 1998, 351 (May 30), 1650-1652.
Jaboulay, *Lyon M/ed*, 1906, 107, 575-577.
A.Jakobsen, A Second Opinion In Defence of Living Donor Transplant, *Health Policy,* 1990, 16, 123-126.
A.Jakobsen, Living Donor Practices and Processes in Europe, in D.Price and H.Akveld (eds.), Living Organ Donation in the Nineties: European Medico-Legal Perspectives, *EUROTOLD*, 1996, 1-12.
I.Janis and L.Mann, Decision Making: A Psychological Analysis of Conflict, Choice and Commitment, *The Free Press*, 1977 at 11.
B.L.Kasiske et al., Long-Term Effects of Reduced Renal Mass in Humans, *Kidney Int,* 1995, 48, 814-819.
J.P.Kemph, Renal Failure, Artificial Kidney and Kidney Transplant, *Am J Psychiatry*, 1966, 122, 1270-4.
K.V.Johnny et al., Values Gained and Values Lost in Live Unrelated Renal Transplantation, *Trans Proc*, 1990, 22(3) (June), 915-917.

Kennedy and Grubb, Medical Law: Text With Materials, *Butterworths,* 1994, 1087.

Keown, The Gift of Blood in Europe: An Ethical Defence of EC Directive 89/381, *J Med Eth* 1997, 23, 96-100.

Kishore, Organ Donation: Consanguinity Vs Universality - An Analysis of Indian Law, *Trans Proc*, Dec 1996.

D.S.Kittur et al. Incentives for Organ Donation, *The Lancet, 1991,* 338, 1441-1443.

A.Klass, There's Gold in Them Thar Pills, *Penguin*, 1975.

L.Kohlberg, Stage and Sequence: The Cognitive-Developmental Approach to Socialization, in A.Goslin (ed.), Handbook of Socialization Theory and Research, *Rand McNally,* 1969.

W.Kokkedee, Kidney Procurement Policies in the Eurotransplant Region, *Social Science and Medicine*, 1992, 35(2), 177-182.

G.Koostra et al., *Trans Proc*, 1989, 20, 809.

G.Kootstra et al., Twenty Per Cent More Kidneys Through a Non-Heart Beating Programme, *Trans Proc,* 1991, 23, 910-911.

Mukesh Kosla *This Week*, 1989, September 24, 51.

Kostakis et al., *Trans Proc*, 1990, 22, 1432-1433.

H.Kreis, Chapter 10 in Y.Englert (ed.), Organ and Tissue Transplantation in the European Union: Management of Difficulties and Health Risks Linked to Donors, *Martinus Nijhoff,* 1995.

Kropotkin, Modern Science and Anarchism, Freedom Press, 1912.

D.Kubrin, Newton's Inside Out: Magic, Class Struggle and the Rise of Mechanism in the West, in H.Woolf (ed.), The Analytic Spirit, *Cornell*, 1981.

N.G.Kutner et al., End Stage Renal Disease Treatment Modality and Patient Quality of Life, *Am J Nephrol,* 1986, 6, 396-402.

D.Lamb, Organ Transplants and Ethics, *Routledge*, 1990.

The Lancet, (editorial), 1982, ii, 696.

The Lancet, 1998, 351, 1868, 30.

W.Land, The Problem of Living Organ Donation: Facts, Thoughts and Reflections, *Trans Int*, 1989, 2, 168-179.

D.Laskow et al., Analysis of 22 Years Experience of Living Related Transplantation, *Clin Trans*, 1991, 179-191.

Law Commission Report on Mentally Incapacitated Adults, *HMSO,* 1993, Paper No. 129 and Law Com No. 231, *HMSO*, 1995.

V.Lent et al., Nephropathy in Remnant Kidneys: Pathological Proteinuria After Unilateral Nephrectomy, *J Urol,* 1994, 152, 312-6.

Levey et al., Kidney Transplantation From Unrelated Living Donors, *New Eng J Med*, 1986, 314, 914.

Lewis, Kidney Donation by a 7 Year Old Identical Twin Child: Psychological, Legal and Ethical Considerations, *J. Am. Acad. Child Psychiat, 1974,* 13, 221 at 228-232.

Lidz and Meisel, Informed Consent and the Structure of Medical Care, in Presidents Commission, Making Health Care Decisions, *Washington D.C. Government Printing Office,* 1982 at 333-340.

R.Lifton, Nazi Doctors: Medical Killing and the Psychology of Genocide, *Basic Books*, 1986.

Lillich Transplanting Organs from Living Donors: An International Regime or More Free Enterprise, *Finnish Yearbook of International Law*, 1990.

P-L.Liu et al., Renal Function in Unilateral Nephrectomy Subjects, *J.Urol* 1992, 147, 337-9.

Hilde Lorentzen and Florence Paterson, The Use of Living Donors For Kidney Transplants: Second Order and Third Order Decision Making, copy available from OSC, FNSP CNRS, 49 Rue de L'Universite 75007 Paris.

E.R.Maher et al., Mortality and Morbidity of Long Term Haemodialysis, *Lancet*, 1987, i, 452-453.

Mason & McCall-Smith, Law and Medical Ethics, *Butterworths,* 1991, 245.

J.K.Mason, Legal Aspects of Organ Transplantation, in C Dyer (ed.), Doctors, Patients and the Law, 1992.

R.Matesanz and B.Miranda (1992) Organizacion Nacional de Transplantes, in *Transplant,* 4.

S.McLean, A Patients Rights to Know, *Dartmouth*, 1989.

J.P.Merrill et al., Successful Homotransplantation of the Kidney Between Non-Identical Twins, *N.Engl.J.Med,* 1960, 262, 1251.

P.Michelson, Medical Risk and Benefit in Renal Donors: The Use of Living Donation Reconsidered, in Land and Dossetor (eds.), Organ Replacement Therapy: Ethics, Justice and Commerce, 1990, *Springer-Verlag*, 32-39.

P.Michelson, Effect of Transplantation Laws on Organ Procurement, in J.L.Touraine (ed.), Organ Shortage the Solutions, *Kluwer*, 1995, 34.

J.S.Mill, On Liberty, *Penguin*, 1982.

J.S.Mill, Utilitarianism, *Routledge*, 1863.

I.J.Miller et al., Impact of Renal Donation, Long Term Clinical and Biochemical Follow-Up of Living Donors in a Single Centre, *Am J Med,* 1985, 79, 201-208.

B.Miranda et al., Integrated Ways to Improve Cadaveric Organ Donation, *Trans Proc*, 28(1), 1996, 96-97.

D.Morgan, *J.S.W.L.*, 1990, 204.

P.J.Morris (ed.), Kidney Transplantation, 1988.

P.Morris and B.St George et al., Psychosocial Complications in Living Related Kidney Donors: An Australian Experience, *Trans Proc,* 1987, 19, 2840-2844.

J.Murray et al., Successful Homotransplantation Between Identical Twins, *Surg Forum*, 1955, 6, 432.

D.M.Narkun-Burgess et al., Forty-five Year Follow-up After Uniphrectomy, *Kidney Int,* 1993, 43, 1110-1115.

J.S.Najarian et al., 20 Years or More of Follow-up of Living Kidney Donors, *The Lancet* 1992, 340, 807-810.

B.New et al., A Question of Give and Take, Kings Fund Institute, 1994, Research Report 18.

New Engl J Med, 1998, 339(2) at 119-136.

New York Task Force, 1988, 20.

Linda Nielson, Living Organ Donors: Legal Perspectives From Western Europe in D.Price and H.Akveld (eds.), Living Organ Donation in the Nineties: European Medico-Legal Perspectives, *EUROTOLD*, 1996, 58-71.

K.Norrie, Human Tissue Transplants: Legal Liability in Different Jurisdictions, *I.C.L.Q.*, 1985, 42, 442 at 447.

Nuffield Council on Bioethics, Animal-to-Human Transplants: The Ethics of Xenotransplantation, *Nuffield Council on Bioethics*, 1996.

Nys, Desirable Characteristics of Living Donor Transplant Laws, in D.Price and H.Akveld (eds.), Living Organ Donation in the Nineties: European Medico-Legal Perspectives, *EUROTOLD*, 1996, 114-124.

D.A.Ogden, Consequences of Renal Donation in Man, *Am J Kidney Dis*, 1983, 2, 501-511.

G.R.Park et al., Organ donation (letter) *BMJ*, 1993, 306, 145.

T.Patel, France's Troubled Transplant Trade, *New Scientist*, 1993, 3 July, 12-13.

N.B.Paull, Safeguarding Donors: First, Do No Harm, *J Am Blood Res Ass*, 1993, 11 (Spring), Table 4.

G.Pennings, Ch22, in Y.Englert (ed.), Organ and Tissue Transplantation in the European Union: Management of Difficulties and Health Risks Linked to Donors, *Martinus Nijhoff*, 1995.

Persijn, How Severe is Organ Shortage in Eurotransplant?, in J.L.Touraine (ed.), Organ Shortage the Solutions, *Kluwer*, 1995 at p9.

T.G.Peters, Life or Death: The Issue of Payment in Cadaveric Organ Donation, *JAMA*, 1991, 266, 1302-1305.

J.Piaget and B.Inhelder, The Psychology of A Child, *Basic Books*, 1969.

R.J.Ploeg et al., Living Unrelated Kidney Donation: An Under-utilised Resource? *Trans Proc*, 1993, 25(1), 1532-4 at 1533.

D.P.T.Price, Organ Transplant Initiatives: The Twilight Zone, *J Med Eth*, 1997, 23, 170-175.

D.P.T.Price, The Voluntarism and Informedness of Living Donors, in Price and Akveld (eds.), Living Organ Donation in The Nineties: European Medico-Legal Perspectives, *EUROTOLD*, 1996, 98-115.

D.P.T.Price, The Texture and Content of Living Donor Transplant Laws and Policies, *Trans Proc*, 1996, 28(1), 378-379 at 379.

D.P.T.Price and A.Garwood-Gowers, Transplantation From Minors: Are Children Other People's Medicine, *Contemporary Issues in Law*, 1996, 1(1), 1-27.

J.M.Prottas and H.L.Batten, Neurosurgeons and The Supply of Human Organs, *Health Affairs*, 1989, 119-131.

J.Prottas, Buying Human Organs - Evidence that Money Doesn't Change Everything, *Transplantation*, 53(6), 1371-1373.

J.Prottas and H.Batten, The Attitudes of the American Public, Report to the Health Care Financing Administration, April 1986.

Radcliffe-Richards, For Him That Hath Not, in W.Land and J.Dossetor (eds.), Ethics, Justice and Commerce in Organ Replacement Therapy, *Kluwer*, 1990.

S.Raja et al., Liver Transplant From Live Donors *Lancet,* 1989, ii, 497.

A.Rand, Atlas Shrugged, *Penguin Books*, 1985.

F.Rapaport et al., *Trans Proc*, 1991, 23, 899-900.

K.Reemstra, Ethical Problems With Artificial and Transplanted Organs: An Approach to Experiental Ethics, in E.F.Torrey (ed.), Ethical Issues in Medicine, *Little Brown,* 1968.

K.Reemstra, Xenotransplantation: The Ethical and Legal Ramifications, *Medical Law Review*, 1998, Spring (6), 42-61 at 44

W.Reich, The Mass Psychology of Fascism, Souvenir Press, 1997.

A.Rettig, Artificial Kidneys and Artificial Hearts, *Sthrn Cal Law Rev*, 1991, 65, 503-28.

Re Y commentary, Med L Rev 205-207 at 207.

A.Rich, Of Women Born: Motherhood as Experience and Institution, *Bantam*, 1979.

G.Robertson, Informed Consent to Medical Treatment, *LQR*, 1981, 102.

G.Robertson, Organ Donation by Incompetents and the Substituted Judgement Doctrine, *Columbia LR*, 1976, 76, 48.

P.Rodriguez, Paying Donors and the Ethics of Blood Supply, *J of Med Eth,* 1989, 20, 31-35.

C.R.Rogers, Some Learnings From a Study of Psychotherapy With Schizophrenics, *Pennsylvania Psychiatric Quarterly,* 1962, 3-15.

G.Routh, Elective Ventilation For Organ Donation - The Case Against, *Care of The Critically Ill,* 1992, 8, 60-61.

Rychlak, The Psychology of Rigorous Humanism, *Wiley,* 1977 at 193.

H.H.Sadler et al., *Semin,* 1971, 3, 86.

Sadler et al., in Simmons et al., The Gift of Life: The Social and Psychological Impact of Organ Transplantation, *John Wiley & Sons*, 1977, p502.

Saks, Social Psychological Contributions to a Legislative Sub Committee on Organ and Tissue Transplants, *American Psychologist,* 1978 (July), 680-690.

P.E.Sartwell, Iatrogenic Disease: An Epidemiological Perspective, *International Journal of Health Services,* 1974 (winter), 89-93.

Joe C Savage, *Kentucky Law Journal*, 1970, 58, 132.

R.Schlumpf et al., Transplantation of Kidneys From Non-Heart-Beating Donors: Protocol, Cardiac Death Diagnosis and Results, *Trans Proc*, 1996, 28(1), 107-100.

S.H.Schwartz, Elicitation of Moral Obligation and Self sacrificing Behaviour: An Experimental Study of Volunteering to be a Bone Marrow Donor, *J of Personality and Soc Psych*, 1970, 15, 283-293.

R.A.Sells, Voluntarism and Informed Consent, in De Charro et al. (eds.), Systems of Donor Recruitment, *Kluwer,* 1992, 87.
L.R.Shaw et al., *The Lancet,* 1991, 338, 678-681.
T.Sherwood et al., Renal Angiography Problems in Live Donors, *Br J Radiol* 1978, 51, 99-105.
N.E.Simmonds, Central Issues in Jurisprudence, *Sweet and Maxwell,* 1986.
R.Simmons, *Trans Proc,* 1977, 9, 143.
R.G.Simmons, C.R.Anderson, Social-Psychological Problems in Living Donor Transplantation, in J.L.Touraine et al. (eds.), Transplantation and Clinical Immunology XVI, *Elsevier Science Publishers,* 1983, 47-57.
R.G.Simmons et al., Gift of Life, *Transaction Books,* 1987 at 245.
R.G.Simmons et al., Donors and Non Donors: The Role of the Family and The Physician in Kidney Transplantation, in W.Land and J.Dossetor (eds.), Organ Replacement Therapy: Ethics, Justice and Commerce, *Springer Verlag,* 1991 at p108.
Simmons and Karnstra-Hennen, The Living-Related Kidney Donor: Psychological Reactions When the Kidney Fails, *Dialysis and Transplantation,* 1979, 8(6).
R.G.Simmons, S.D.Klein, R.L.Simmons, The Gift of Life: The Social and Psychological Impact of Organ Transplantation, *John Wiley & Sons,* 1977.
P.A.Singer et al., *New Engl J Med,* 1990, 321, 620.
Skegg, Law, Ethics and Medicine, *Oxford University Press,* 1984, 85.
Skegg, Law, Ethics and Medicine: Studies in Medical Law, *Clarendon Press,* 1988.
M.D.Smith et al., *Am J Kid Dis,* 1986, 8(4), 223-233.
A.Spital et al., The Living Kidney Donor, *Arch Intern Med,* 1986, 1993.
Spital, Unconventional Living Kidney Donors: Attitudes and Use Among Transplant Centers, *Transplantation,* 1989, 48(2), 243-248.
R.Spital, M.Spital and A.Spital, The Donor's Decision in Renal Transplantation: A Cost Benefit Analysis, *Am J Kid Dis,* 1987, IX(5 May), 396-403.
Spital et al., The Living Kidney Donor: Alive and Well, *Arch Intern Med,* 1986, 146 at 1993.
Sollinger et al., *Transplantation,* 1984, 38, 664-668.
A.Somerville, Medical Ethics Today: It's Practice and Philosophy, *BMA,* 1993.
Stauch et al., Sourcebook on Medical Law, *Cavendish,* 1998.
Jonathon Stoye, No Clear Answers on Safety of Pigs as Tissue Donor Source, *The Lancet,* 1998, 352, Aug 29, 666-667.
T.S.Szasz, Law, Liberty and Psychiatry: An Inquiry Into The Social Uses of Mental Health Practices, *MacMillan,* 1963.
The Sunday Times 1995, 30 July.
D.E.R.Sutherland, *Trans Proc,* 1985, 17, 110.
D.E.R.Sutherland, *Trans Proc,* 1985, 17, 1503.
D.E.R.Sutherland et al., Medical Risks and Benefit of Pancreas Transplants From Living Related Donors, in W.Land and J.Dossetor (eds.), Organ Replacement Therapy: Ethics, Justice and Commerce, *Springer Verlag,* 92-101.

T.Talseth et al., Long Term Blood Pressure and Renal Function in Kidney Donors, *Kidney Int*, 1986, 29, 1072-1076.

Taylor et al., Renal Transplantation in the United Kingdom and Ireland - The Centre Effect, *The Lancet,* 1985, i, 798-802.

P.I.Terasaki et al., High Survival rates of Kidney Transplants From Spousal and Living Unrelated Donors, *New Eng J Med,* 1995, 333(6), 333-336.

B.Teo, Organs For Transplantation: The Singapore Experience, *Hastings Centre Report,* 1991, Nov-Dec:10-3.

P.M.Ter Wee et al., Pair Tested Renal Reserve Filtration Capacity in Kidney Recipients and Their Donors, *JASN,* 1994, 4, 1798-1808.

Tilney and Kirkman, Consideration of Kidney Donation Using Living Related Sources, *Transplantation and Clinical Immunology,* 1985, 16, 207-213.

R.Titmuss, The Gift Relationship, *Pantheon Books,* 1971.

The Council of The Transplantation Society, 1985 Guidelines, *The Lancet*, 1985, 2, 715-6.

The Transplantation Society, The Statement of the Committee on Morals and Ethics, Reprinted in Appendix 1 of WHO's Legislative Responses To Organ Transplantation, *Martinus Nijhoff,* 1994.

UKTSSA 1991 Annual Report.

UKTSSA 1992 Annual Report.

Ullmann, *Ann.Surg*, 1914, 60, 195-219.

Unger, *Berl.Klin.Wschr*, 1909, 1, 1057-60.

P.S.Veitch, Recent Initiatives From the British Transplant Society, in D.Price and H.Akveld (eds.), Living Organ Donation in the Nineties: European Medico-Legal Perspectives, *EUROTOLD*, 1996, 19-23.

J.A.Velosa et al., *Trans Proc,*1985, 17, 100.

F.Vincenti et al., Long Term Renal Function in Kidney Donors, Sustained Compensatory Hyperfiltration With No Adverse Effects, *Transplantation,* 1983, 36, 626.

Wakeford and Stepney, *Br J Surg,* 1989, 76(5), 435-439.

D.M.Walker, Principles of Scottish Private Law, *Clarendon Press*, 1982 (3rd edn), Vol 1.

M.J.Waples et al., Living Donor Nephrectomy: A 20 Year Experience, *Urology,* 1995, 45(2), 207-210.

Jim Warren, Financial Incentive Controversy Continues, *Dialysis and Transplantation*, March 1993, 156-158.

Weiland et al., Information on 628 Living-Related Kidney Donors at Single Institution With Long Term Follow-Up in 472 Cases, *Trans Proc,* 1984, 16, 5-7.

R.West, Organ Transplantation, *Office of Health Economics*, 1991, 26.

L.Westlie et al., Quality of life in Norwegian Kidney Donors, *Nephrol Dial Transplant*, 1993, 8, 1146-1150.

S.L.Williams et al., Long Term Renal Function in Kidney Donors: A Comparison of Donors and Their Siblings, *Ann Intern Med,* 1986, 105, 1-8.

H.Wilms, Indication for Living Donation in Kidney Transplants, *Trans Proc,* 1988, 20, 797.

World Health Organization, Legislative Responses To Organ Transplantation, *Martinus Nijhoff,* 1994.

T.Yasamura et al., Experience With 246 Living Related Donor Nephrectomy Cases at a Single Institution in Japan, *Jpn J Surg,* 1988, 18, 252-258.

Index

For Product Safety Concerns and Information please contact our EU
representative GPSR@taylorandfrancis.com
Taylor & Francis Verlag GmbH, Kaufingerstraße 24, 80331 München, Germany

www.ingramcontent.com/pod-product-compliance
Ingram Content Group UK Ltd.
Pitfield, Milton Keynes, MK11 3LW, UK
UKHW020158200926
475702UK00004B/513
* 9 7 8 0 3 6 7 1 4 8 7 1 3 *